IMAGES
of America

MOUNT SPOKANE

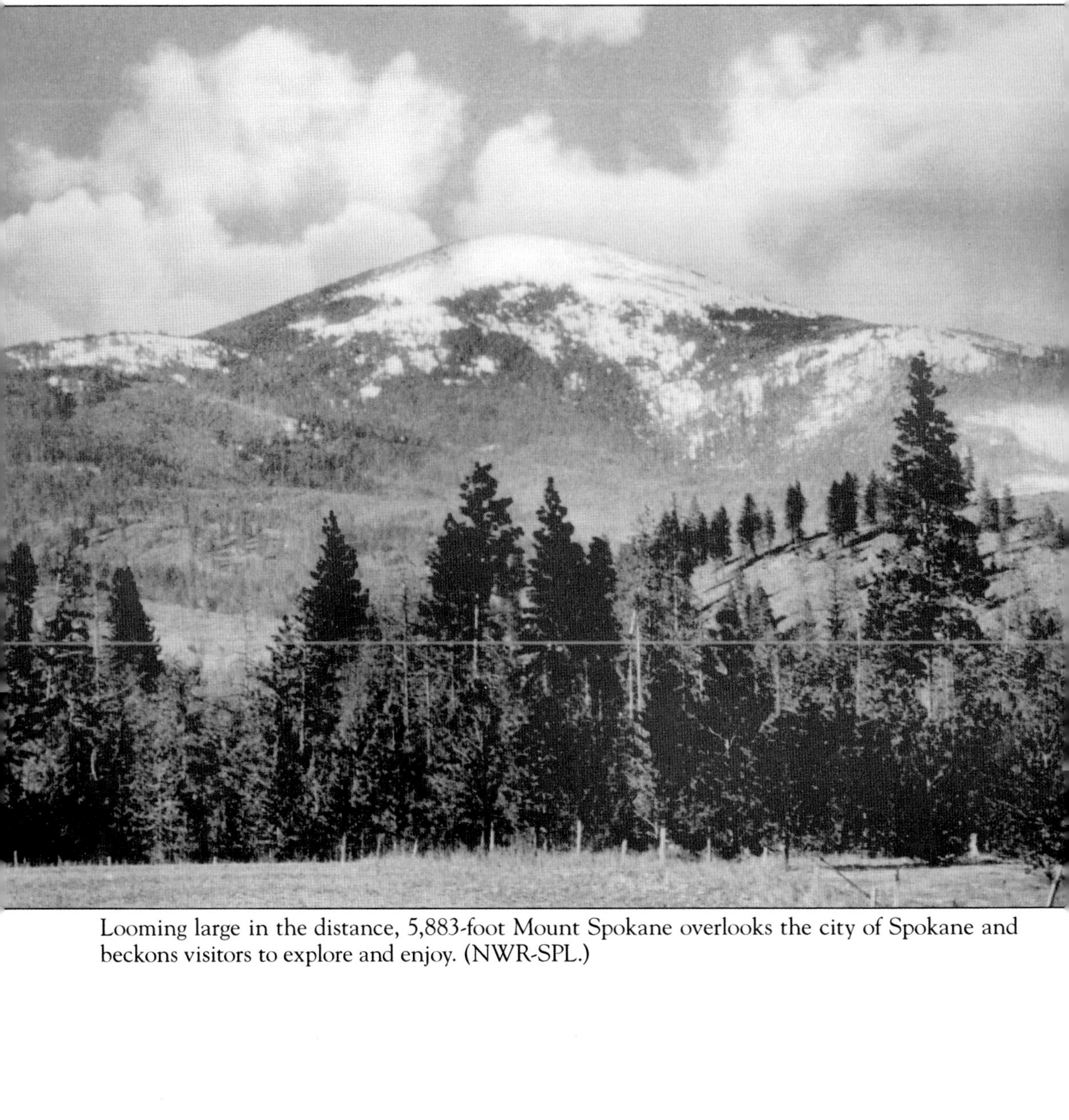

Looming large in the distance, 5,883-foot Mount Spokane overlooks the city of Spokane and beckons visitors to explore and enjoy. (NWR-SPL.)

On the Cover: The Mount Spokane Lodge operated from 1940 until it was destroyed by fire on January 23, 1952. (Tony and Suzanne Bamonte.)

IMAGES
of America

MOUNT SPOKANE

Duane Becker

ARCADIA
PUBLISHING

ISBN 978-0-7385-9543-6

Published by Arcadia Publishing
Charleston, South Carolina

Printed in the United States of America

Library of Congress Control Number: 2011944276

For all general information, please contact Arcadia Publishing:
Telephone 843-853-2070
Fax 843-853-0044
E-mail sales@arcadiapublishing.com
For customer service and orders:
Toll-Free 1-888-313-2665

Visit us on the Internet at www.arcadiapublishing.com

This book is dedicated to Lynn Sailor, my late brother-in-law, who first introduced me to Mount Spokane, and to my wife, Terri Becker, who suggested I write a book on Mount Spokane for Arcadia Publishing. Terri's encouragement and help with this project have been greatly appreciated.

Contents

ACKNOWLEDGMENTS

Special thanks go to following people and organizations for permission to use photographs and maps: Terri Becker for taking the modern-day photographs (Terri); Tony and Suzanne Bamonte (TSB); Northwest Room, Spokane Public Library (NWR-SPL); Leo's Studio (Leo); Washington State Digital Archives (WSDA); AAA of Washington, formerly AAA Inland Automotive Association (AAA); Greater Spokane, Inc. (GSI); Inland Power and Light Company (Inland); Duane Broyles (DB); Dean Ladd (DL); Charles and Larry Haley (Haley); Museum of North Idaho (MNI); Fire Lookout Museum–Ray Kresek (RK); Lynn Sailor (LS); Hearn Bros. Printing (Hearn); Walter Knopp (WK); Mount Spokane Ski Patrol, Donna Larson (SSP); Gonzaga University Library (GUL); Boy Scouts of America (BSA); Spokane Nordic Ski Education Foundation, www.spokanenordic.org, Jane McDonald (JM); Friends of Mount Spokane State Park, www.mountspokane.org, Cris Currie (CC); Jeanne Bartle (JB); and Tom Frost (TF). Please note that map drawings are by Russ Rask (RR) and that some images are from the author's collection (AC). In addition, thanks go to the Mount Spokane Ski and Snowboard Park, Brad McQuarrie, and Kristin Whitaker, www.mtspokane.com. A thank you also goes to Loulou Kneubuhler. Lastly, Patty Geaudreau, Evelyn Reed, and Winnie Sundseth helped with proofreading.

Introduction

At 13,919 acres, Mount Spokane is the largest state park in Washington. For years, the park has been a popular winter and summer recreation area. Today, skiing, snowboarding, snowmobiling, hiking, mountain biking, horseback riding, and berry picking round out visitors' time. Mount Spokane and the surrounding foothills are part of the southern extension of the Selkirk Mountains. The Selkirk Mountains extend from this area to the north and well up into Canada. The terrain around the Mount Spokane area is rugged and heavily timbered. From an average elevation of 2,125 feet to 5,883 feet at the summit, Mount Spokane covers a range of habitats, including stream, mountain, and subalpine. Ponderosa pine, Douglas fir, tamarack, and subalpine fir make up the majority of the softwoods. Birch, mountain maple, and other hardwoods can be found as well as hundreds of plant species. Mount Spokane is within the Little Spokane River watershed with other creeks feeding Newman, Hauser, and Spirit Lakes. Animals and birds, including moose, elk, bear, deer, cougar, mountain blue jays, and hawks, are plentiful.

Prior to 1955, the geology of the mountain was not studied to any extent. There have been numerous geologic studies of the surrounding areas, including the Spokane Valley (the 1909 Calkins study) and Latah (the 1926 Pardee and Bryan study). A portion of the eastern half of Mount Spokane was included in a report on the geology of Kootenai County, Idaho (the 1940 Anderson study). Geologist A.E. Weissenborn began mapping the Mount Spokane 15-minute quadrangle; fieldwork started in late 1958 and continued part-time until completion in 1972. Weissenborn's study and another one completed in 1966 by geologist Allan B. Griggs concluded that several areas of Mount Spokane are made up of old rock from the Precambrian age. The Precambrian age is the oldest geologic time period. It is believed that Mount Spokane, one of the oldest mountains in the area, was part of the old continental shelf. The area of Mount Spokane consists of quartz, granite, potassium feldspar, some garnet, and several other types of rock. Although many have speculated and there have been rumors, Mount Spokane is not volcanic in origin.

Geologists began to take notice in 1955 with the discovery of uranium on the west slope of Mount Spokane. Over the years, there have been many occurrences of uranium in the area. Mining is prohibited within the state park boundaries; however, private land around the mountain has been mined. The largest share of uranium came from the Daybreak Mine on the northwest slope of Mount Spokane. Another uranium-mining area was just east of the Daybreak Mine and called Morning Star Uranium, Inc. Both areas provided excellent quality uranium, with the Daybreak location having one of the highest concentrations of autunite uranium.

The first road that was constructed to the mountain was built mainly using hand tools and horses. One man in particular was responsible for the road; his name was Francis Cook. Some of Francis Cook's many business activities included the development of Spokane's first park on the south hill, later to be named Manito Park. He was the president of the Washington Territorial

Legislature from 1879 to 1880, as well as the publisher of Spokane's first newspaper, the *Spokan Times*. The original spelling was Spokan. Cook was actively involved in transportation projects in and around Spokane as well as being a substantial landowner and developer. Francis Cook; his wife, Laura; and family lived quite comfortably in Spokane until the financial depression of 1893. The Cook family lost their home to creditors and then moved to a piece of property they owned north of Spokane. From his new home, Cook had an exceptional view of the mountain, which in those days was called Mount Carlton. He became fascinated and, in 1908, purchased land at the summit. His goal turned to building a road up the mountain to the summit. At first, Cook spent his time deciding on a route and working with property owners to secure rights for the road. Over a period of 10 years, beginning in 1909, he blazed a road up the mountain almost to the summit, working only during the summer and with family help. Cook advertised nonstop to Spokane citizens and businessmen about the mountain and the outstanding views. Within a few years, the public began to take notice of the mountain and called the road "Cook's Auto Road." With interest in the mountain growing, Cook was instrumental in getting its name changed from Mount Carlton to Mount Spokane. After petitioning for the name change and with governmental approval, Cook and the citizens of Spokane finally had a mountain named after their city in 1912. During the summer months, the public became fascinated, and automobile trips to the mountain became popular. Francis Cook died on June 29, 1920, at the age of 69. He lived to see the interest in Mount Spokane grow.

In 1899, the Washington State Good Roads Association was formed. By 1911, the association had lobbied the state legislature to gain its support of a state highway program to be paid for by state funds. With almost no good-quality roads in Washington State, there was a need for improving what roads the state did have and constructing new roads. One of the plans called for a highway to be built from Spokane to Seattle, called the Sunset Highway, with advertised side trips in various areas. The businessmen and citizens of Spokane, as well as the Good Roads Association, believed that the road to Mount Spokane should be included as one of the advertised side trips.

On July 8, 1927, the land around the summit of Mount Spokane was transferred from the county to the state, and officially, Mount Spokane became a Washington State park. Many prominent Spokane businessmen and citizens began to donate land acreage to the state park.

Skiing was very popular in Spokane during this time, with major ski events held at Moran Prairie and Wandermere. But skiers wanted a longer ski season than the areas around the city could provide. They began to look farther north to Mount Spokane. For years, many thought that the slopes of Mount Spokane would be a great skiing area that would definitely extend the ski season. By the winter of 1931, plans were being drawn up to quickly transform Mount Spokane into a skiing destination.

In 1933, the Civilian Conservation Corps (CCC) arrived on Mount Spokane. The CCC boys went to work building roads, trails, and picnic areas. They constructed the Vista House and the Mount Spokane Lodge and improved and widened Cook's Auto Road. Construction of the modern-day Mount Spokane Park Drive road was completed by the CCC.

With Cook's Cabin and its rope tow, plus several ski clubs in operation, Mount Spokane became a winter destination. The Mount Spokane Lodge was constructed and opened in 1940. Construction of a double chairlift followed in 1946. This was Washington State's first chairlift and the first double chairlift ever used. With several smaller ski cabins built by the ski clubs, skiing at Mount Spokane was more popular than ever. In 1950, construction was started on a large addition to the Mount Spokane Lodge. Tragedy struck when a fire ripped through the lodge and addition in January 1952, shortly before the new portion of the lodge was to be opened. Nothing remained of the lodge except the concrete foundation. Soon after, the entire ski operation moved from the south face of the mountain to a more weather-sheltered area on the east slopes. The 1956 skiing season opened with a new lodge and chairlift. Skiers loved the new area, and attendance over the next several years was at capacity. Four additional chairlifts were constructed on Mount Spokane.

A fire lookout tower was in operation on the summit from 1934 until 1994 under the supervision of the Washington State Department of Natural Resources. Through the years, the Bonneville

Power Administration, Avista Power, the Washington State Patrol, and Spokane's KXLY-TV have maintained their transmitters, towers, and equipment at the summit with special permits from the State of Washington.

Nordic cross-country skiing has been popular at Mount Spokane for a long time. The Inland Empire Nordic Club took the leading role in developing the cross-country ski program at Mount Spokane, and grooming equipment was purchased in 1985. The Selkirk Lodge, also known as the "warming hut," opened in 1989, and today, under the direction of the Spokane Nordic Ski Education Foundation, Nordic cross-country skiing is bigger than ever at Mount Spokane.

Horseback riding has always been a summer activity at Mount Spokane and continues to be today. In the last several years, mountain biking and snowboarding have gained interest and feature many scheduled events and competition meets.

Currently, the ski operations are managed under the direction of the nonprofit Mount Spokane Ski and Snowboard Park. It offers skiing and snowboarding with five double chairs on more than 1,425 acres and 2,000 vertical feet, slopes for all ability levels, and night skiing. The ski school program at Mount Spokane is one of the best in the region. A tubing hill with rope tow, cross-country skiing, snowmobiling, and snowshoeing are all popular in the winter.

Groups like the Friends of Mount Spokane and Mount Spokane 2000 are active in future plans and development of the area. As of 2012, there are plans to build a new multipurpose four-season lodge at Mount Spokane and to extend the downhill ski and snowboard operations with the construction of another chairlift.

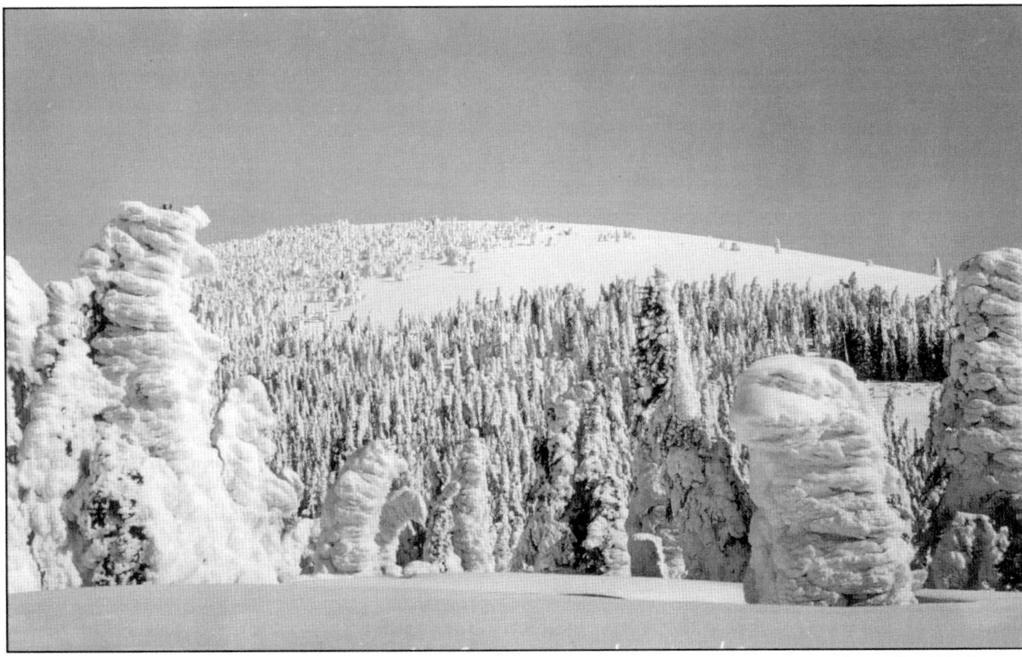

The summit of Mount Spokane is pictured from the Mount Kit Carson area. (NWR-SPL.)

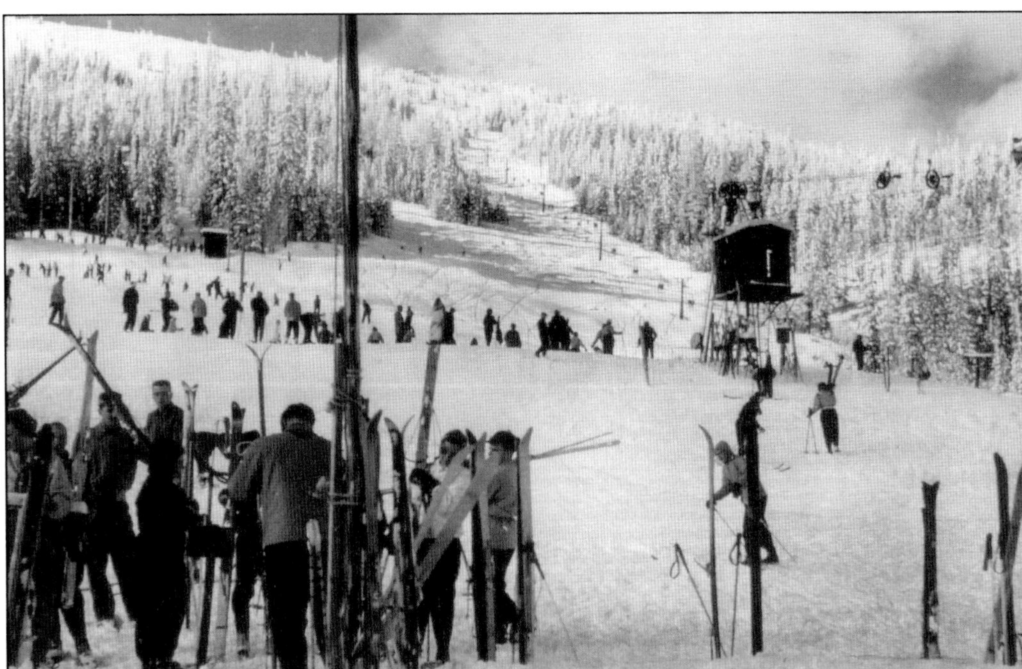

Skiing has always been popular at Mount Spokane, including this great skiing day in the late 1950s. (SSP.)

One

The Road to the Mountain

The first road from the base of Mount Spokane to a short distance from the summit was built by Spokane businessman Francis Cook. By the summer of 1909, Cook owned several hundred acres of land on Mount Spokane, including the summit. He began searching for the best route to build a road to the mountaintop. Cook arranged to buy the road right-of-way from property owners and, with the help of his sons Silas, Frank, and Chester, he started clearing brush and trees for the new road. Daughter Florence placed the survey stakes, while her father sited the way using his level. It was all elementary and crude, but after several summer seasons, the road began to take shape. Later, Cook employed a crew of men to help the family with the road.

Cook built two cabins, the first on the way to the mountain and the second near the summit. The cabin closest to the summit was used to sleep in during construction of the road. The road for the most part was nothing more than a wide trail with many difficult spots to pass due to muddy washouts. But each year, the road was improved. After 1910, automobiles began making the trip to Mount Spokane. Cook charged a 50¢ fee per automobile to use the road. He also offered saddled ponies and campsites to rent. These fees were the only compensation that Francis Cook ever received for his work on the road. Cook continued working during the summers, cutting brush and removing tree stumps. The road ended at the second cabin, which was called Cook's Cabin. From there, a hiking trail to the summit would start.

Francis Cook died in 1920, with the road complete to within 700 feet of the summit. With the help of his family, friends, and business leaders, the roadwork continued. Eventually, the county and then the state took over the maintenance of the road. Cook's original survey and grade was checked by state engineers and found to meet their specifications. The state continued to use Cook's original route for the road.

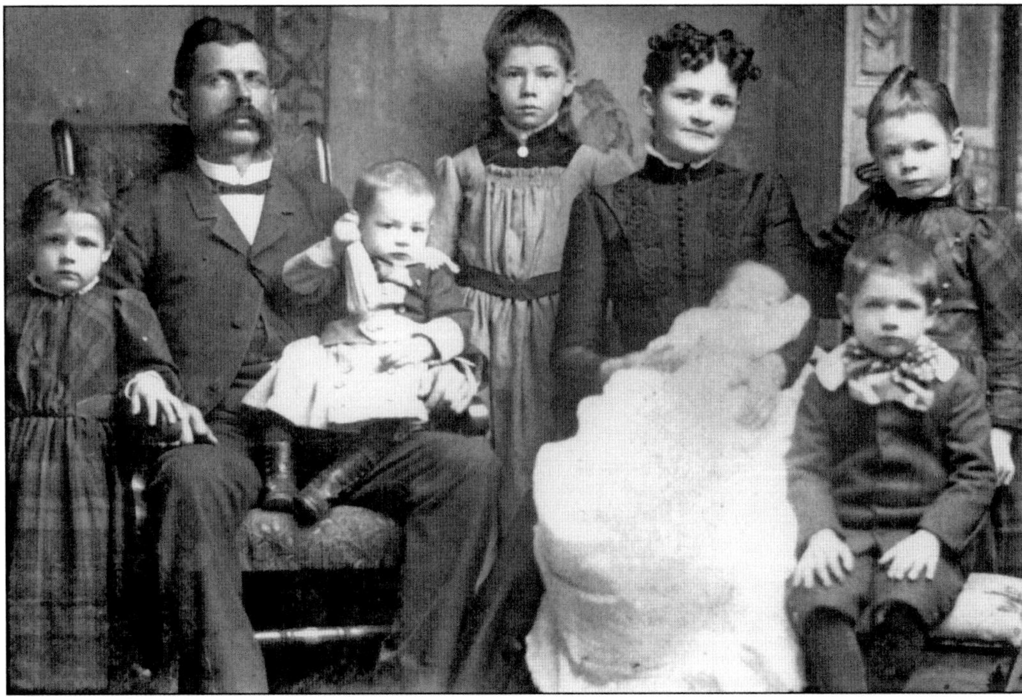

The history of Mount Spokane would not be complete without the Cook family, pictured here in 1890. From left to right are Clara; Francis, holding Frank; Katie; Laura, holding Chester; Silas; and Laura May. The Cooks would eventually have 11 children. Francis, with the help of the children, surveyed and cleared brush and trees while building the road up the mountain. (TSB.)

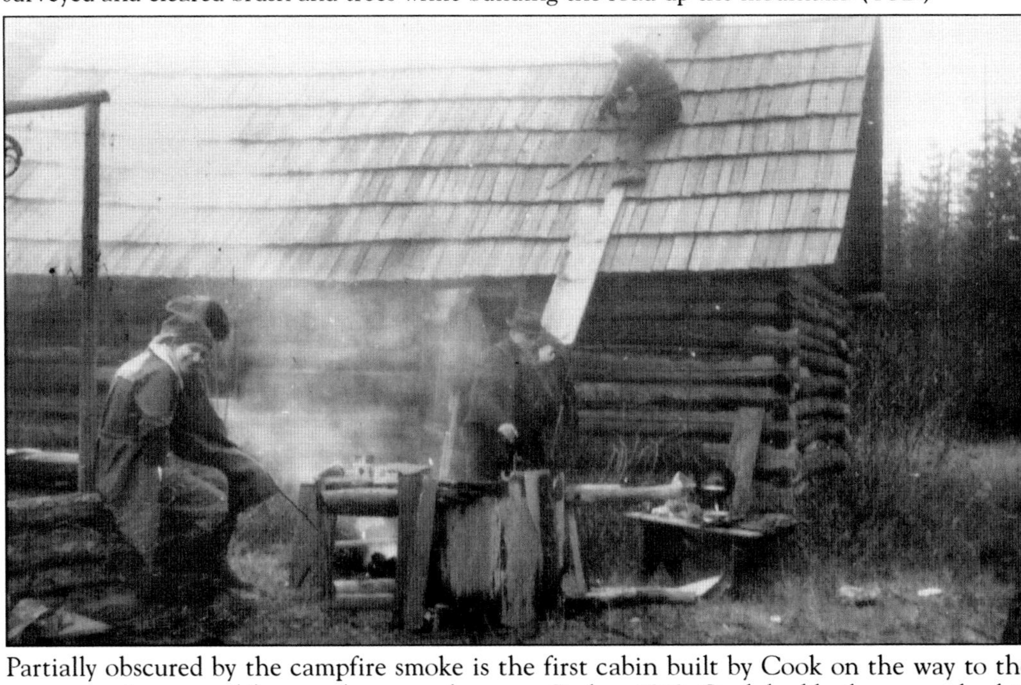

Partially obscured by the campfire smoke is the first cabin built by Cook on the way to the mountain. It was used for a work area and storage. By late 1912, Cook had built a second cabin near the summit, which would become a landmark at Mount Spokane. (TSB.)

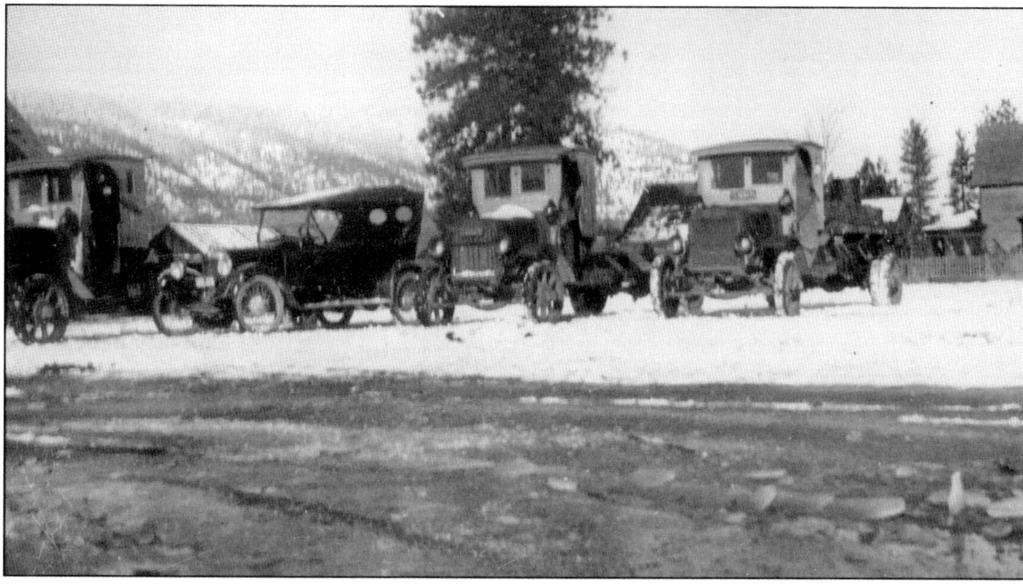

This image depicts part of the ongoing traffic headed to Mount Spokane. By the end of 1915, Cook had a passable wagon road that would support automobiles most of the way to the summit. Cook kept no records or reports of the building of his road. During interviews with newspaper reporters, he would mention the construction just enough to let the public know where the terminus was. (TSB.)

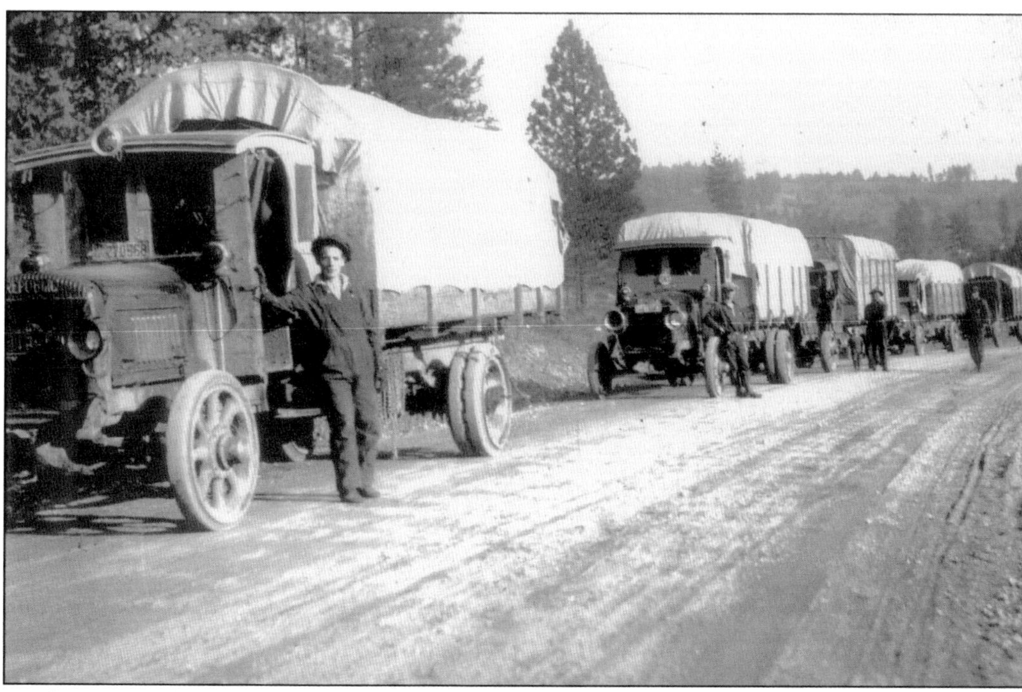

Work crews and a truck convoy are seen headed for Mount Spokane to work on the Cook's Auto Road. Later on, Francis Cook would employ a small road construction crew. Traffic increased dramatically during the 1920s and even more so in the upcoming years. (TSB.)

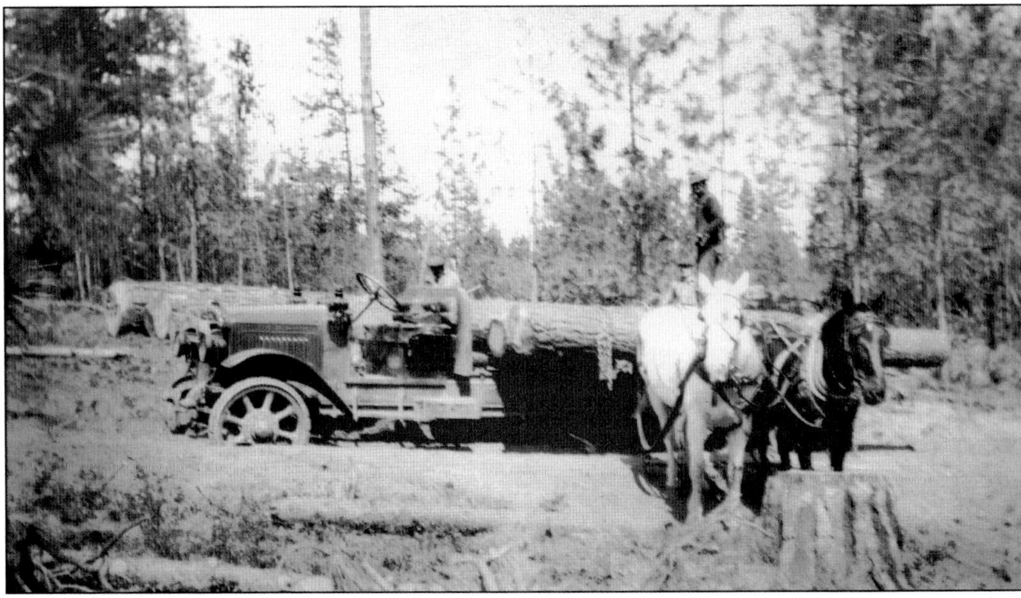

Building the road was hard work and often required the use of horses and trucks. By 1920, automobile-touring schedules were published in the Spokane newspapers featuring the trip to Mount Spokane. The automobile-touring season was generally from late June to early October. Reports from those early days often mention soft spots and mud on the road in the middle of July. (TSB.)

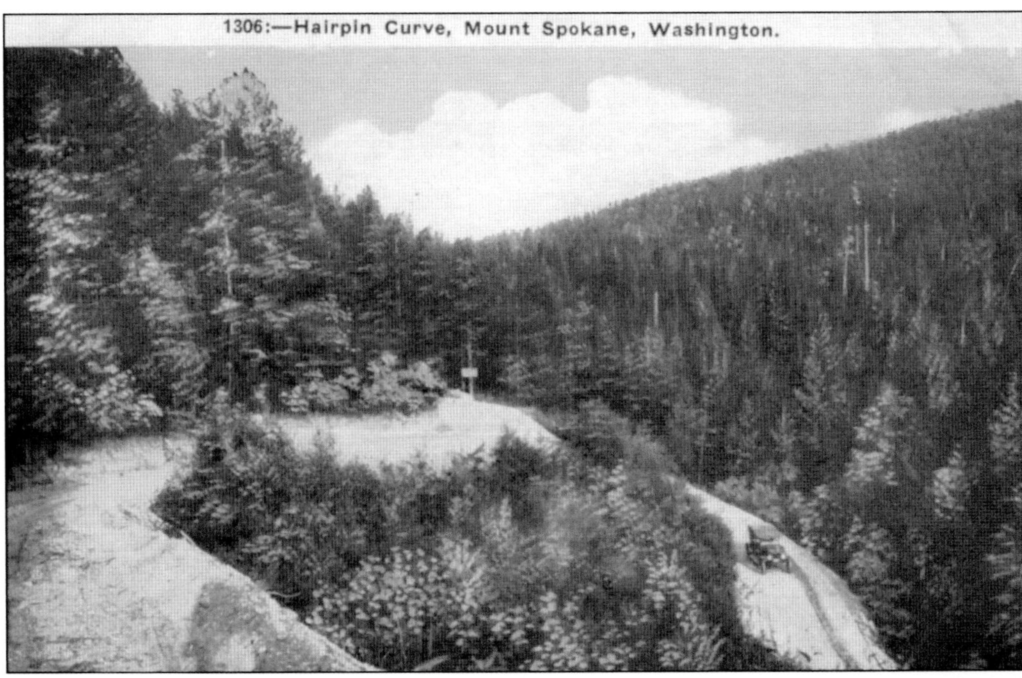

This is a very rare linen postcard image. Note the vehicle on the right heading down the hill. Steep, sharp switchbacks were very common near the top of the mountain. By 1920, almost every motorist in Spokane made the trip up to Mount Spokane during the summer months. The distance from downtown Spokane at Howard and Riverside to the cabin was listed as 34 miles. (DB.)

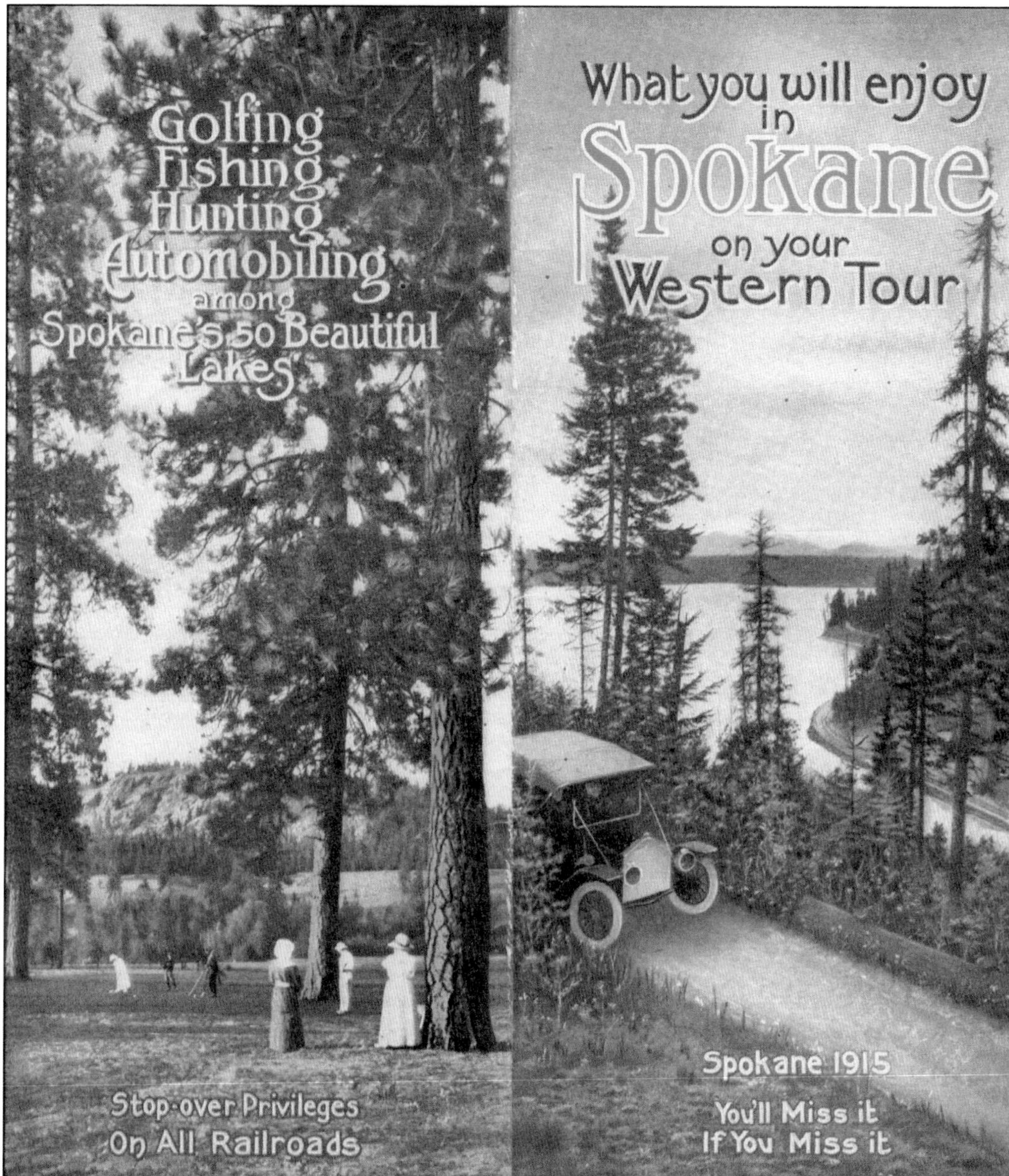

This is the pamphlet for the 1915 Spokane Chamber of Commerce. The businessmen and citizens of Spokane felt the road to Mount Spokane should be included in promotional pamphlets and brochures as an advertised automobile-touring trip. With the introduction of the Ford Model T in late 1908 and Chevrolet in 1911, other makes and models of cars soon followed. The automobile was gaining in popularity. During the 1910s, several national and regional expositions involving automobile-touring races around the country, including Washington State, stirred the imagination and boosted enthusiasm of everyone. Sales of automobiles increased, and day trips with the automobile became a family adventure. (GSI.)

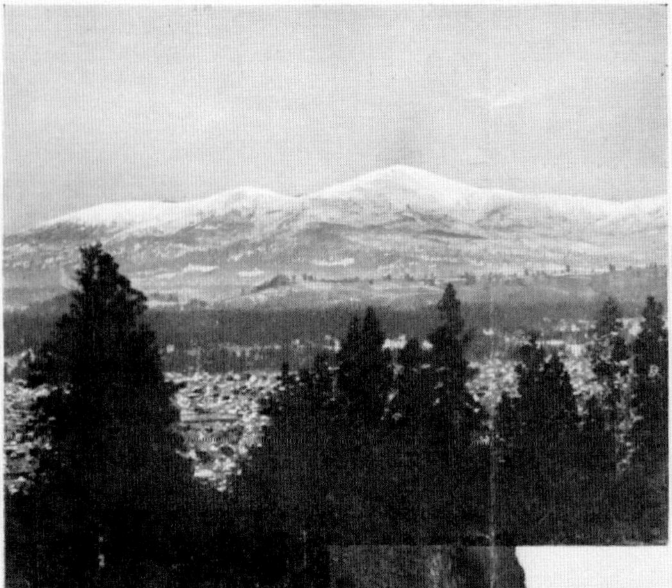

Spokane the Beautiful, and Beautiful Mount Spokane

which produces 30 per cent of the lead output of the United States. At Kellogg, Idaho, are the mine and mills of the Bunker Hill and Sullivan, the largest lead-silver mine in the world. This is a veritable city underground.

Immediately south of Spokane and stretching away to the Bitter Root mountains are the famous grain fields of the Palouse country. A coat of many colors is draped over the hills that rise and fall endlessly like the smooth swells of the sea. Stubblefields of bright yellow swing in long strips up the slopes and vanish over the crest of the rise. A combined harvester in action is worth a journey in itself. The Palouse country can be reached by steam or electric railroad and by automobile. From the summit of Steptoe Butte, 65 miles from Spokane, a matchless view of the Palouse country is available.

On the Palouse trip visitors can obtain an idea of the vast lumbering industry of the Spokane country by visiting the mill of the Potlatch Lumber Company, at Potlatch, Idaho, 75 miles south of Spokane. This is the largest lumber mill in the world.

Twenty miles north of the city towers Mount Spokane, 6,000 feet into the clouds. An automobile road has conquered its height to within easy

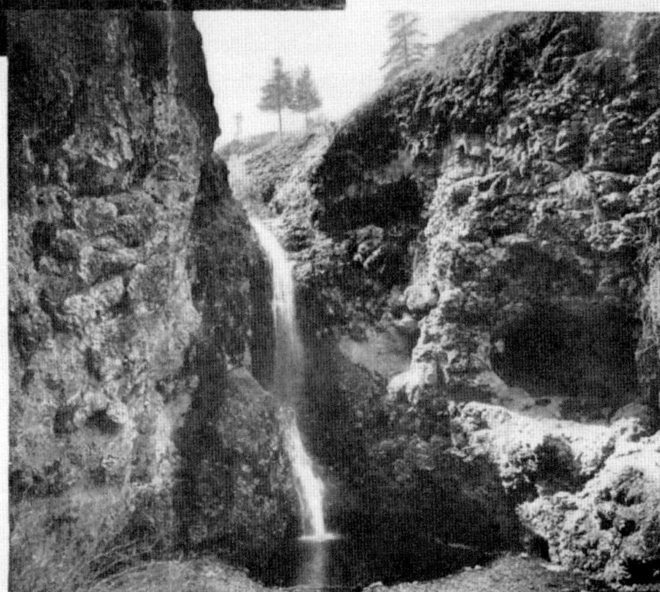

Indian Canyon, in One of Spokane's 43 Parks. Tribal Home of the Spokane Indians for Generations

Page Four

With the cover featured on the previous page, here is a page from the 1915 Spokane Chamber brochure featuring a photograph of Mount Spokane. The brochure mentions the fact that Mount Spokane is just north of the city and that the automobile road ascends the mountain with an easy walk to the summit. The brochure continues, "from its summit can be seen portions of the states of Washington, Oregon and Idaho, and the province of British Columbia. Within range of the naked eye is a varied panorama of scenery and industry—seventeen lakes and rivers, great forest, broad acres of farms and orchards, and scores of towns. High above all other mountains in the Spokane country, this peak affords an unobstructed view in all directions as far as the human eye can penetrate." (GSI.)

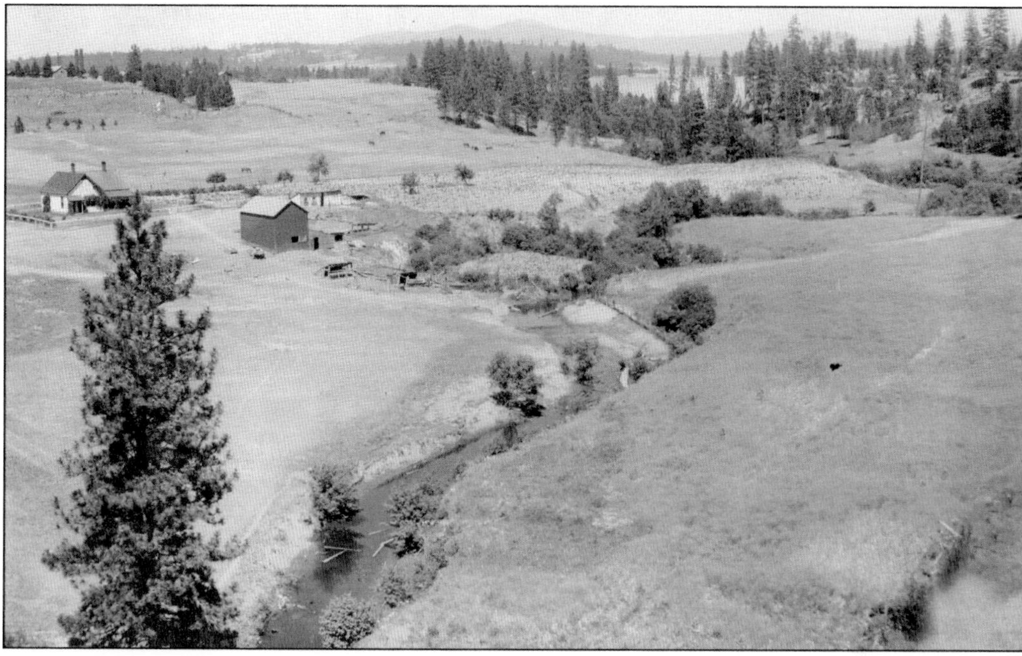

This is the type of wooded area and farmland that the road to Mount Spokane traversed through. The mountain in the distance can be seen with Deadman Creek in the foreground. Later in 1937, a second road, now called the Mount Spokane Park Drive, was opened to Mount Spokane following this creek bed. Automobile traffic increased almost immediately as people began to use this improved and easier grade. (TSB.)

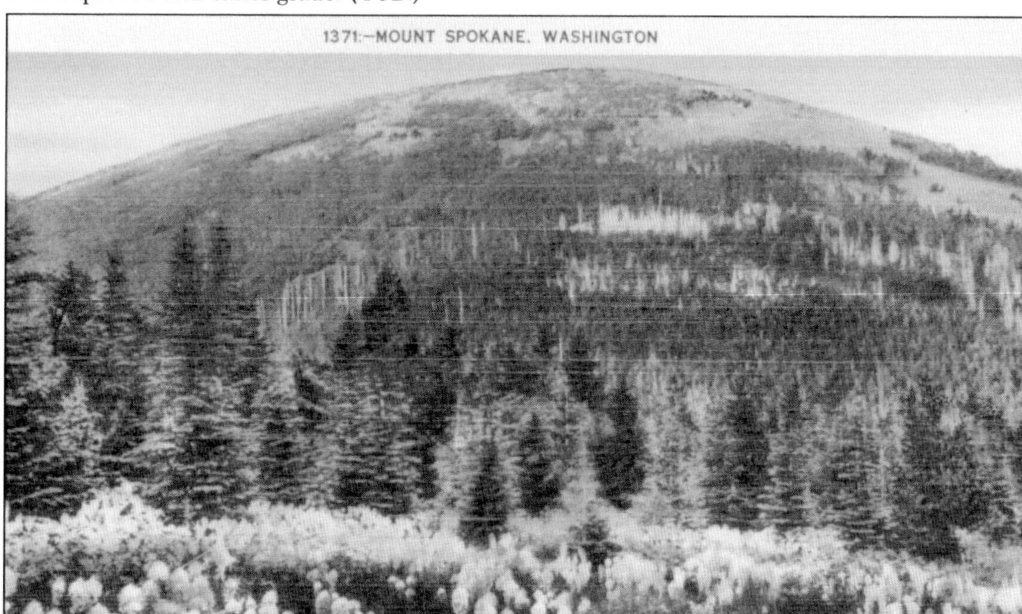

This is a very old linen-type postcard from the 1920s with mountain wildflowers in full bloom. These mountain scenes were popular. More and more people would make the summer trip to the mountain, and by the 1930s it was one of the most popular day-trip designations. The interest in developing Mount Spokane was very strong. (DB.)

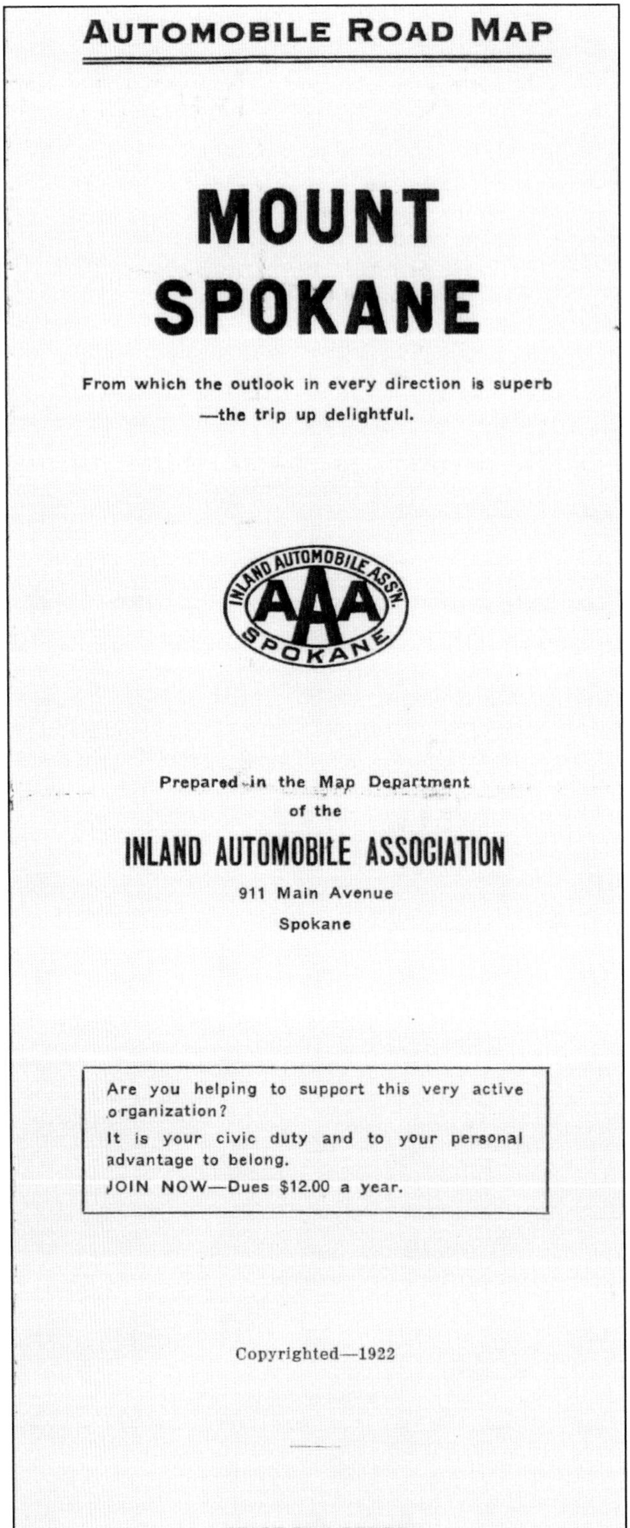

AUTOMOBILE ROAD MAP

MOUNT SPOKANE

From which the outlook in every direction is superb —the trip up delightful.

Prepared in the Map Department of the

INLAND AUTOMOBILE ASSOCIATION

911 Main Avenue

Spokane

Are you helping to support this very active organization?

It is your civic duty and to your personal advantage to belong.

JOIN NOW—Dues $12.00 a year.

Copyrighted—1922

PRICE TEN CENTS

Spokane's Inland Automobile Association produced an automobile road map in 1922 showcasing the route from the city of Spokane to the mountain. This brochure with the map was handed out to many automobile owners around the Spokane area throughout the 1920s, and almost all made the summer day trip to the mountain. During the 1920s, there were articles on automobile tours in the Spokane newspapers almost on a weekly basis. Maps and articles were produced from the AAA of Spokane and the Spokane Chamber of Commerce. Mount Spokane was well publicized, and people could not get enough. (AAA.)

LOG OF MOUNT SPOKANE TRIP

Miles
0.0 Howard and Riverside, go east to Division St.
0.5 Division St., turn left.
0.8 Cross Spokane River.
1.4 Mission Avenue, turn right.
2.1 Hamilton St., turn left.
2.5 Illinois Ave., turn right.
3.5 Spokane River on right.
4.0 Fiske St., turn left.
5.1 South city limits of Hillyard (Market St.)—Drive slowly thru city.
6.3 North city limits of Hillyard. Straight ahead following pavement. (St. Michael's Scholasticate to the right).
7.6 Straight ahead.
9.4 Straight ahead.
10.0 MEAD, straight ahead.
10.4 Straight ahead. (View of Mt. Spokane on the right).
11.0 Cross Deadman Creek on high bridge.
12.6 End of pavement—straight ahead—Road to right leads to Greenbluff Prairie.
13.1 Bear left—railroad on right.
14.1 Bear left.
14.4 Underhead crossing at Dean. Go slow.
15.2 Turn right across G. N. railroad tracks--Use Care.
15.5 Turn left.
16.0 Straight ahead.
16.6 Straight ahead.
17.0 Turn right.
18.0 Straight ahead.
19.5 School on right.
20.0 Straight ahead.
21.0 Big Meadows ahead.
21.6 Turn right.
22.6 Turn left. (Greenbluff road to the right).
23.4 School—turn right.
24.9 Mt. Spokane Sign Board—beginning of Mt. Spokane road.
25.3 Spring No. 1.—Farm house on left.
25.6 Straight ahead.
28.4 Spring No. 2.
28.9 Spring No. 3.
29.0 Spring No. 4.
29.2 Switchback—abrupt left turn—Caution.
29.3 Spring No. 5 on right.
30.8 Spring No. 6.
33.6 Sharp curve to left.
34.3 Cook's cabin—Spring No. 7.

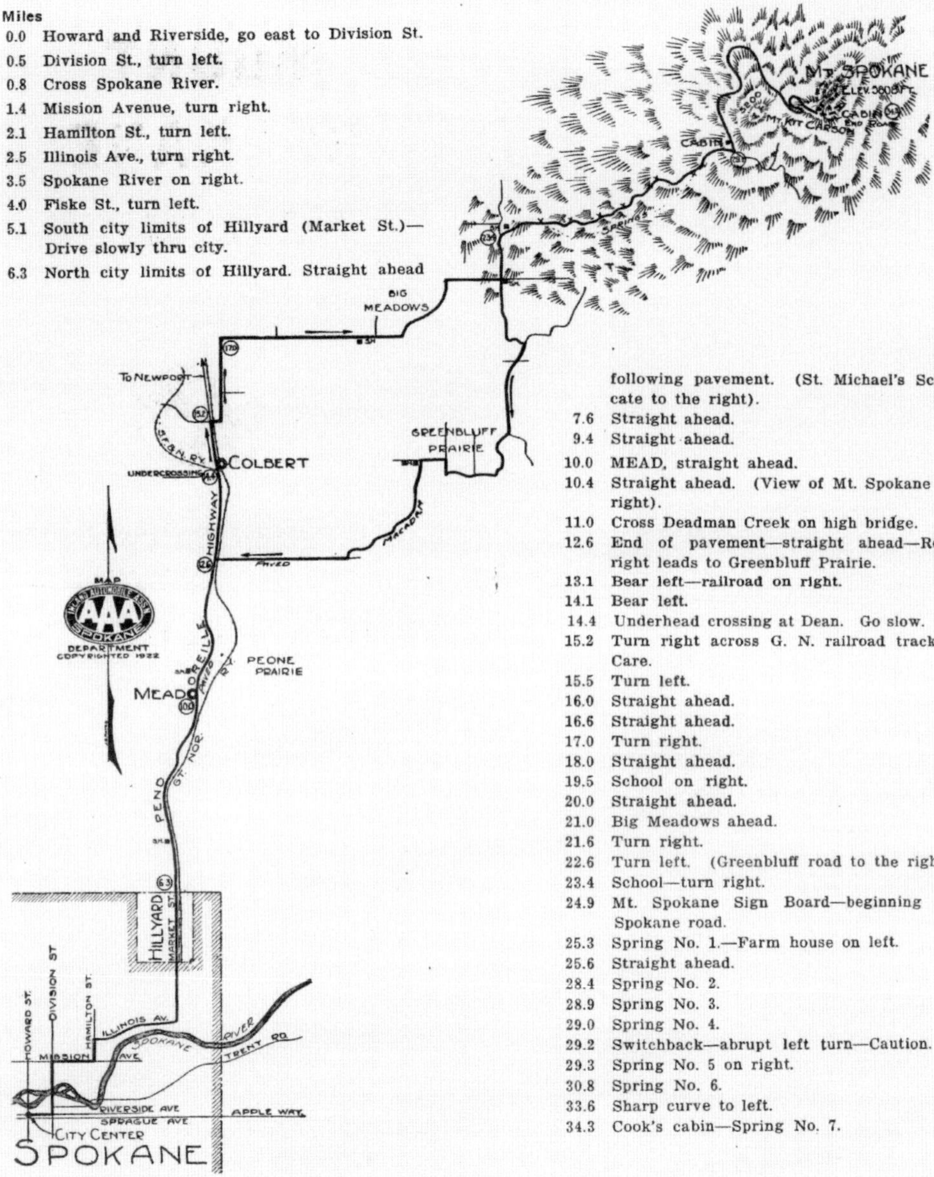

The map from the brochure on the left shows the mileage and points of interest along the route. The first road, called Big Meadows Road, is what Francis Cook extended up the mountain and called Cook's Auto Road. Later, a second section of road was constructed from the Pend Oreille Highway just south of Colbert and was called the Day Mount Spokane Road. It would join with the Cook's Auto Road. In the 1920s, automobile traffic increased dramatically, and it was suggested to use the Day Mount Spokane Road on the way up and the Big Meadows Road for the return trip. In 1937, the Deadman Creek Road was opened and became the main route to Mount Spokane. The older Big Meadows/Cook's Auto Road was still popular and would be used as secondary road for many years to come. (AAA.)

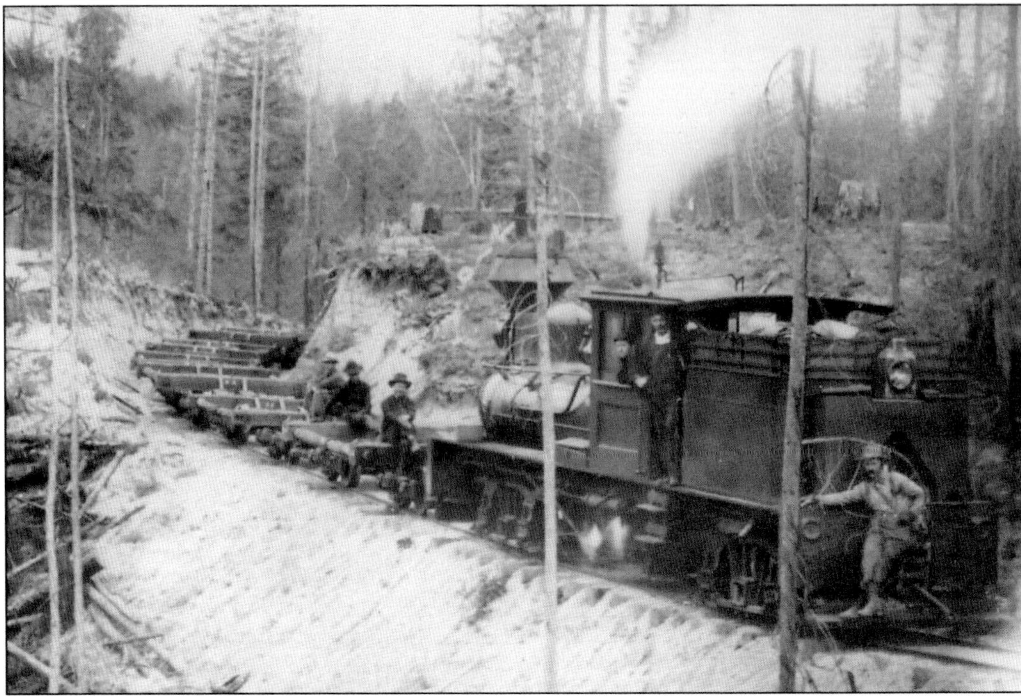

In 1905, Francis Cook tried to finance the construction of a railroad up the west side of the mountain, only to fail because of lack of investors. During the 1920s, the Edwards and Bradford Sawmill at Elk, Washington, successfully built a Shay logging railroad from its mill in Elk to the slopes of Mount Spokane to harvest timber and then ship it on the railroad back to the mill in Elk. This logging railroad had extended around Mount Spokane to the southern slope of the mountain. Later, parts of the Deadman Creek Road were built on portions of this old railroad bed. (Above, AC; below, Hearn.)

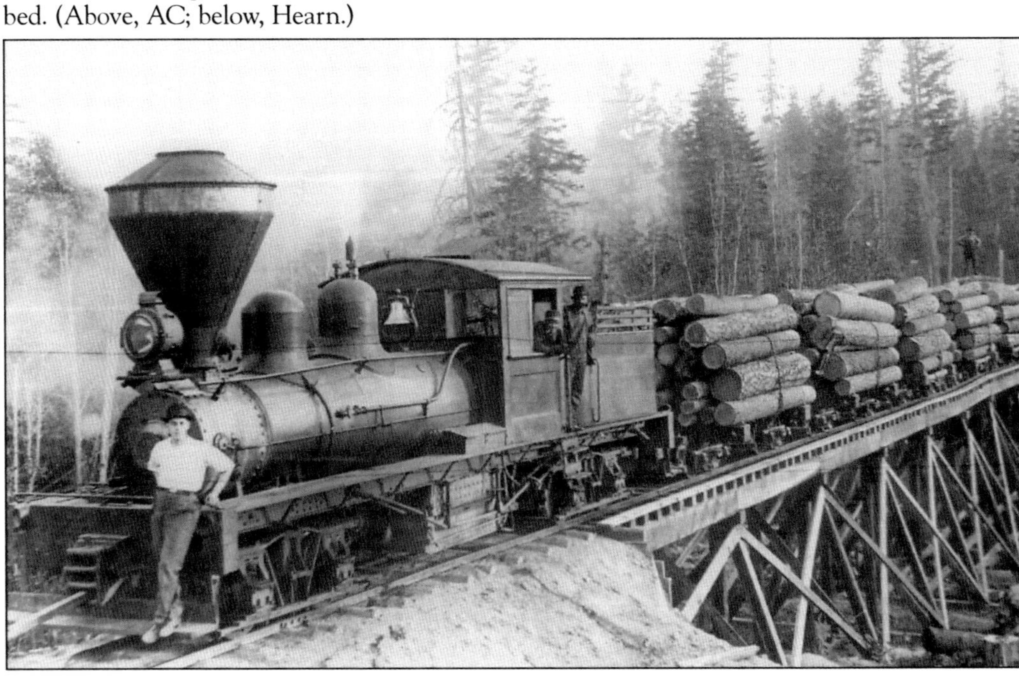

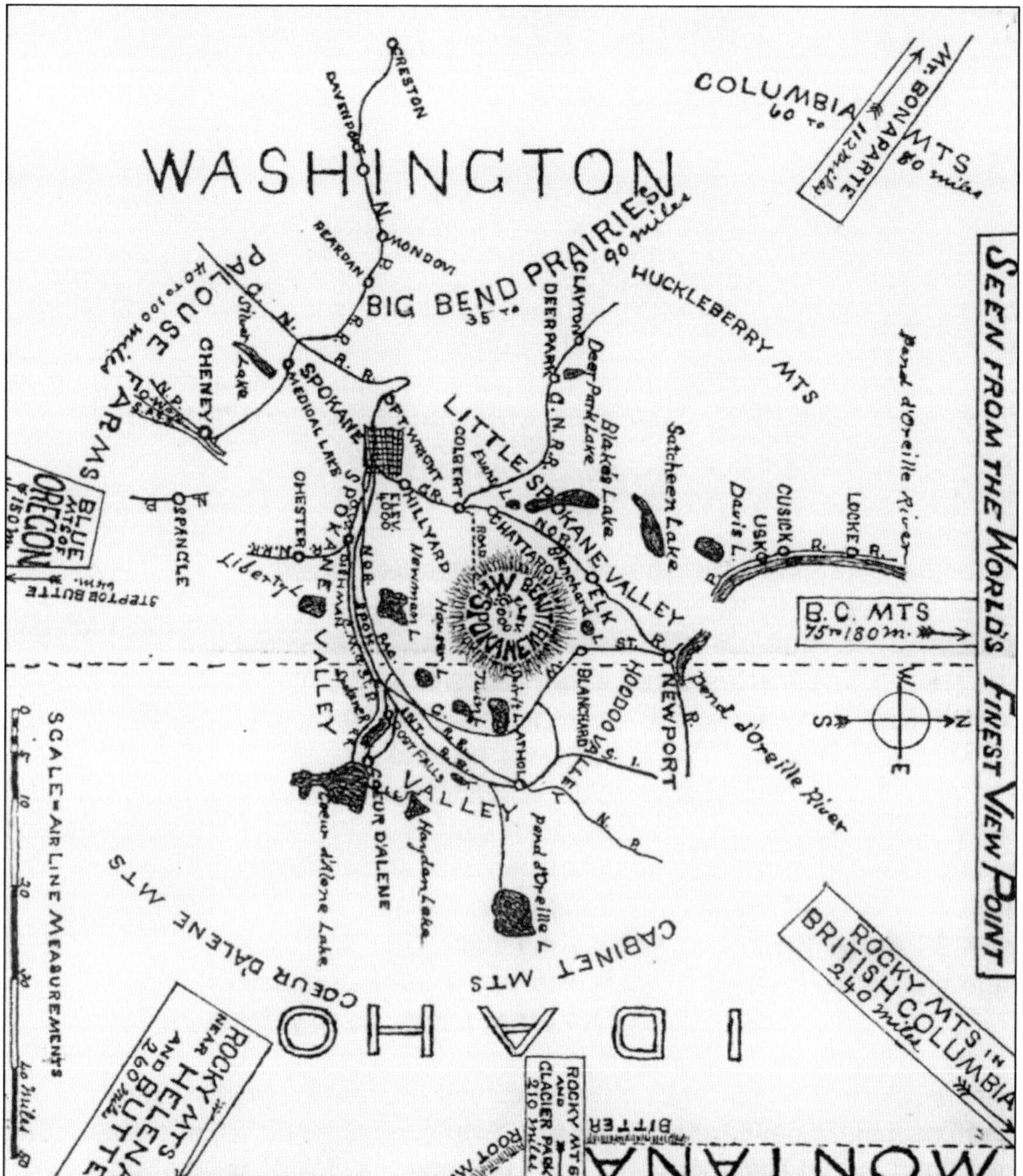

Francis Cook drew this c. 1916 map of the Mount Spokane area with his personal comments added. For some time, it was the only map of the Mount Spokane area. On the sides of the map is text (not included here) that describes the summit's views. The text mentions that the scenes are incomparably beautiful on a clear winter day and that the air was invigorating and healthful. The park entrance fee is listed as 50¢ with saddled ponies for rent at 50¢ per hour. The text concludes with the fact that the beauty of Mount Spokane is unparalleled and that all people should see it. It is believed that Francis Cook handed this map out to citizens for free. (Courtesy of Doris J. Woodward and the Cook family.)

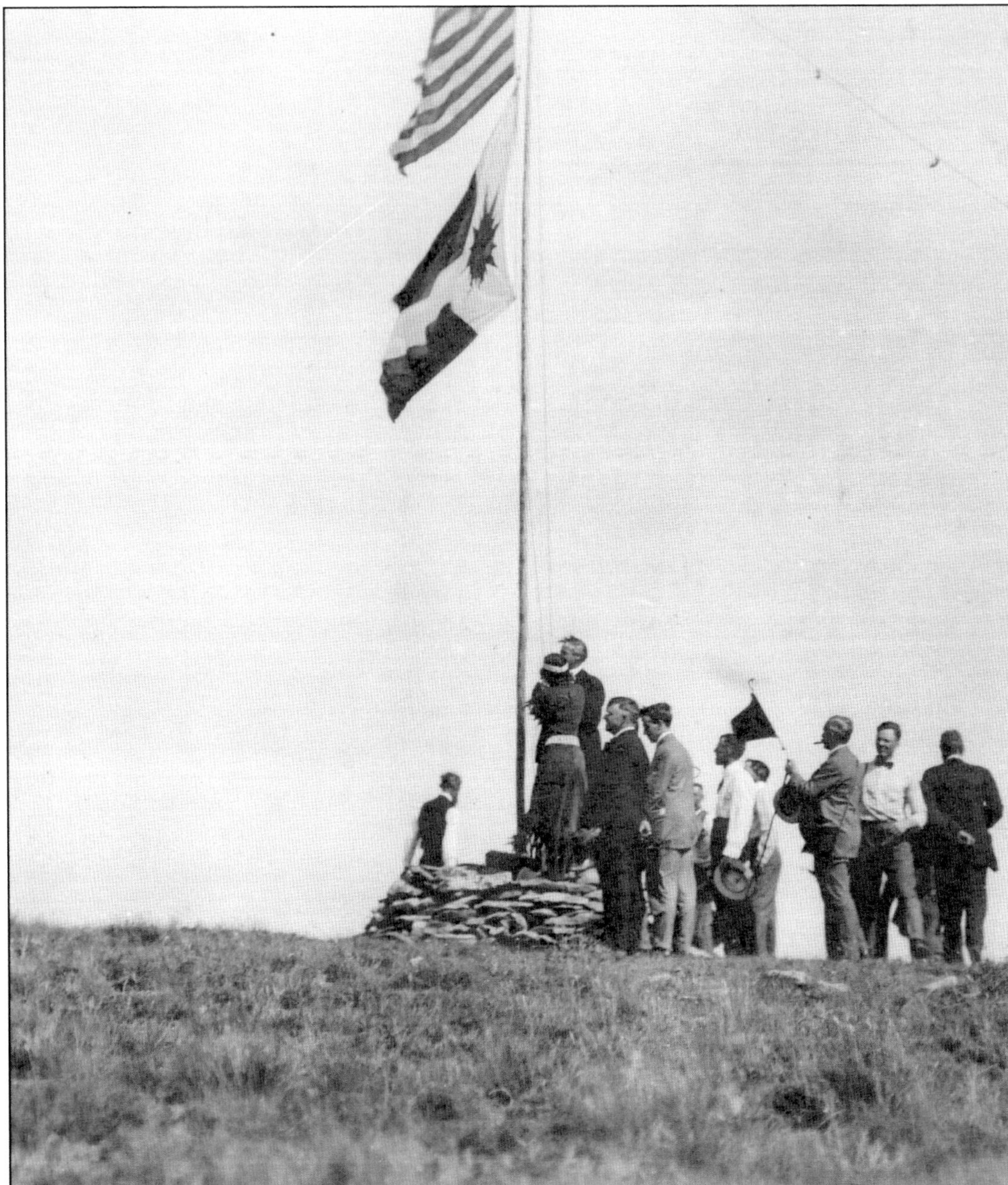

This photograph shows the official August 23, 1912, name-change ceremony at the summit of Mount Spokane with flags flying in the breeze. Prior to 1912, Mount Spokane had several different names. While surveying the boundary between the United States and Canada, the Boundary Commission issued reports and maps from 1859 to 1861 of surveyed areas. On a map of the Spokane country, the mountain location is shown with an Indian name "Mount Checolsum." Other early names were "Mount Baldy" and "Mount Carlton." After 1912, the Mount Spokane name became official. (NWR-SPL.)

Two

The Early Years

With the help of Francis Cook and the citizens of Spokane, the mountain was officially dedicated as Mount Spokane on August 23, 1912. Dignitaries, officials, and citizens made their way up Cook's Auto Road as far as they could drive their automobiles. From that point, they hiked to the summit for the mountain's name-change ceremony planned for 2:00 p.m.

Washington State governor Marion E. Hay, Spokane mayor W.J. Hindley, and Miss Spokane Marguerite Motie were among those on hand. At the summit, a flagpole was erected with both the national and city flags. Governor Hay and Miss Spokane said a few remarks, several dynamite cartridges were set off to mark the occasion, and Mount Carleton, alias "Old Baldy," officially became Mount Spokane.

The county did very little at first, but by the 1930s improvements began on sections of road to the mountain. Before he died, Cook legally transferred his land owned at Mount Spokane to the county with the understanding that the area would be established as a county park for all to visit and enjoy. Business and civic leaders in Spokane began to lobby the state to take the area over as a state park. Several years of meetings with state officials finally paid off. On July 8, 1927, the area of Mount Spokane officially became a Washington State park. A dedication was planned for Saturday, August 20, 1927, on the summit. This dedication was a large event with over 400 people in attendance. Those on hand for the dedication included Washington State officials, Spokane County commissioners, Spokane businessmen, and citizens.

People became aware of the picturesque wintertime landscape near the summit. Photographs and postcards began to be produced featuring Mount Spokane. It is safe to say that every subject, countryside, and city image has graced a postcard. Mount Spokane is no exception. By the 1940s, postcards of the summit and ski areas were common.

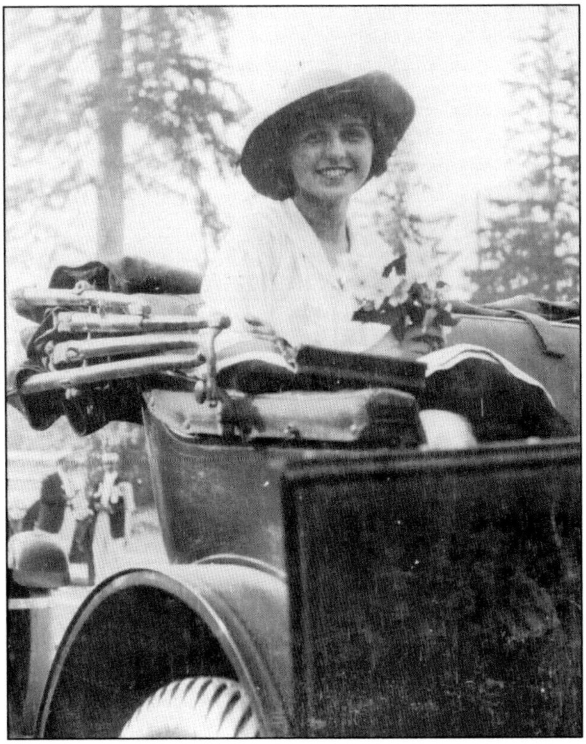

Miss Spokane Marguerite Motie is seated in the automobile on the trip to the mountain for the name-change and dedication ceremony. The City of Spokane during this time had an official hostess, who represented the city on official duties and attended civic events throughout the city and the Inland Empire. Marguerite was the city's first Miss Spokane and she, along with Spokane's mayor, represented the citizens of Spokane. Shown here is a very early Spokane Chamber of Commerce brochure advertising the Spokane country and Mount Spokane in particular. On this front page, the City of Spokane's own Miss Spokane welcomes the traveler to the area. The beauty on Mount Spokane that awaits the traveler is mentioned in the brochure. (Left, TSB; Right, GSI.)

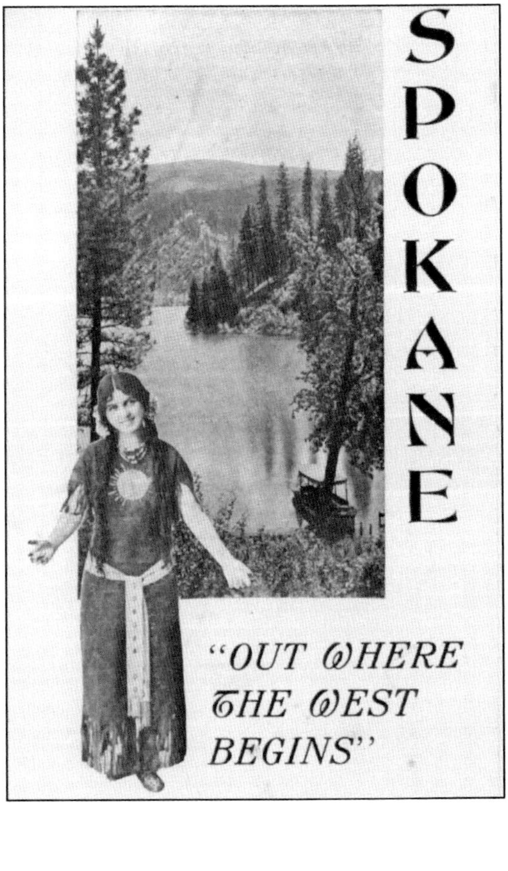

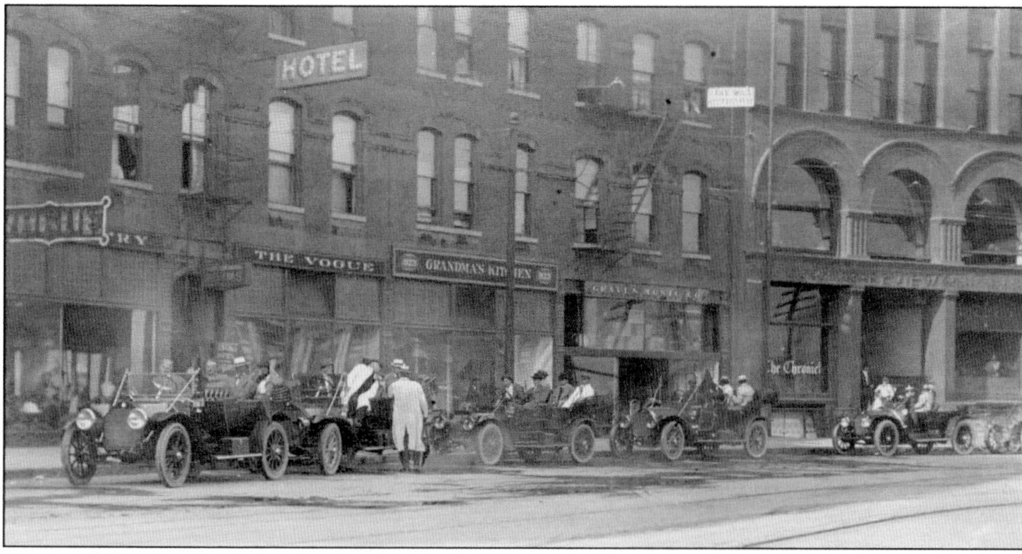

Automobiles await the start of the road trip to the mountain for the name-change and dedication ceremony. During the 1920s, Spokane's local papers, the *Spokane Chronicle* and *Spokesman Review,* both owned by the same publisher, the Cowles family, would showcase feature articles in their newspapers of these automobile trips to the mountain. Gathering the morning of a trip in downtown Spokane in front of the newspaper headquarters, all would convoy as far up the mountain as the existing road would permit. The group would then hike the remaining short distance to the summit. Shown below on the day of the name-change and dedication ceremony, Francis Cook is standing holding a flag and vase on the right, while Washington State governor Marion E. Hay is seated in the automobile behind the driver. (Both, TSB.)

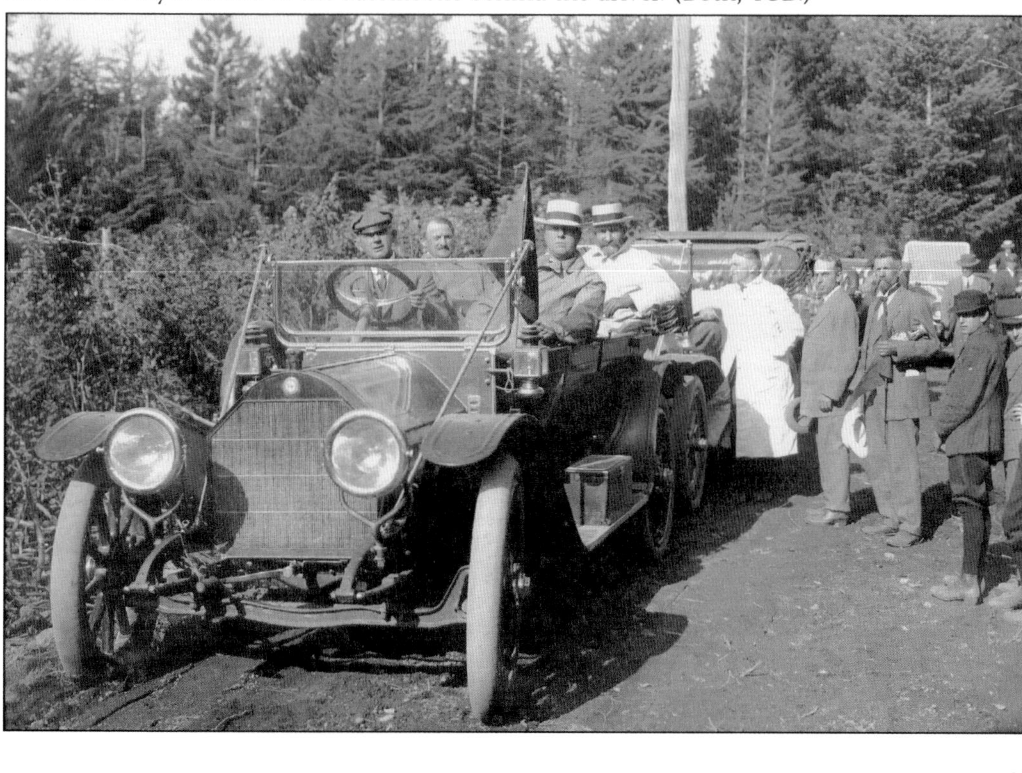

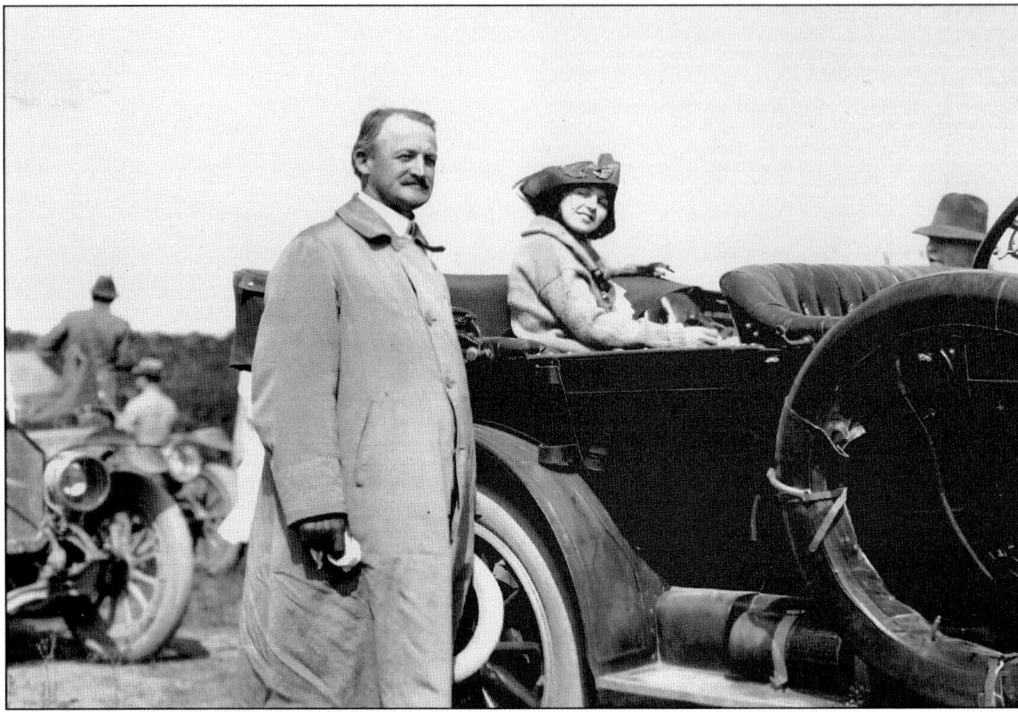

Miss Spokane is seated with Governor Hay alongside the motorcade. The photograph below shows the officials and dignitaries gathered at the summit in a small shelter, which was constructed of poles and a white canvas roof. Resting under the shelter, Miss Spokane is the one turning and looking at the camera. (Both, TSB.)

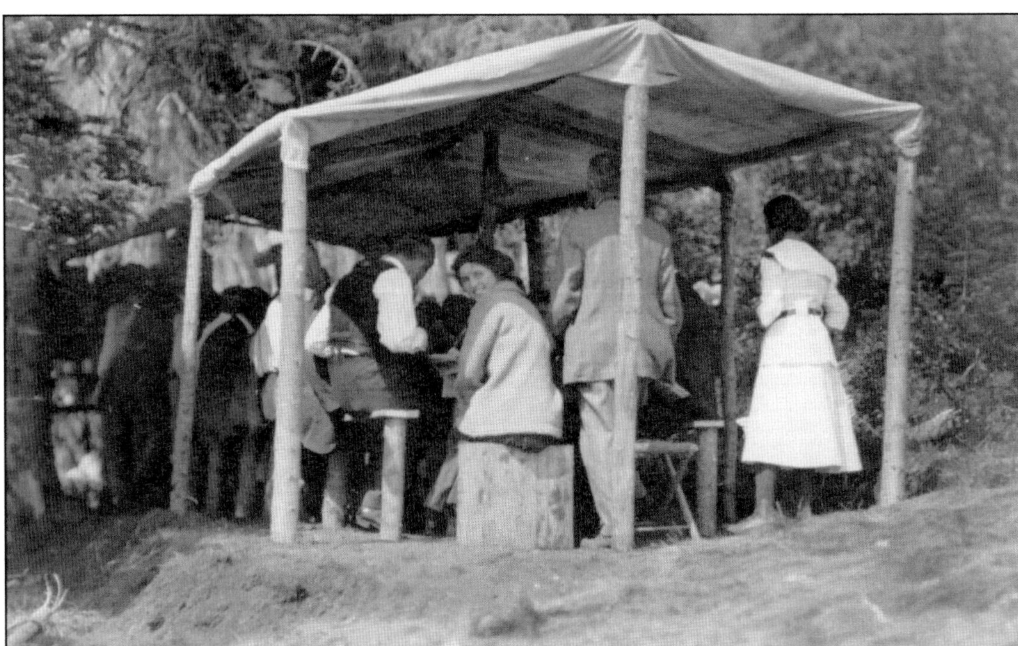

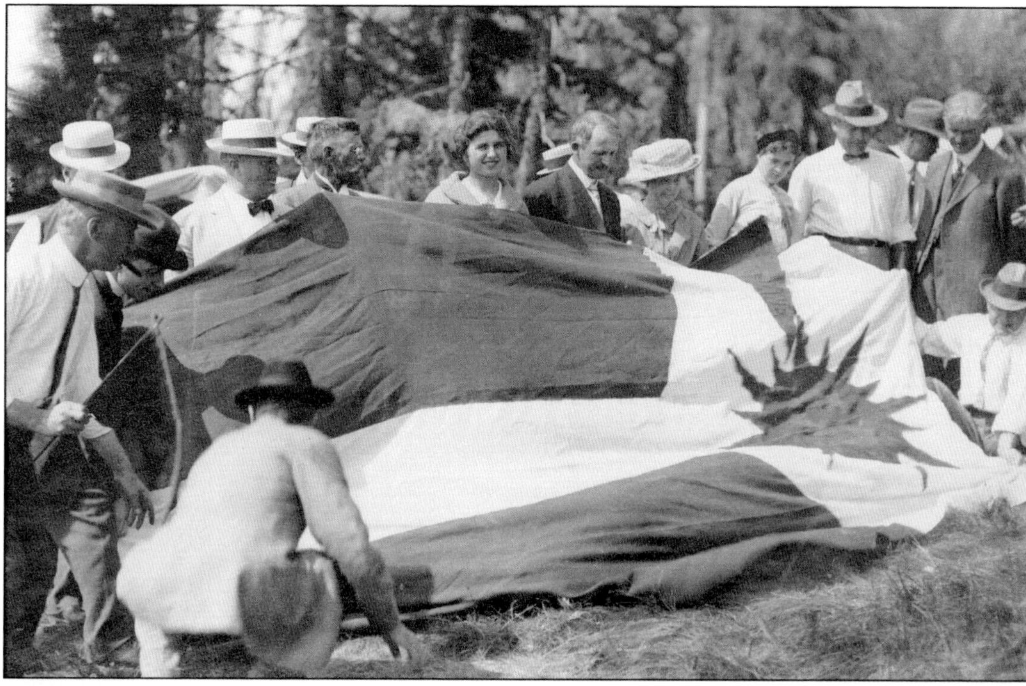

The group attending the ceremony is posing with the City of Spokane's flag. Everyone was proud of the moment and felt honored to be present for the event. The photograph below shows the entire group with the flag. Several members of the Cook family were present. Spokane's Mayor Hindley is standing just above the white portion of the flag on the left. To the right of the mayor is Winnie Cook; Francis Cook is just behind her. From left to right, Emma Cook and Florence Cook are pictured to the right of Francis. Miss Spokane and Governor Hay are shown in the center. Also present, Edith Cook is standing and holding the end of the flag. (Both, TSB.)

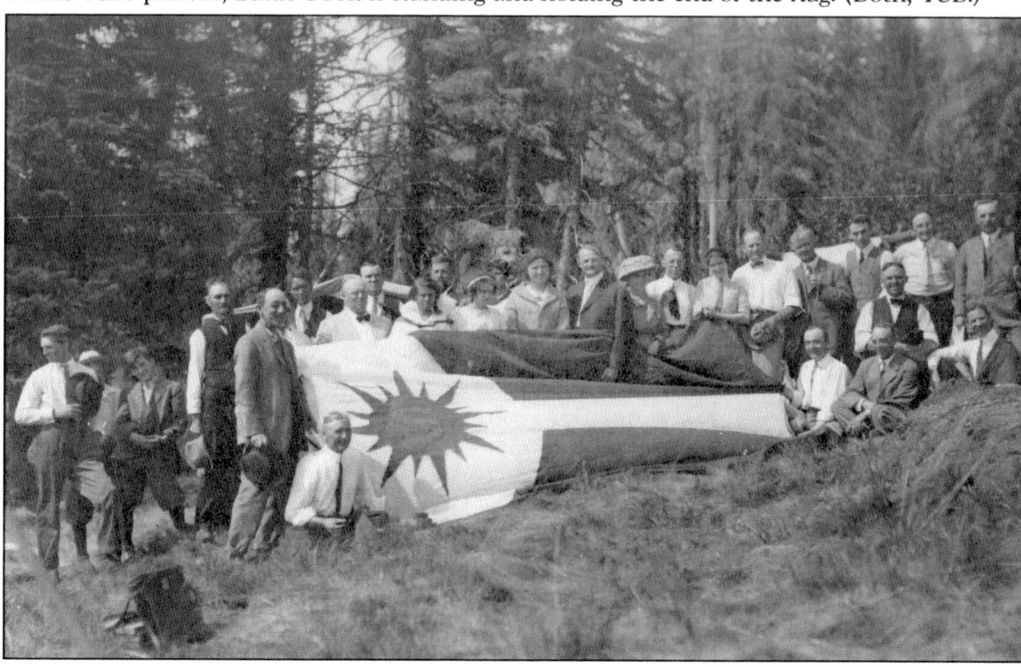

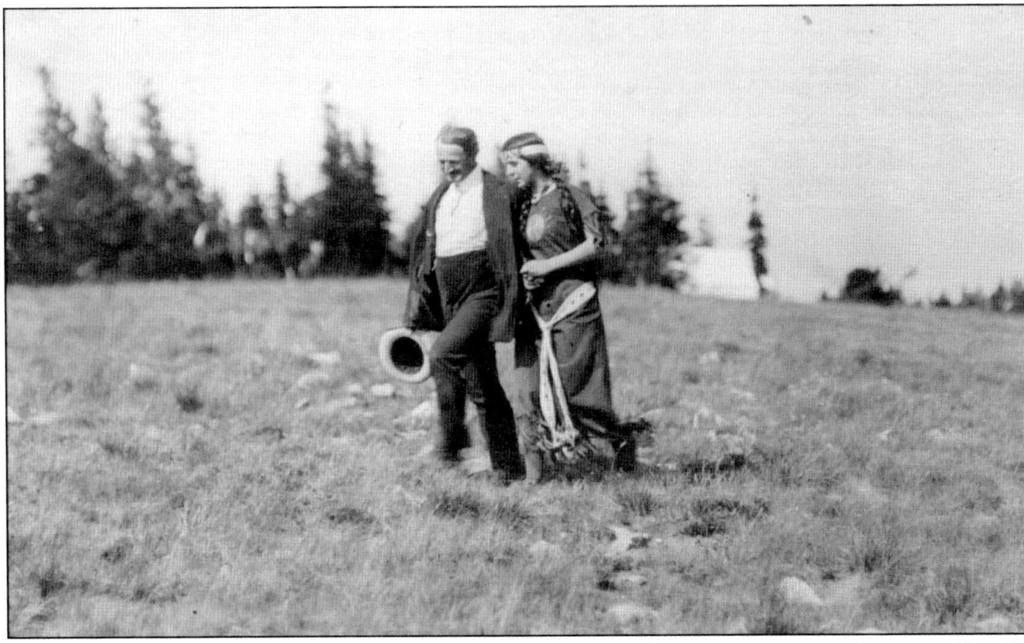

Washington State governor Marion Hay and Miss Spokane Marguerite Motie are taking a stroll at the summit. Note the white-colored roof of the shelter in the background. There were quite a few people who made the trip up the mountain for the dedication. Local reports say the group left the mountain shortly after the conclusion of the ceremony and was back in Spokane by 6:00 p.m. (TSB.)

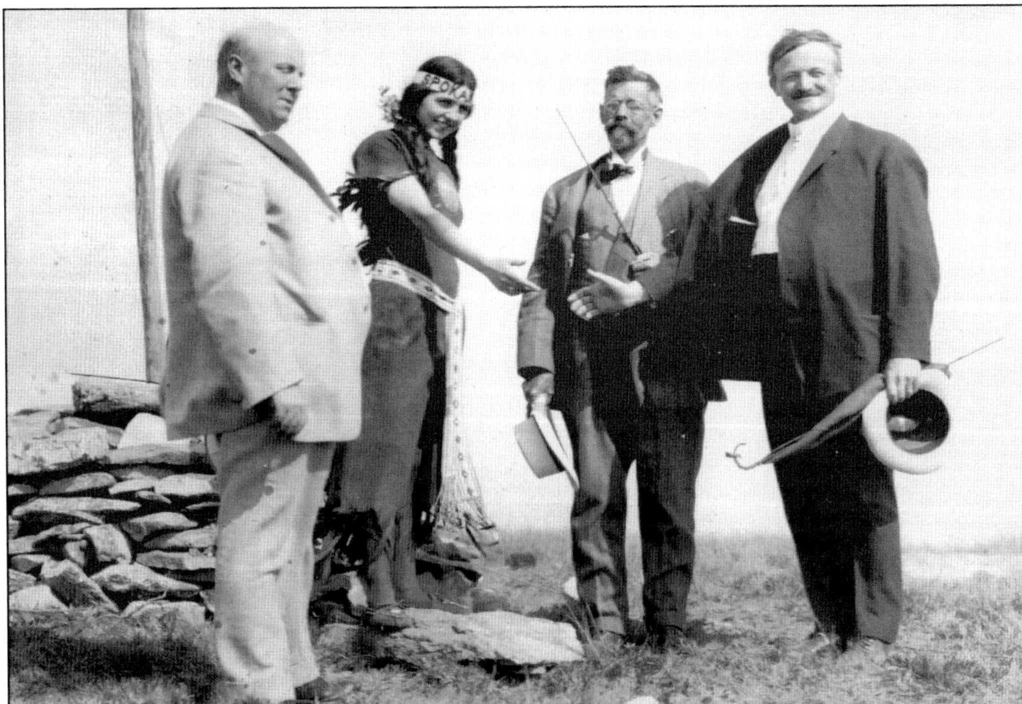

At the base of the flagpole, pictured from left to right, are Spokane's Mayor W.J. Hindley, Marguerite Motie, Francis Cook, and Governor Hay. (TSB.)

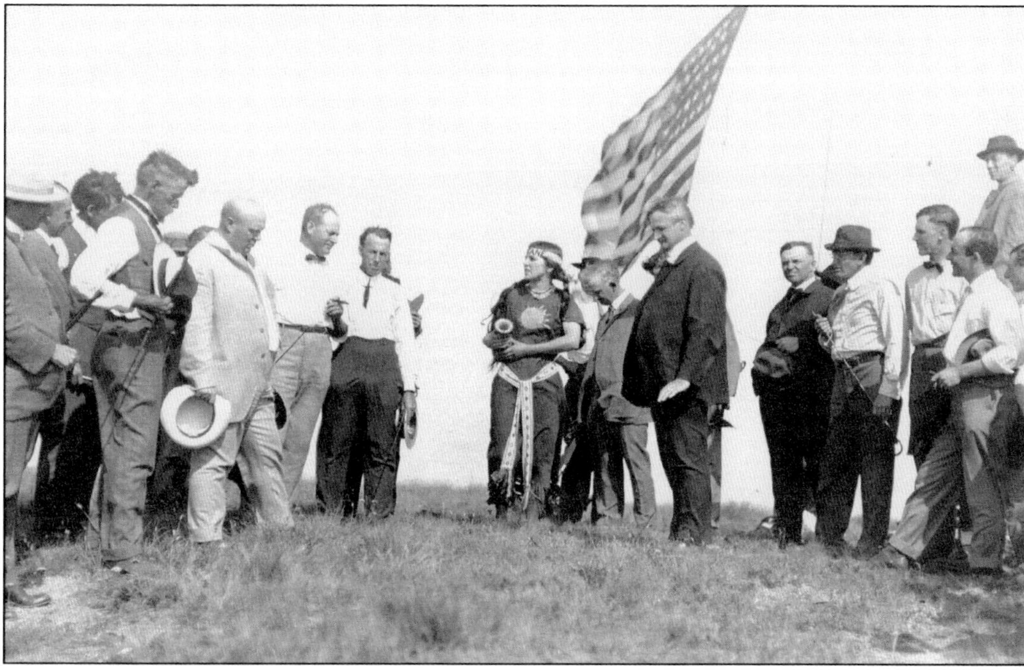

The group at the summit is photographed with the American flag during the final prayer of dedication. Note the small vase that Miss Spokane is holding. This was used to carry water from the Skyline Spring, located near the summit. The water was poured on the ground at the summit for the purpose of christening the mountain. In order to support a temporary flagpole, a rock carrion was hastily built around a pole made from a long log. In the photograph below, the governor and Miss Spokane can be seen posing on the rocks with the others looking on. (Both, TSB.)

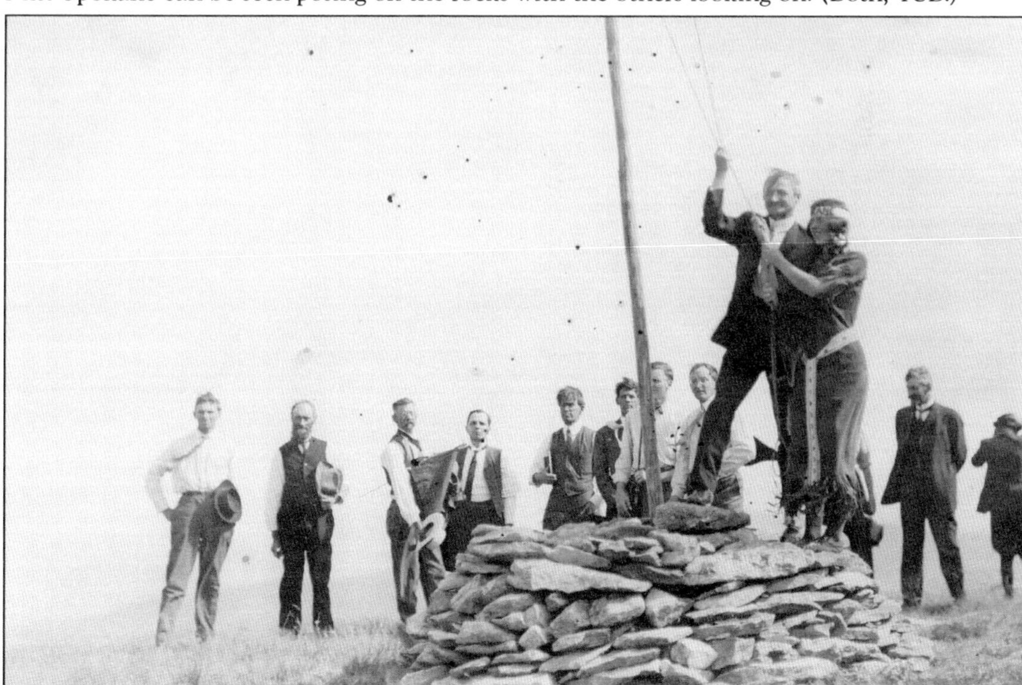

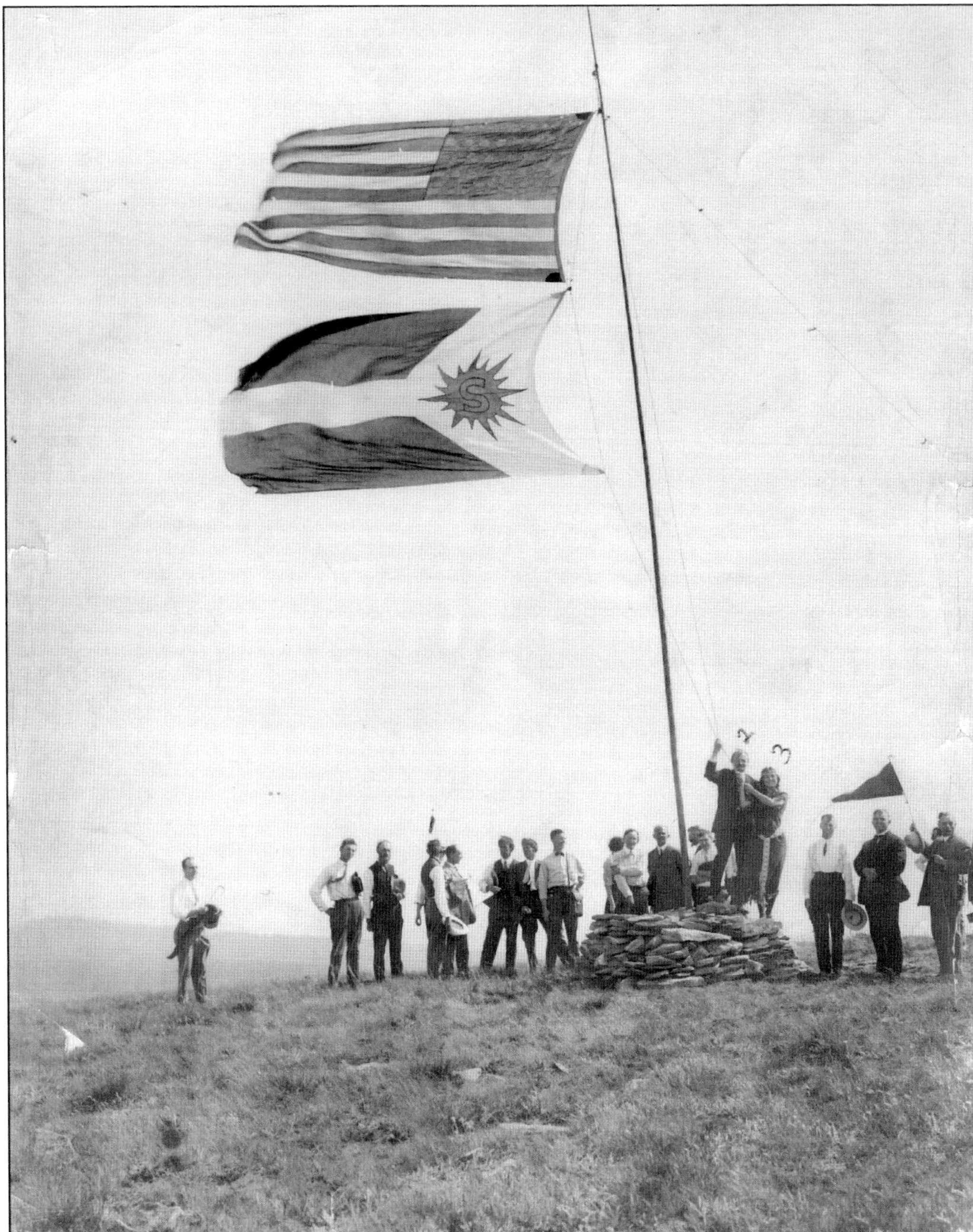

The flags are flying high. The flags of the United States and the City of Spokane are waving in the summer breeze on August 23, 1912, as the governor and Miss Spokane tie off the flag ropes. The next day, Spokane newspapers, the *Spokesman Review* and *Spokane Chronicle*, carried full articles and photographs of the name change to Mount Spokane and dedication. (TSB.)

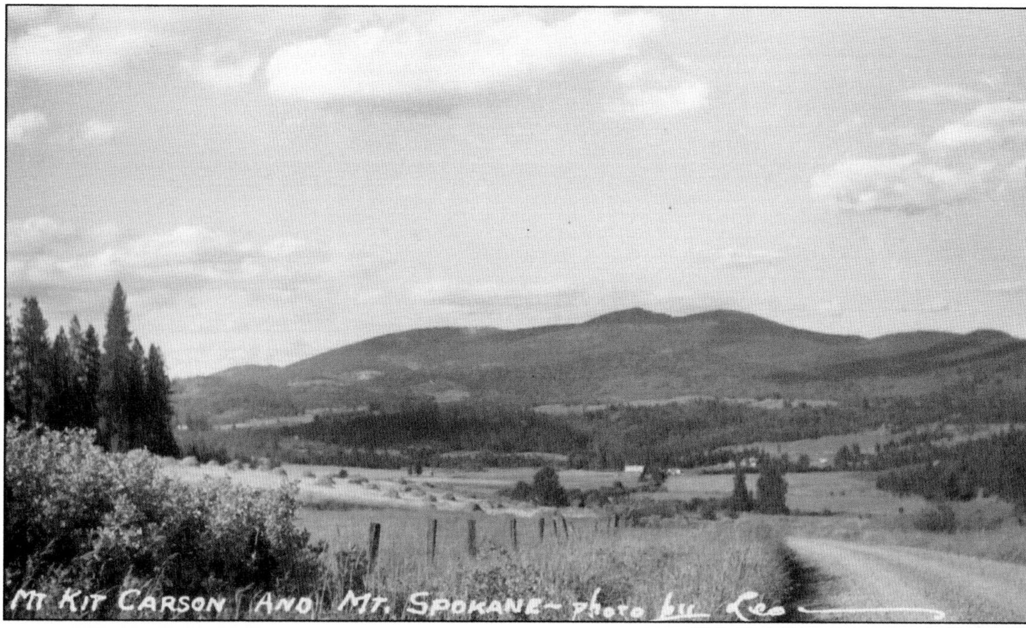

This early photograph was taken at Green Bluff, just northeast of the city of Spokane. This is a good view of the entire chain of mountains around Mount Spokane. Day Mountain is on the left from the angle of the photograph, and what seems to be the tallest is in fact Mount Kit Carson with an elevation of 5,282 feet. Mount Spokane, with an elevation of 5,883 feet, is to the right of Kit. (NWR-SPL.)

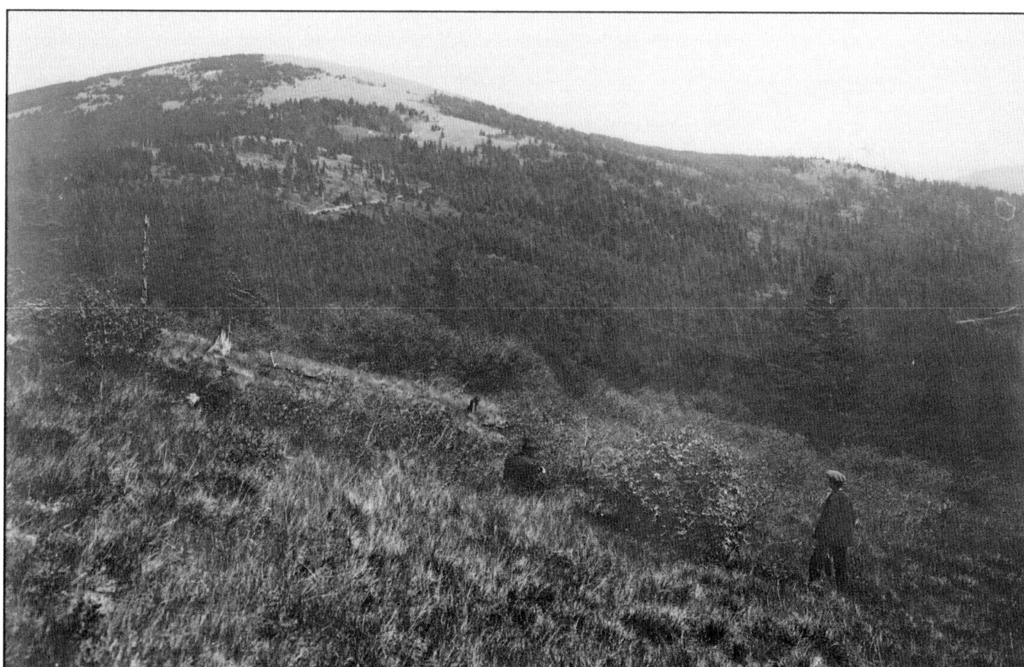

This photograph from the 1920s shows Mount Spokane from Mount Kit Carson. The smaller mountain just below Mount Spokane is Beauty Mountain, and what seems to be a scar on the side of Mount Spokane is the Cook's Auto Road. Note the two men in the foreground. (NWR-SPL.)

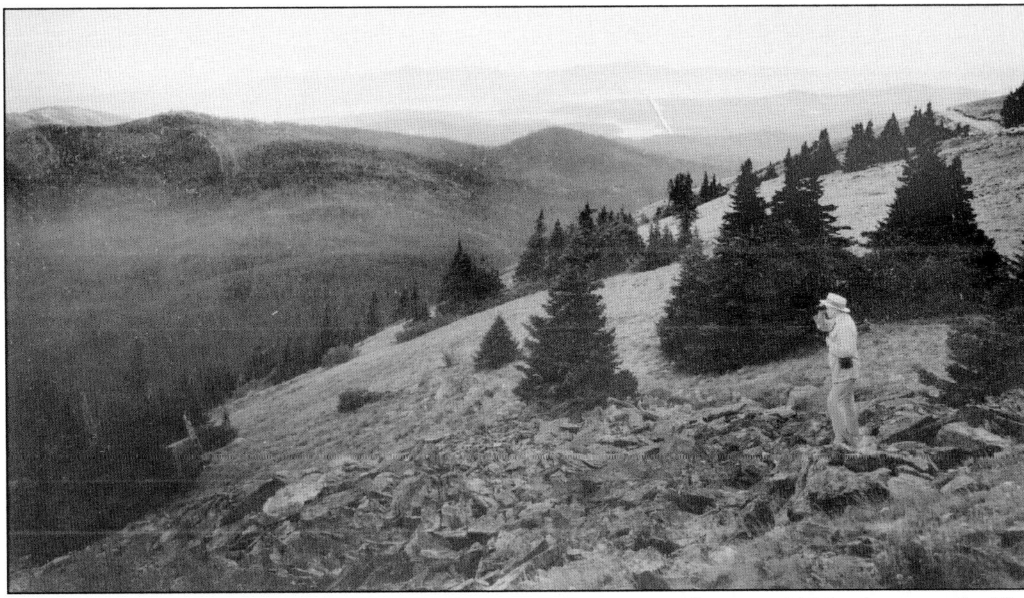

The view from the summit of Mount Spokane can be seen in this rare 1920s photograph. The photograph was taken looking to the south toward Newman Lake with the Spokane Valley in the background. Note the small rocks scattered about, which are typical at the summit. Below is another rare photograph of wildflowers in full bloom on Mount Kit Carson with Mount Spokane in the distance. During this time, there were several photographs featuring wildflowers with Mount Spokane in the background being circulated around the Spokane area, and some were used for postcards. (Both, NWR-SPL.)

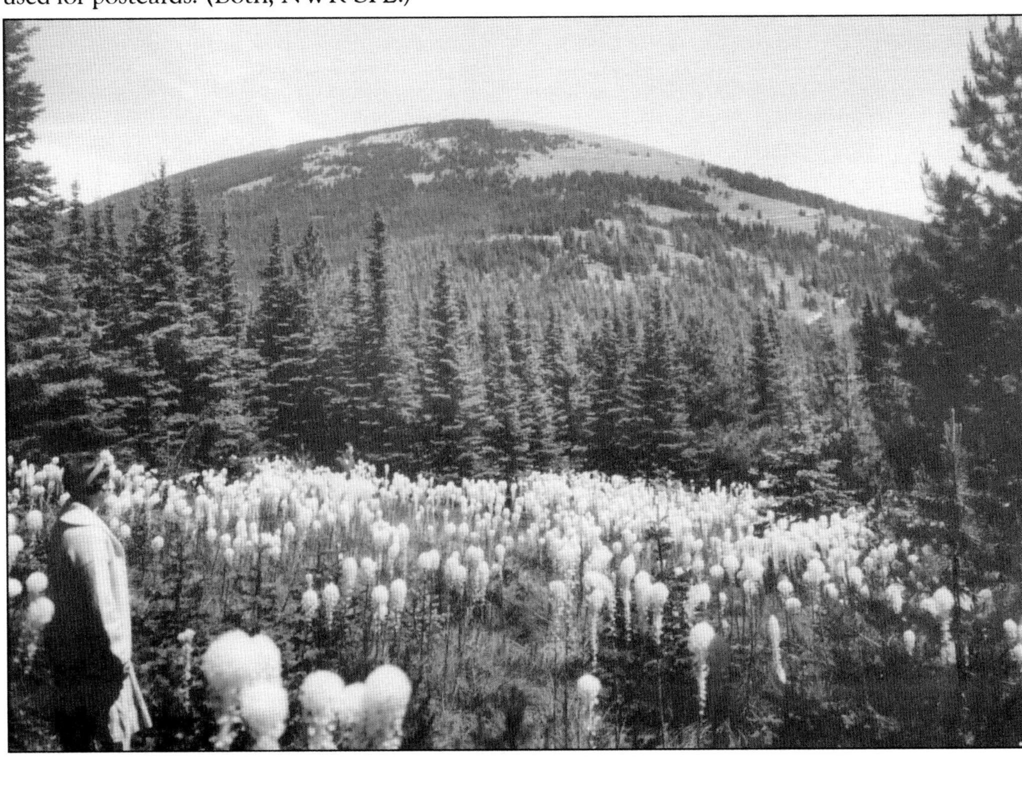

Near the summit, the trees and landscape become so laden with snow and ice that they take on interesting shapes. Skiers and snowshoers on the mountain during the 1920s and 1930s would name the tree shapes according to what they resembled. The *Spokesman Review* and *Spokane Chronicle* photographers, as well as private studios, began to photograph almost anything that was covered by the snow and ice. By the end of the 1950s, there were many photographs taken of the winter landscape near the summit. The photograph at right is of a tree that was named the "Elephant," while the tree photographed below was named "Angel Wings." (Both, NWR-SPL.)

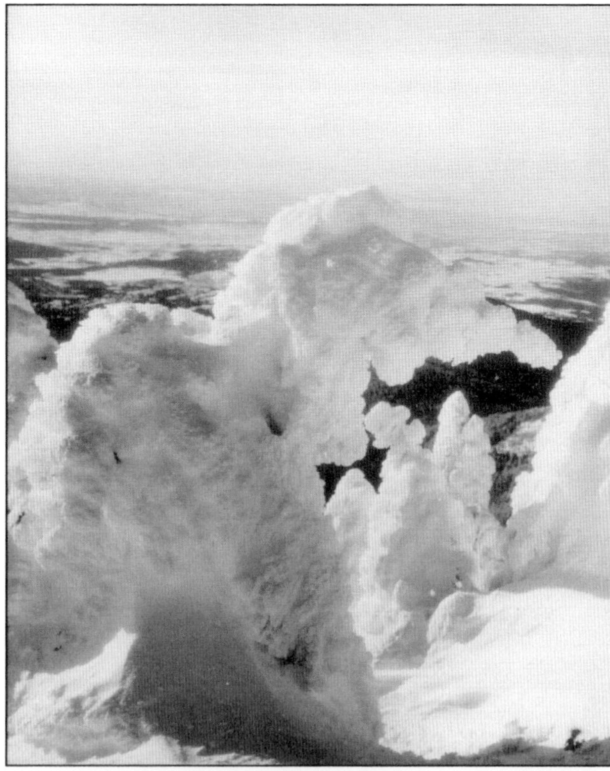

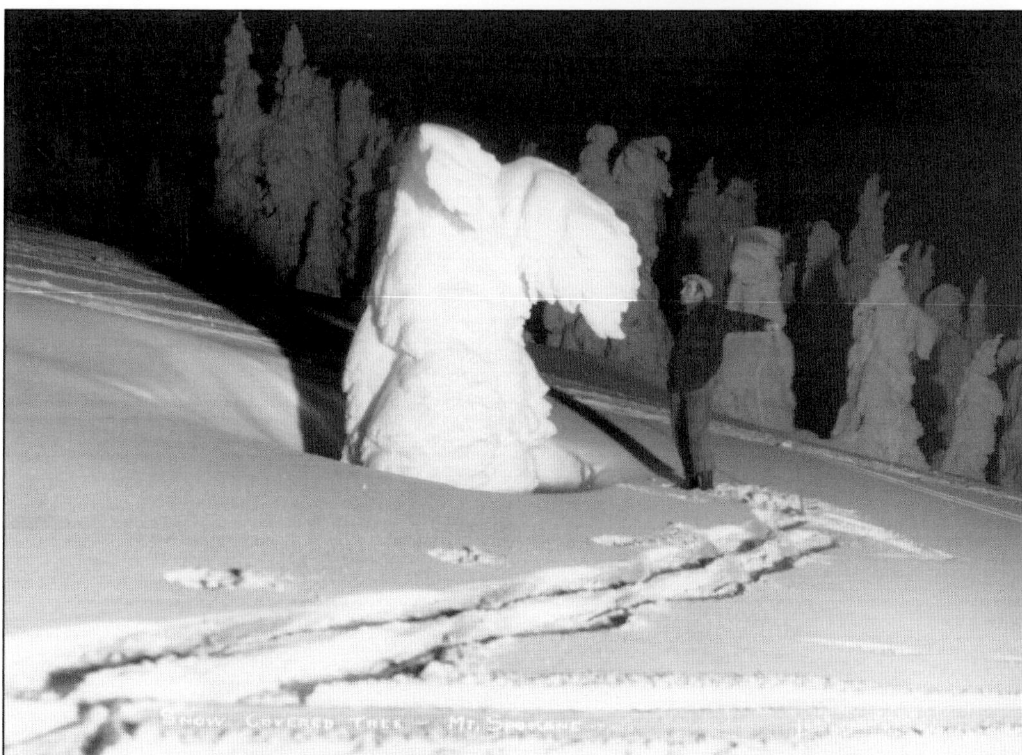

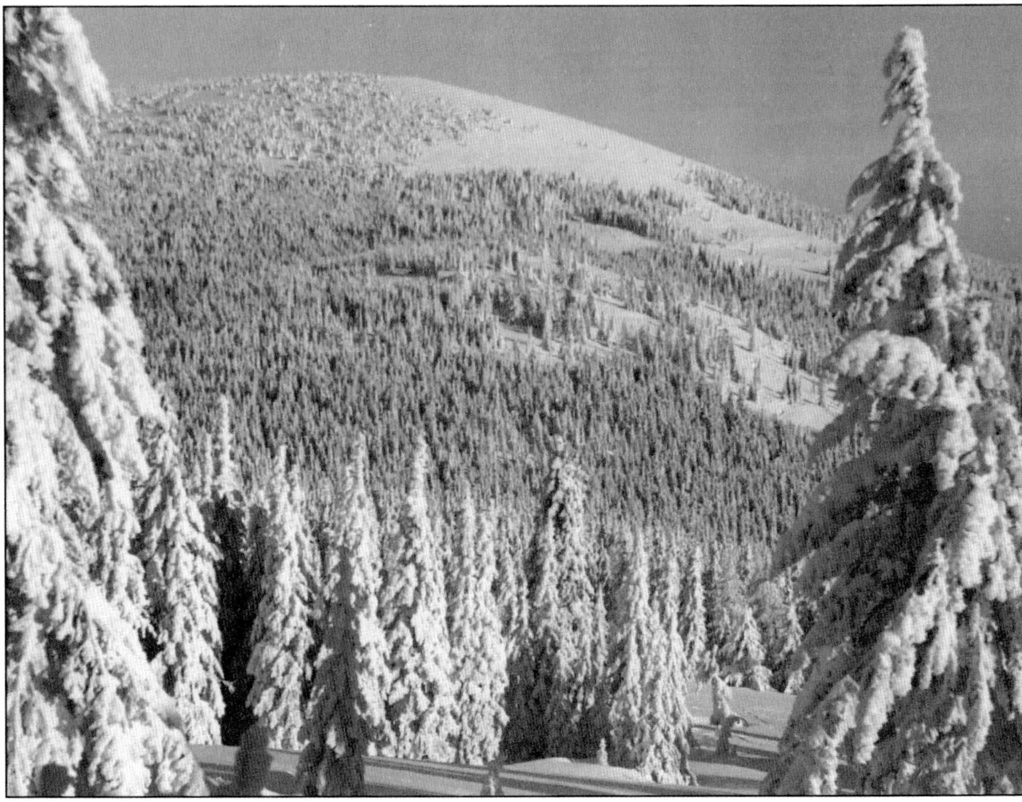

At lower elevations around Mount Spokane, snow can accumulate up to four feet deep from November to April. Above, a winter scene has been cast with the mountain in the background. Farther up the mountain, the snow increases with summit depths averaging from 8 to 12 feet each year. Everything gets coated in snow and ice. Often this wintertime effect is called rime. When snow accumulates on branches, trees begin to take on unique shapes. Below is a tree that has transformed to look like an ocean wave about to overtake a skier. (Above, NWR-SPL; below, Leo.)

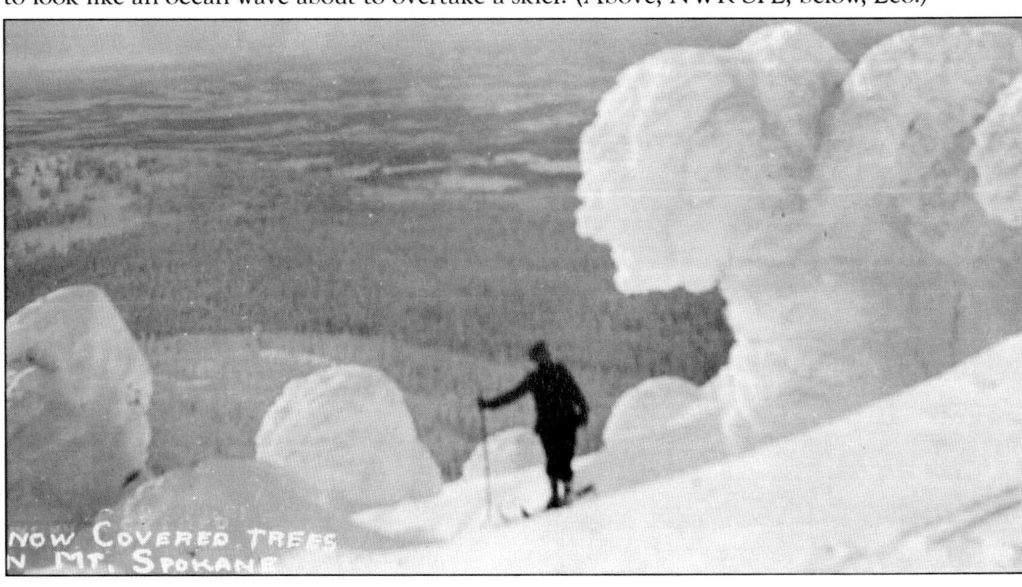

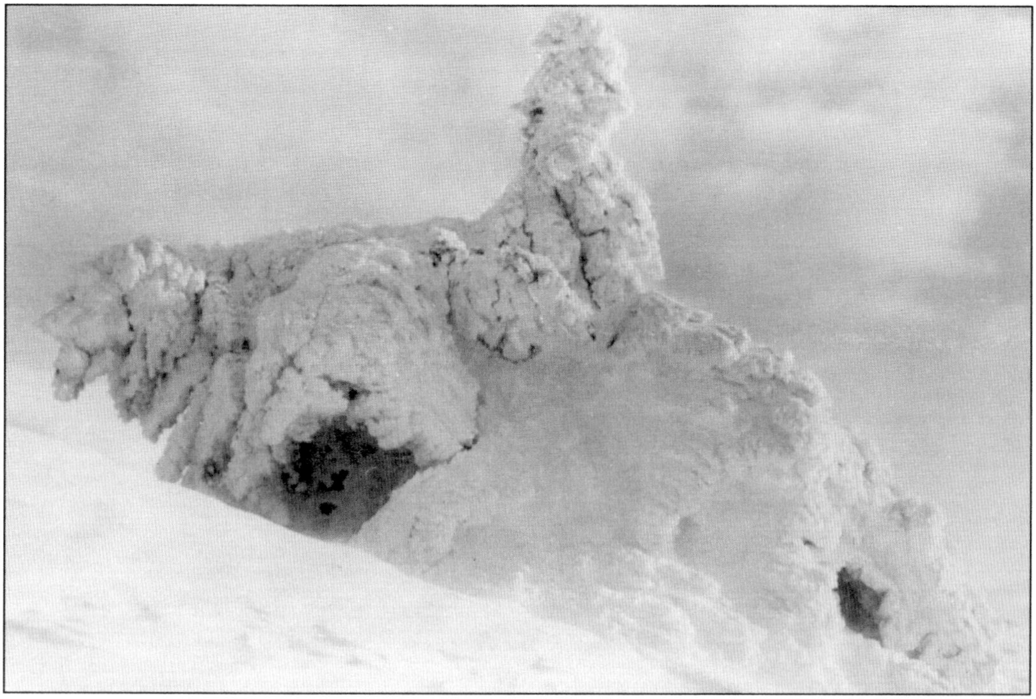

This tree was located near the summit, and the photographer noted its location to go back during the summer months to snap another photograph to compare with the winter scene. Snow has worked its way around every part of the "Rider Tree." Below is the photograph of the "Rider Tree" in the summer. With stark contrast, one can compare the difference that ice and snow make, but yet, the tree maintains its shape to a degree. (Above, NWR-SPL; below, Leo.)

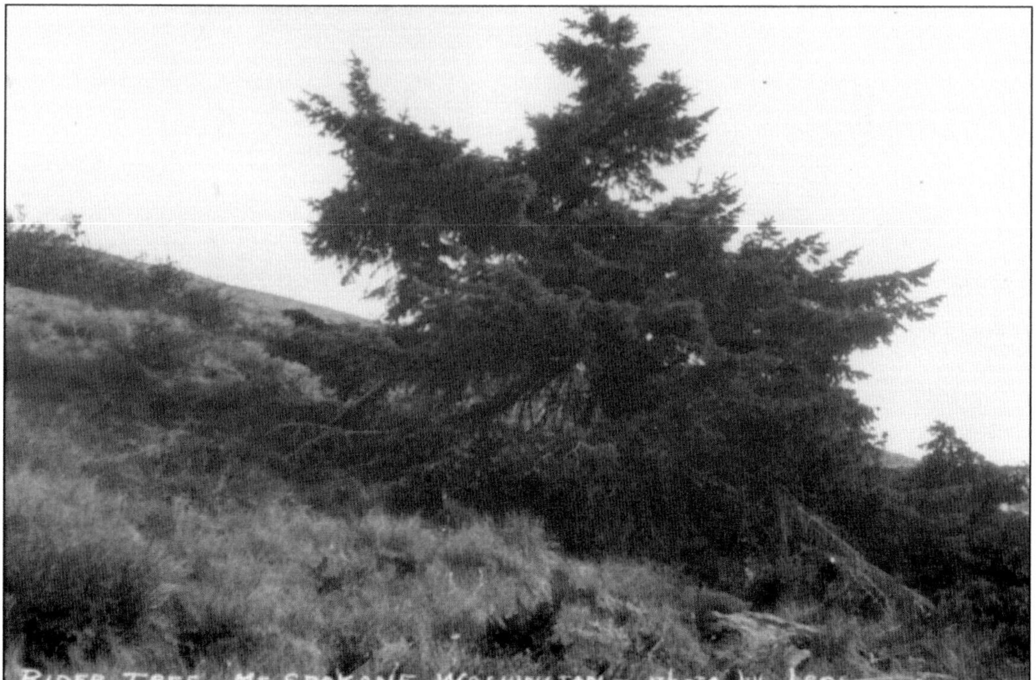

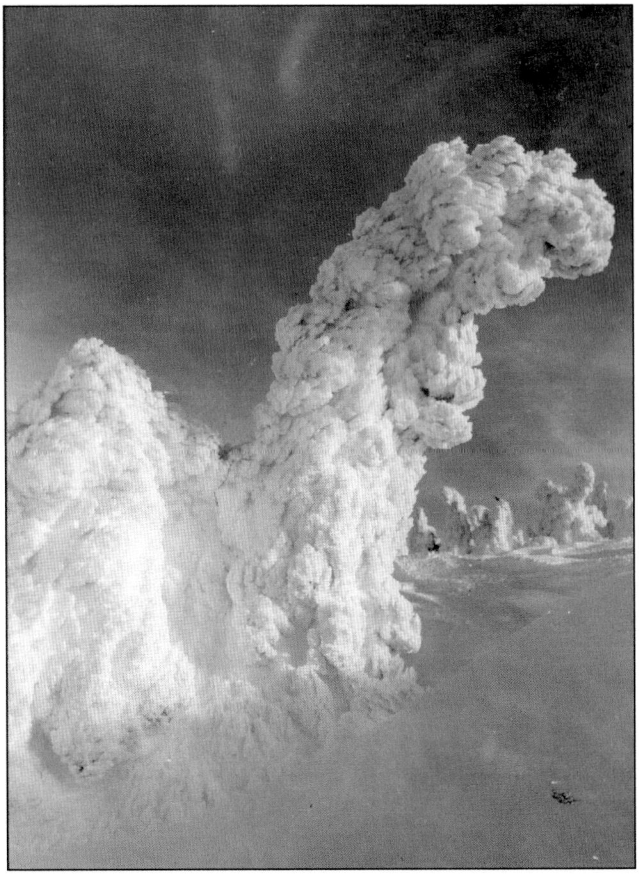

This photograph was taken near the summit, and the tree takes on the appearance of a kneeling camel. These photographs were breathtaking scenes of a fairyland. So much so that *Life* magazine featured a two-page spread of the snow and ice formations atop Mount Spokane. Burton Belknap, a local Spokane amateur photographer, took and submitted the photographs to *Life*. The issue, dated December 12, 1955, included three of his photographs and a short write-up on the winter wonderland summit of Mount Spokane. One photograph was of the Vista House encased in ice, another showed the trees covered in ice crystals, and the third depicted the fire lookout tower swallowed up in ice and snow. At the time, it was reported, Belknap received a call from the *London Daily Mirror* for his photographs to be used in the *Mirror*. (Left, NWR-SPL; below, Leo.)

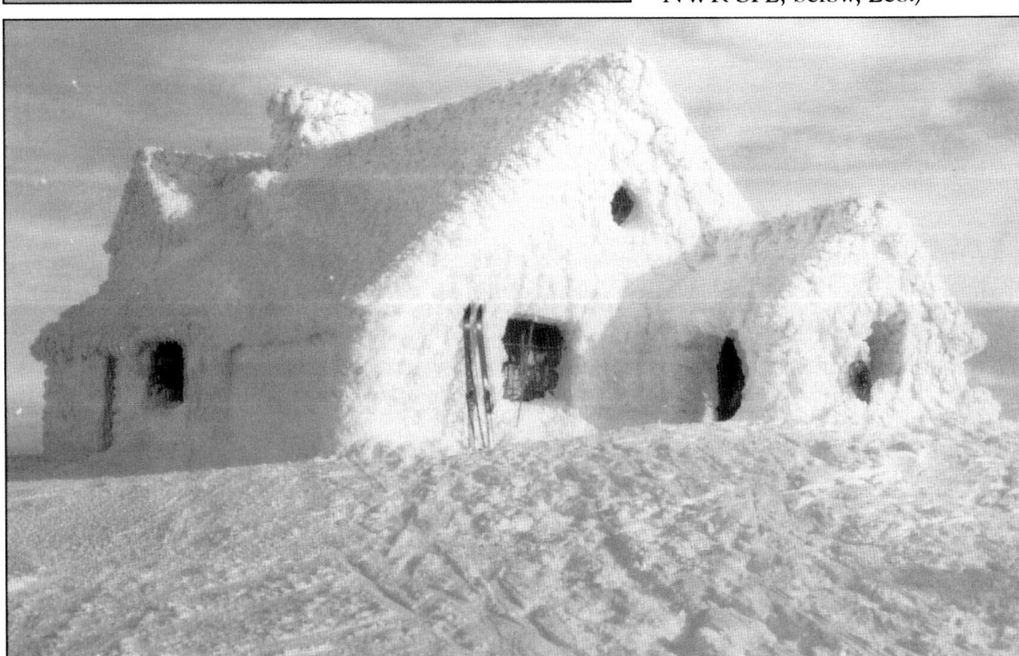

The trees can be encased in snow for weeks at a time, but then, without warning, a steady rain with warm winds can melt the snow and ice. However, within days, the temperature can plummet with another winter snowstorm, dropping several feet of snow. Trees, shrubs, and anything else can be once again frozen solid. Trees laden with snow and ice can form almost any shape. Many times, trees can take on the look of a large scary monster, as shown below. (Both, NWR-SPL.)

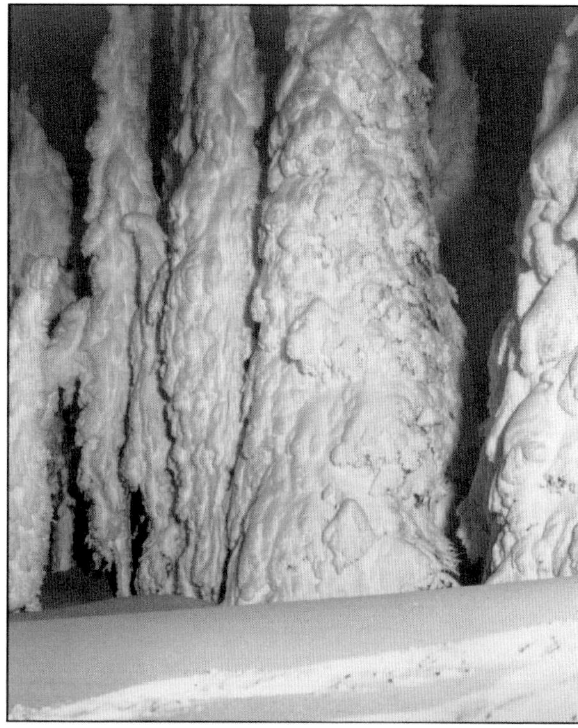

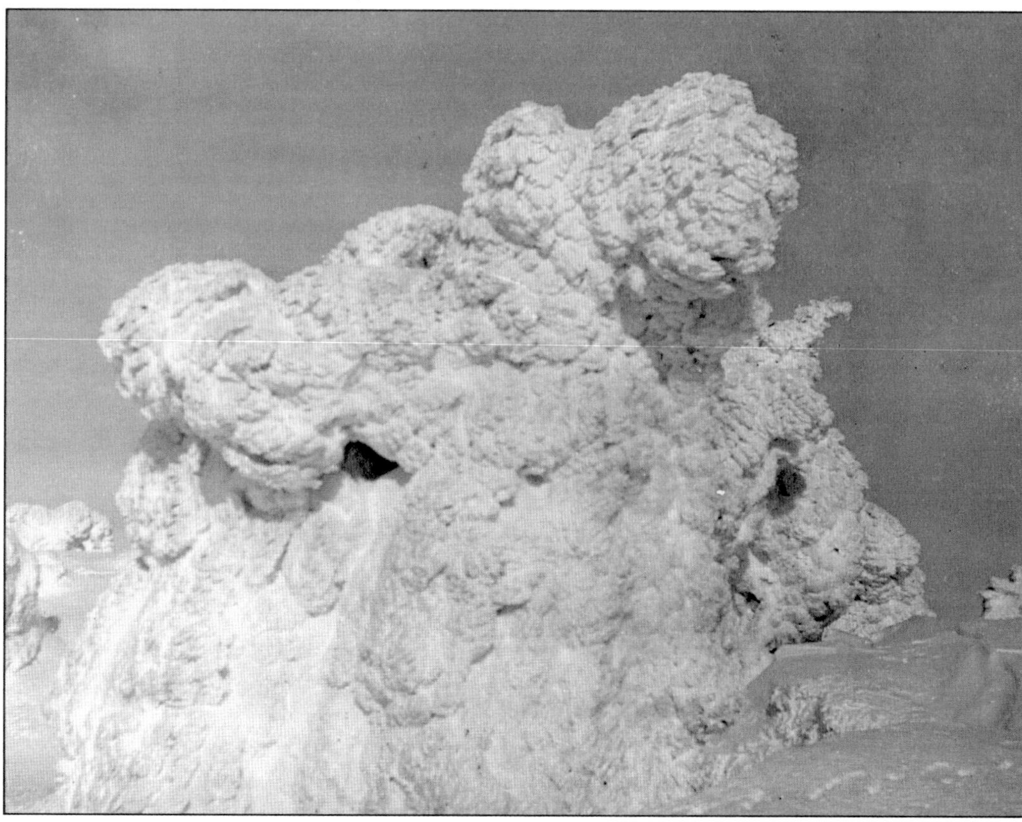

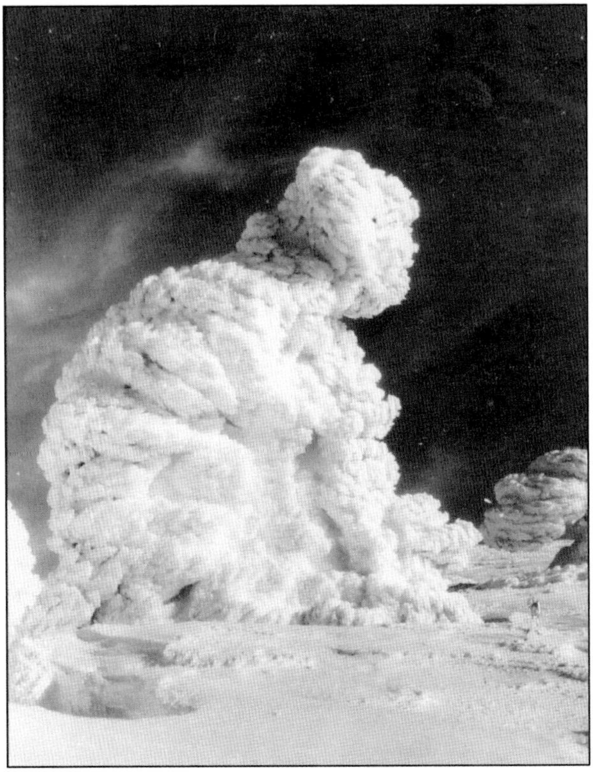

Another photograph of a snow-covered tree resembles a large scary monster that is ready to spring to life. Most of the upper-southern portion of Mount Spokane is treeless, except for the occasional tree or shrub, which gives the appearance of billows of smoke when covered in snow. Wind gusts, sometimes near hurricane force, can have an effect on the displacement of snow and ice. (Both, NWR-SPL.)

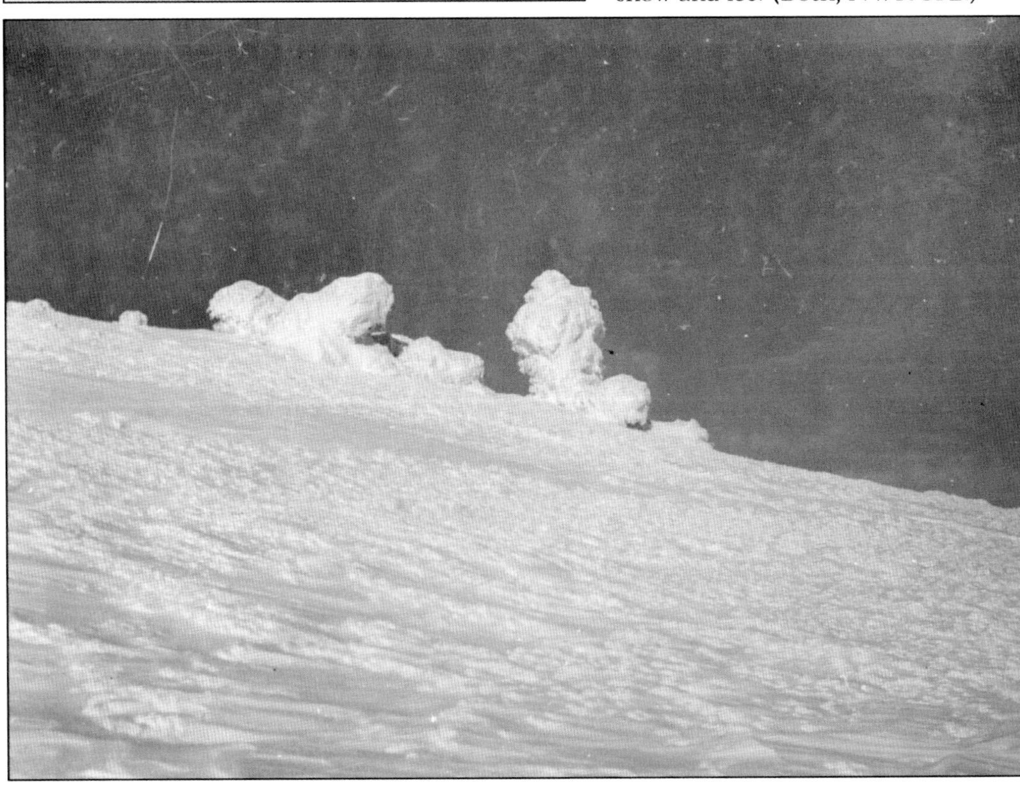

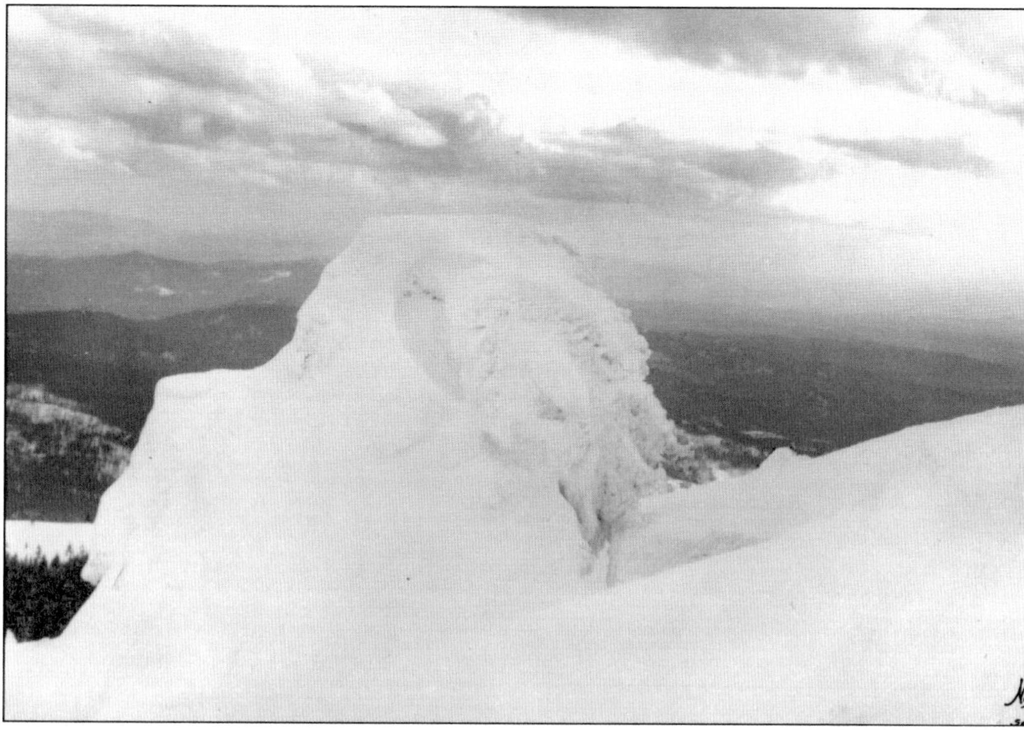

Summit conditions can vary quickly, and the weather is unpredictable. During the winter months, the weather can change from sunshine to snowy conditions almost immediately. With the Vista House being on the summit, it receives its fair share of winter snow and ice. (Above, NWR-SPL; below, TSB.)

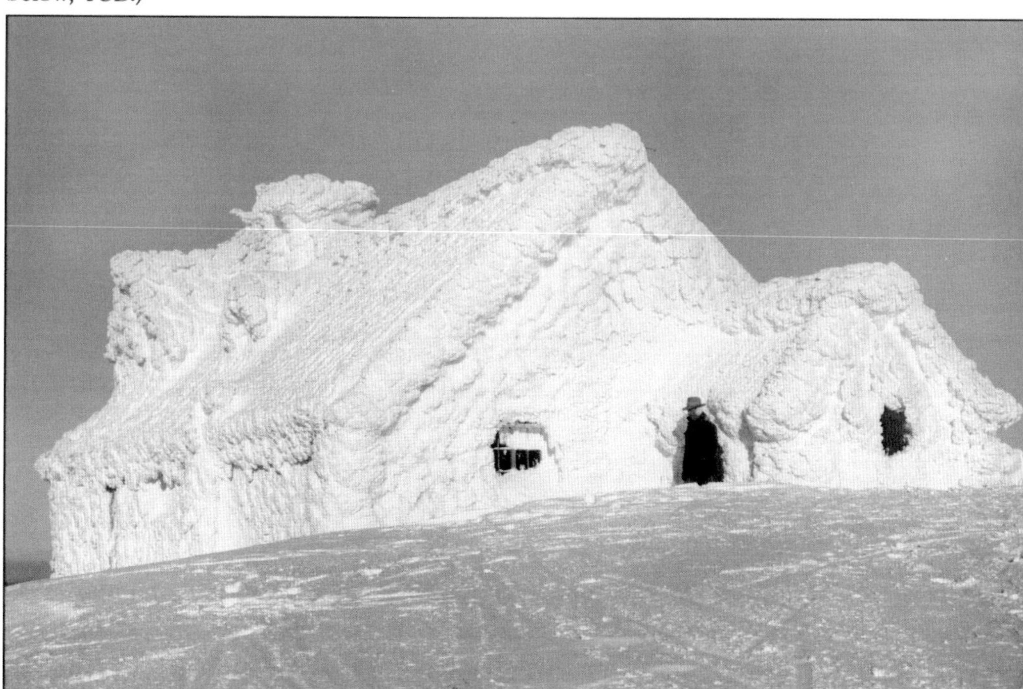

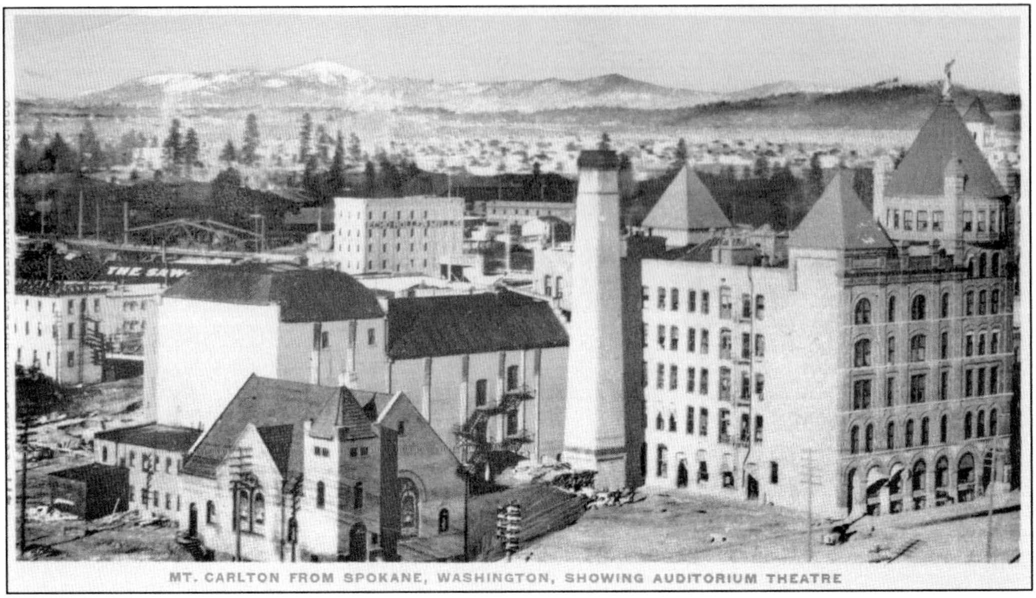

There have been billions of postcards sent through the postal system. The caption on this postcard reads, "Mt. Carlton from Spokane, Washington, showing auditorium theatre." The card is postmarked 1905 and was printed before the name change of Mount Spokane. Shown below is the back of the card, with the 1905 postmark and 1¢ stamp with an image of Ben Franklin. Note the flag cancellation mark and the words at the bottom left: "This side is for address." Postcards have been around for more than 100 years, with the first government postcard being issued in 1873. Private postcards were produced a number of years before the first government-issued one. By the 1890s, photograph postcards became common, and in 1901 the government authorized the use of private-printed postcards. (Both, AC.)

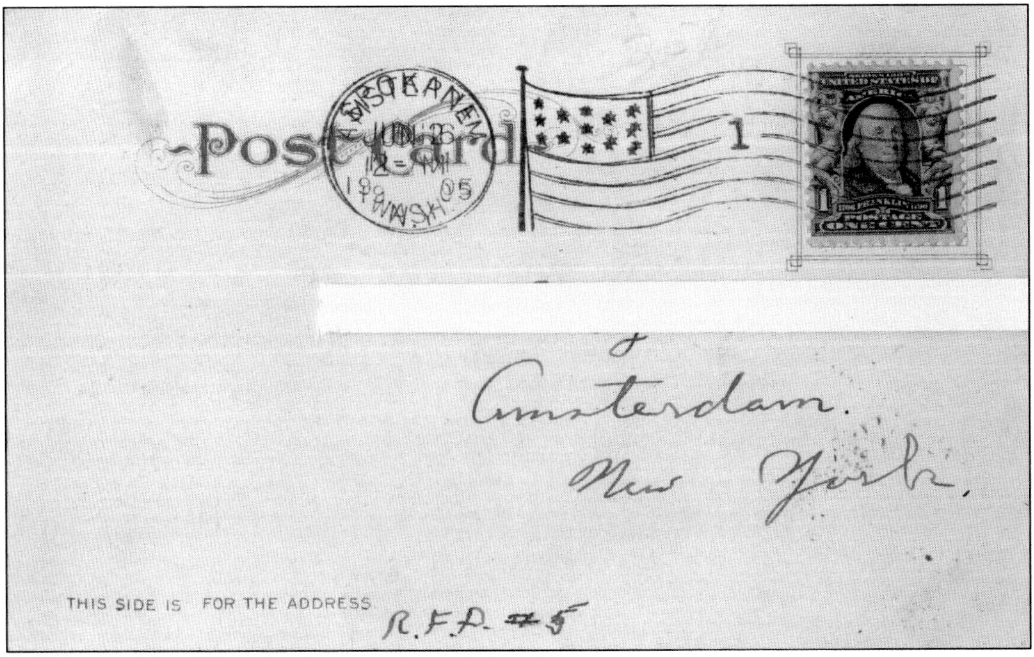

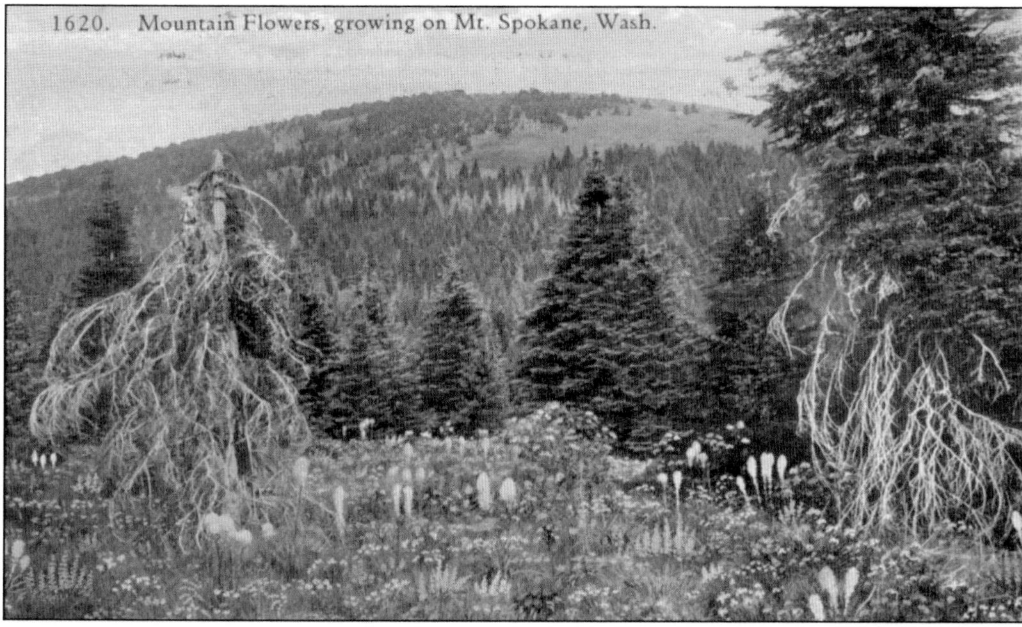

This is a very early postcard image of Mount Spokane; the caption on the card reads, "Mountain Flowers, growing on Mt. Spokane, Wash." Shown below is the back of the postcard. The postcard is postmarked Spokane, Washington, 1932, with one side for the address and the other for a short message. Note the 1¢ postcard stamp with an image of Pres. George Washington. Printed on the bottom of the stamp is "1732 Washington 1932." (Both, AC.)

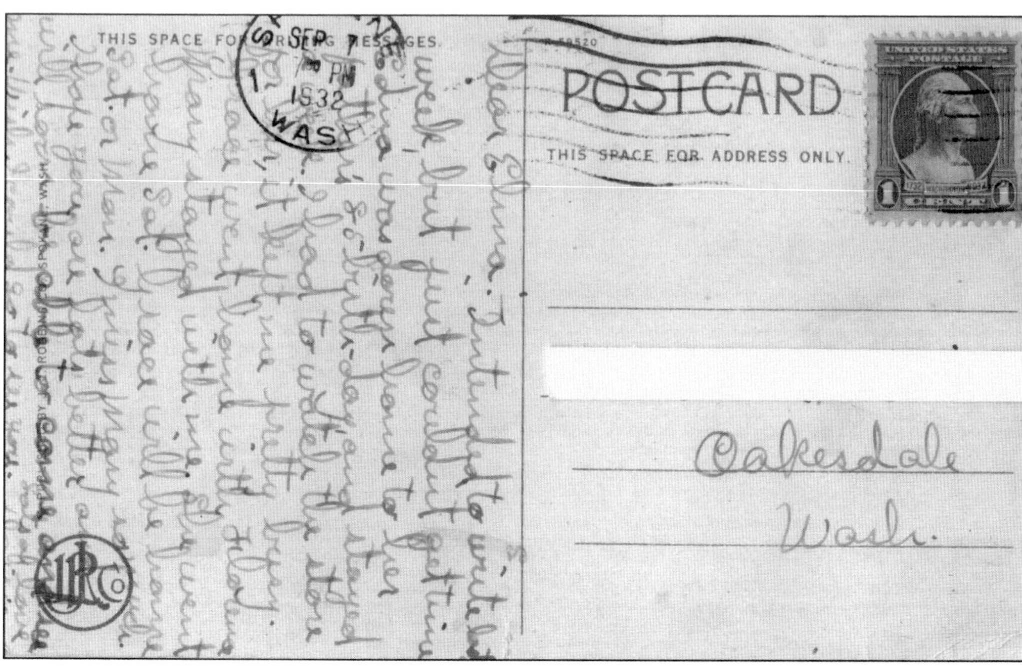

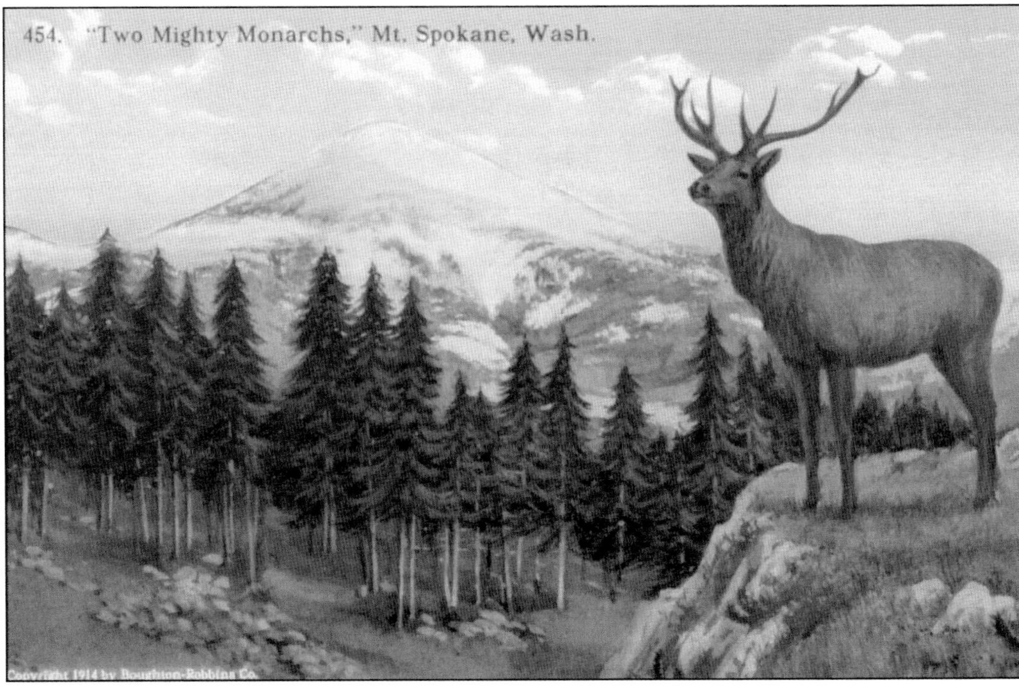

This is a Mount Spokane postcard, titled "Two Mighty Monarchs, Mt. Spokane, Wash." This 1914 postcard features two things that are common around Mount Spokane—trees and elk. The view is very reminiscent of today. The other postcard reads, "Mt. Spokane ('Old Baldy') from Spokane, Washington." This is an early, undated postcard showing Mount Spokane from the city of Spokane. (Both, AC.)

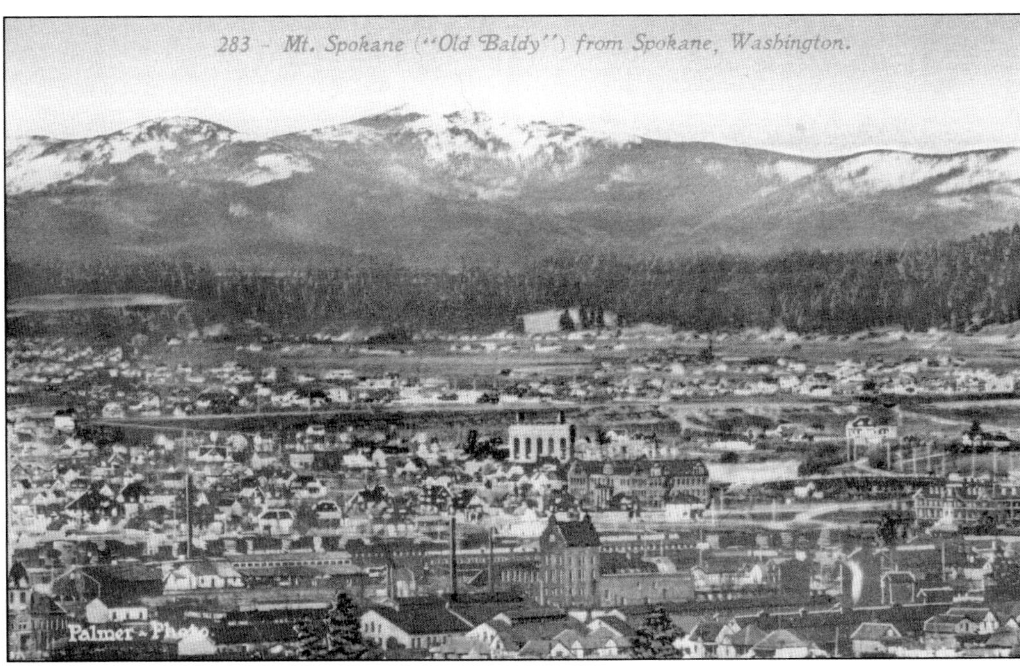

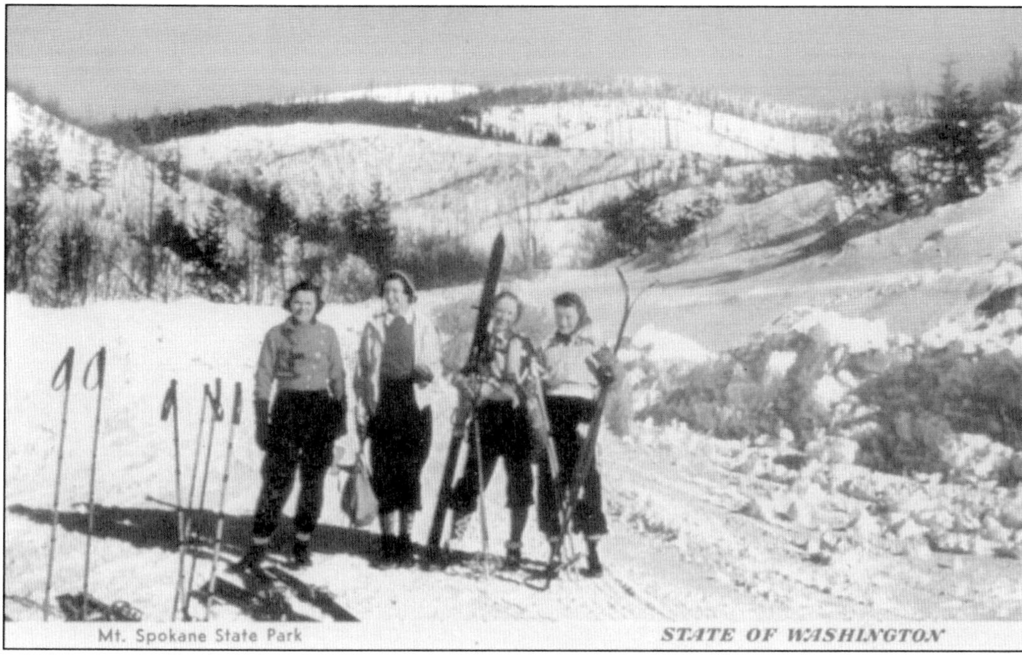

Washington State tourism also got into the postcard business with several postcards being produced in the 1940s and 1950s. These cards captured various scenes from the Washington State parks. These two postcards feature vintage scenes of a group of ladies skiing and another of the Mount Spokane Lodge in the 1940s. (Both, AC.)

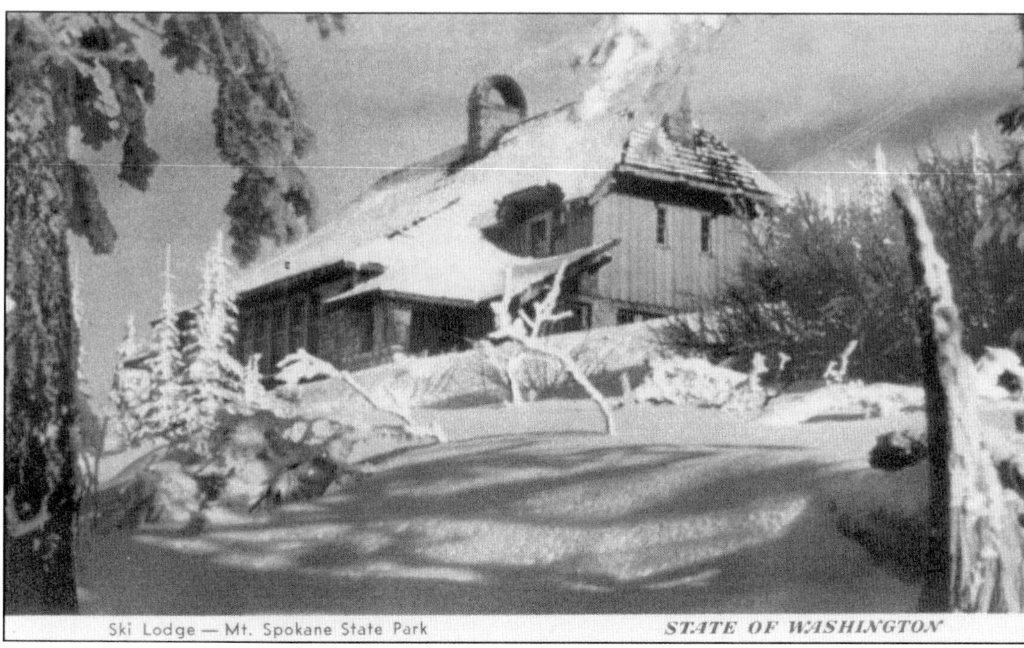

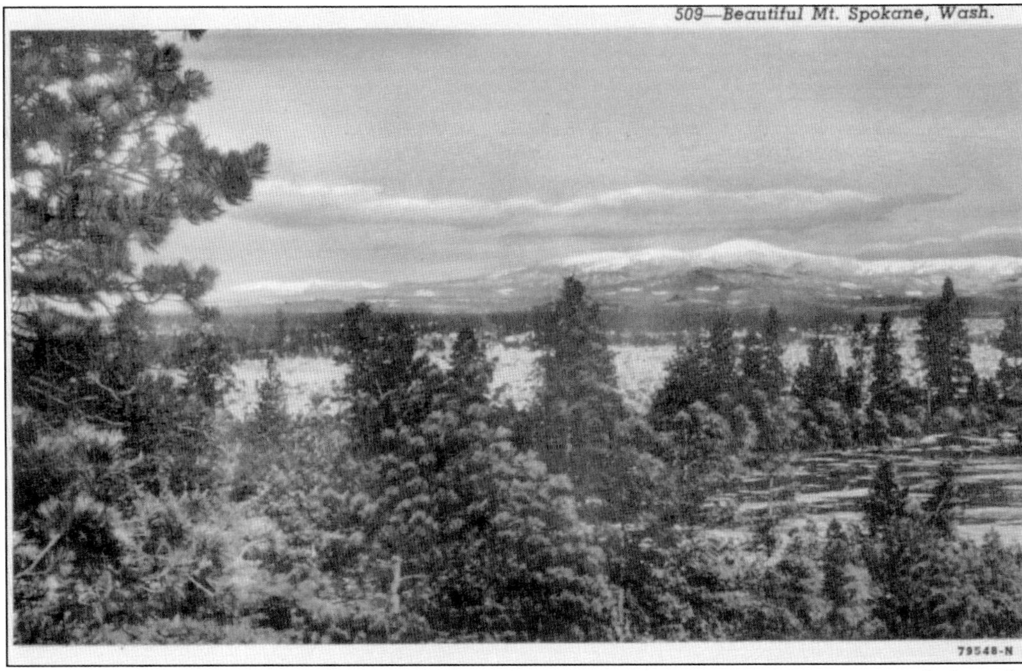

The images found on vintage postcards featured Mount Spokane in a variety ways, including the depiction of the countryside with Mount Spokane in the background and also a view of Spokane Ski Club's cabin on the mountain. Countless numbers of real-photo postcards were being printed and sold all over the world before World War I. Production in the United States began to grow, and soon after the war, the United States became one of the world's largest postcard producers. Colored postcards began by first being hand painted but were later produced with the use of dyes. Photochromes, produced from true colored film, were introduced in 1939. The quality was great, and the materials were inexpensive. Photochromes are still being produced today. (Both, AC.)

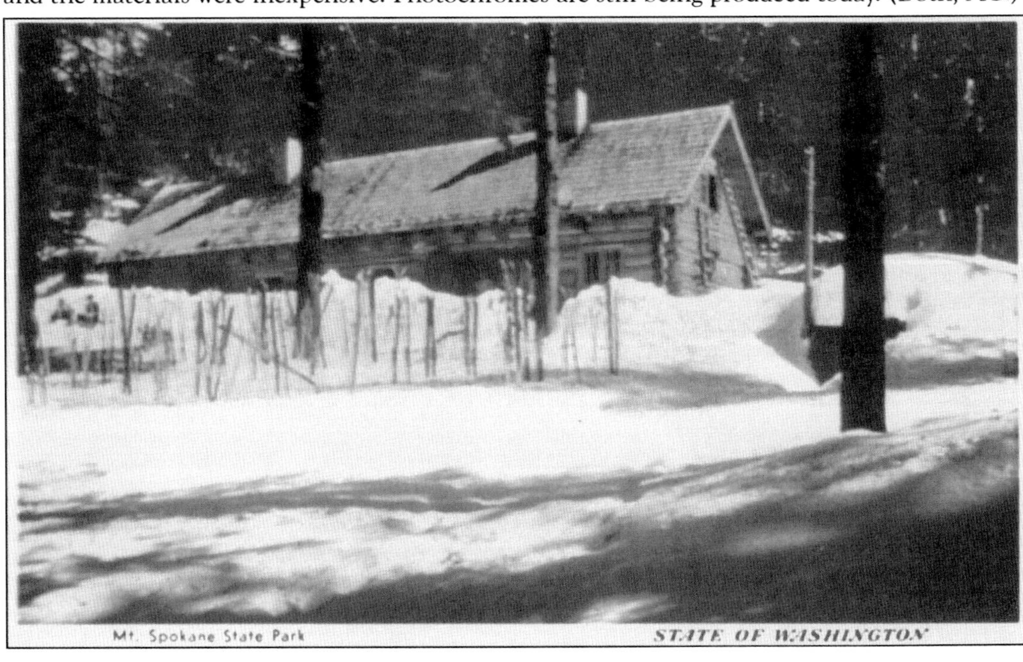

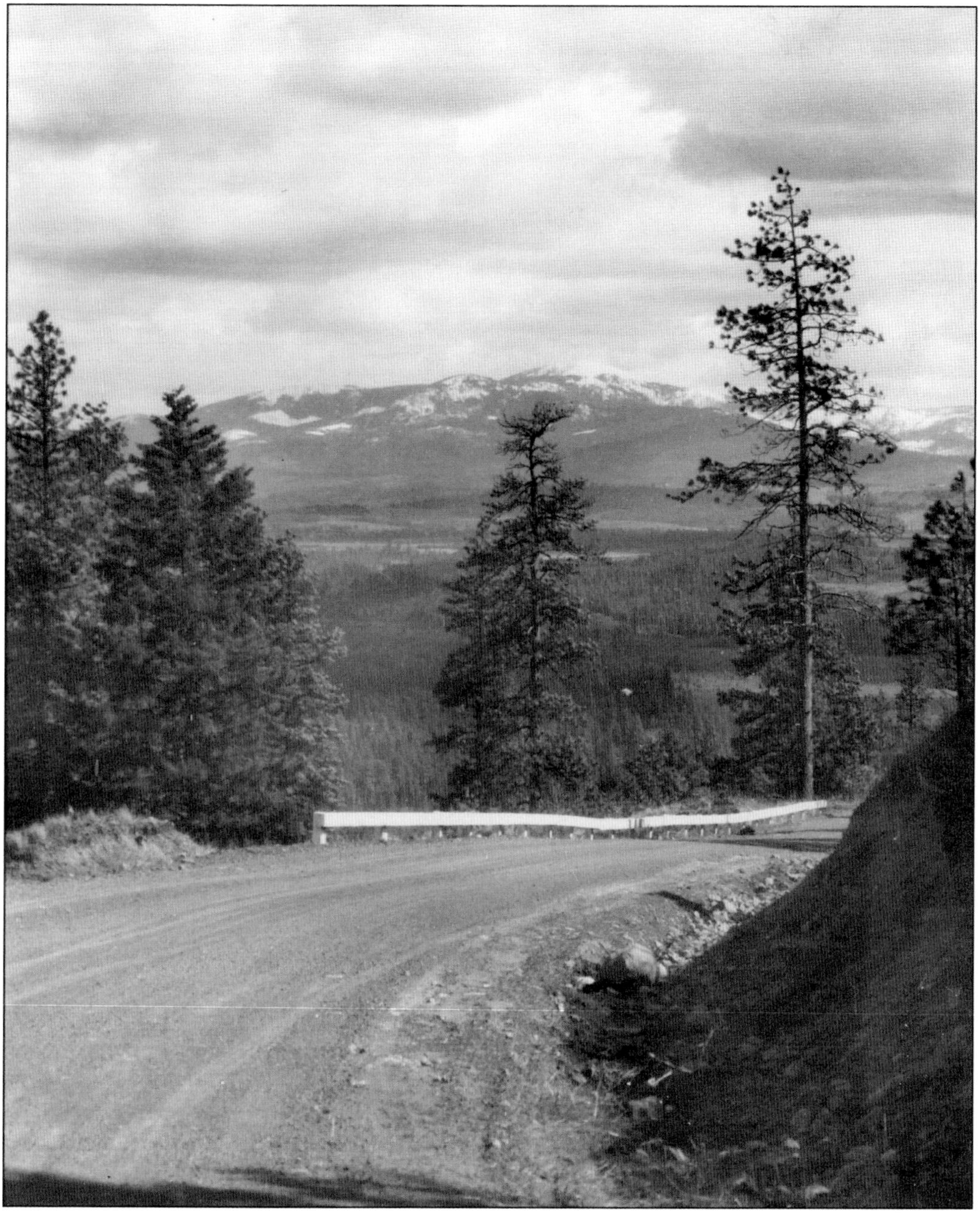

This photograph was taken in the 1920s from the community of Dartford, just north of Spokane, with Mount Spokane in the distance. At the turn of the 20th century, the roads in the Spokane area were rarely maintained. There were no good-quality roads and no plans to improve the existing ones. Washouts and mud were very common in the spring in the Mount Spokane area. In 1899, Samuel Hill, a former railroad executive, saw the need for improving what roads the state did have in addition to constructing new roads. Hill invited around 100 Spokane men to sit down and discuss plans for improving the roads. Only 14 men attended this meeting, but out of it, the Washington State Good Roads Association was formed. Later on, county roads were graded at least once each spring. (NWR-SPL.)

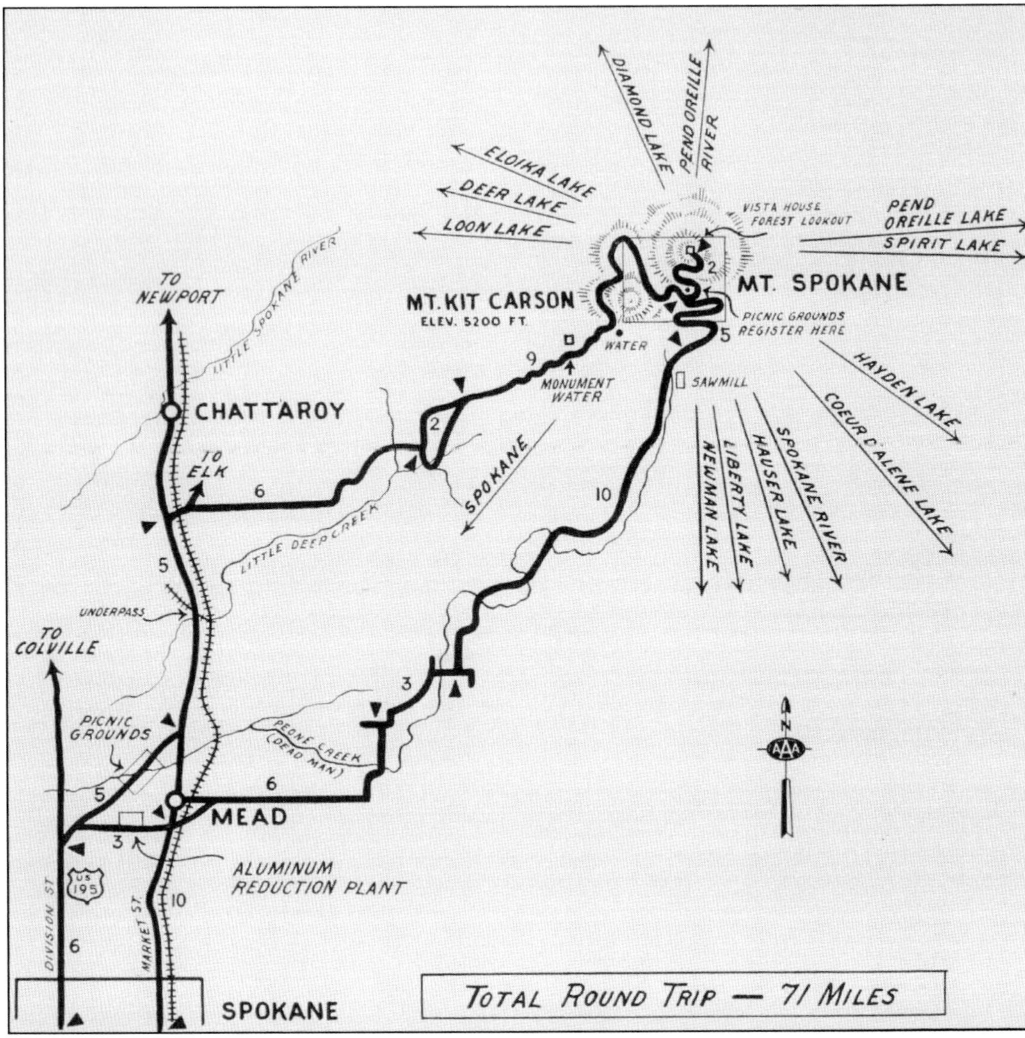

Produced by the Inland Automobile Association, later AAA, this is an early road map that was featured in the Spokane Chamber of Commerce magazine, called *Little Journeys*. Between 1910 and 1960, both organizations produced many pamphlets and brochures on the automobile's trip up the road to the mountain, which included scenic points of interests while visiting Mount Spokane. This early-1950s map shows the roads from the city of Spokane to the mountain. The labeled arrows point to the lakes and rivers that can be seen from the summit. The road furthest north was the first road used from the 1910s to 1937 and was soon called the Day Mount Spokane Road. After 1937, the Deadman Creek Road to the south was opened. Today, the state has closed the Day Mount Spokane Road within the park boundary to automobiles, but it is open to bicyclists, horseback riders, and hikers. The Deadman Creek Road is now called Mount Spokane Park Drive and is the main road used today. (AAA-GSI.)

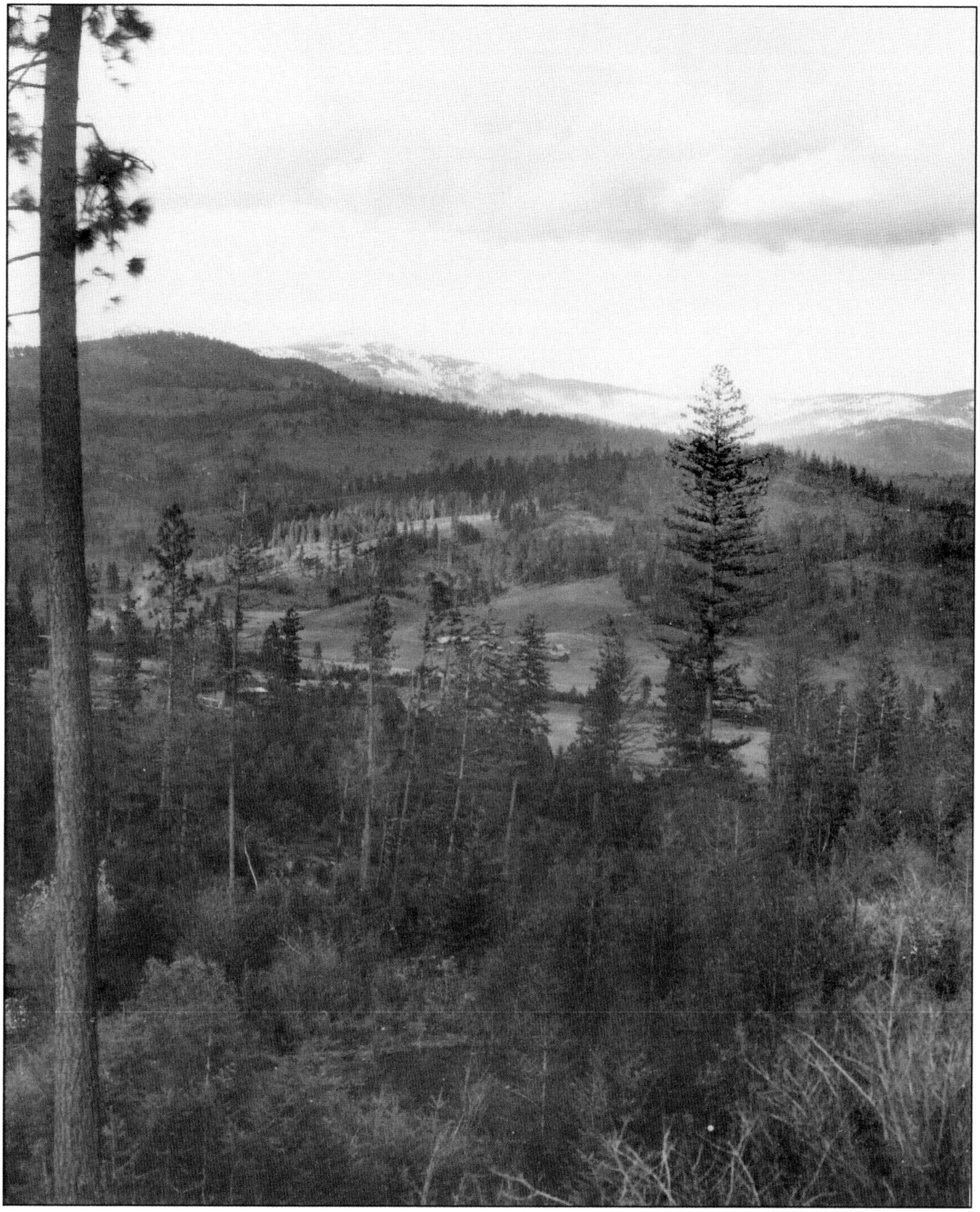

Taken just north of the city of Spokane, this photograph is looking north to Mount Spokane. Most of the area around the mountain was timber, and roads were scarce. Timber and logging have always been a part of the Mount Spokane country. Starting out with local sawmills, especially the Edwards and Bradford Mill at Elk, Washington, the area around Mount Spokane had its share of selective logging over the years. Timber is still prevalent today with ranches and farmland scattered throughout the area. Although this photograph was taken in the late 1920s, the area, except for a few new homes, looks the same. (NWR-SPL.)

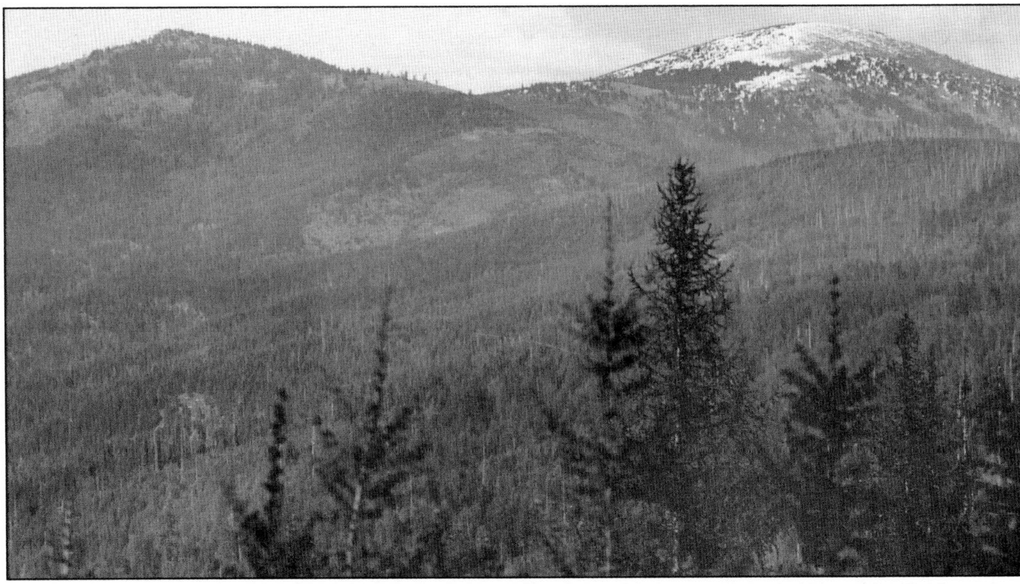

Mount Spokane, with the surrounding countryside, is seen here in 1920. Mount Kit Carson is on the left, and the summit of Mount Spokane is on the right. What looks to be a connecting saddle between the two mountains is Beauty Mountain. The 1929 map was produced by the Inland Automobile Association (AAA of Spokane). Note the highway leaving Spokane and heading north to Newport. This was called Highway 195 on early maps. Today, it is US Highway 2. At Chattaroy, the road to Mount Spokane, called Big Meadows Road, begins. Cook's Auto Road started down Big Meadows Road several miles and continued up toward the summit. It then circled the northwest side of Mount Kit Carson, gaining elevation at a rapid rate but stopping short of the summit. During this time and up to 1937, when the Deadman Creek Road was opened, this was the main route to Mount Spokane. (Above, NWR-SPL; below, AAA.)

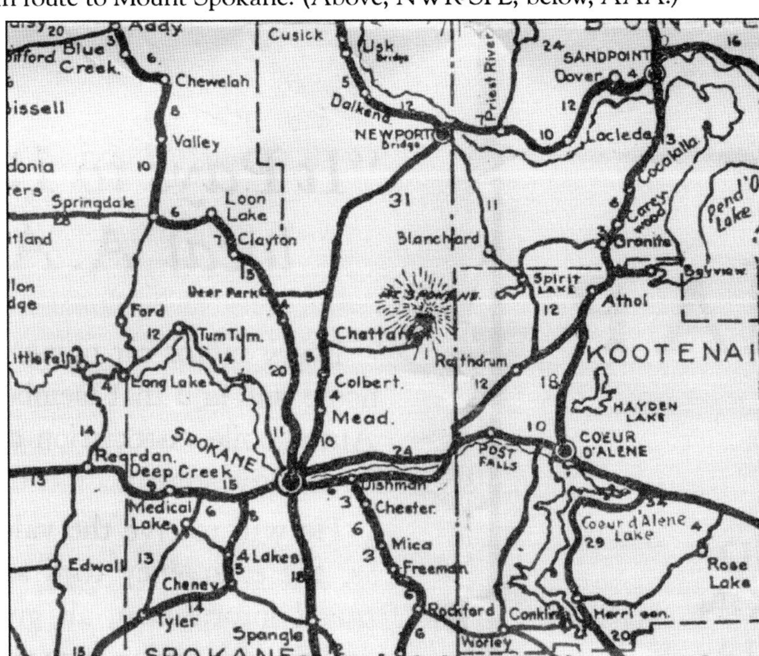

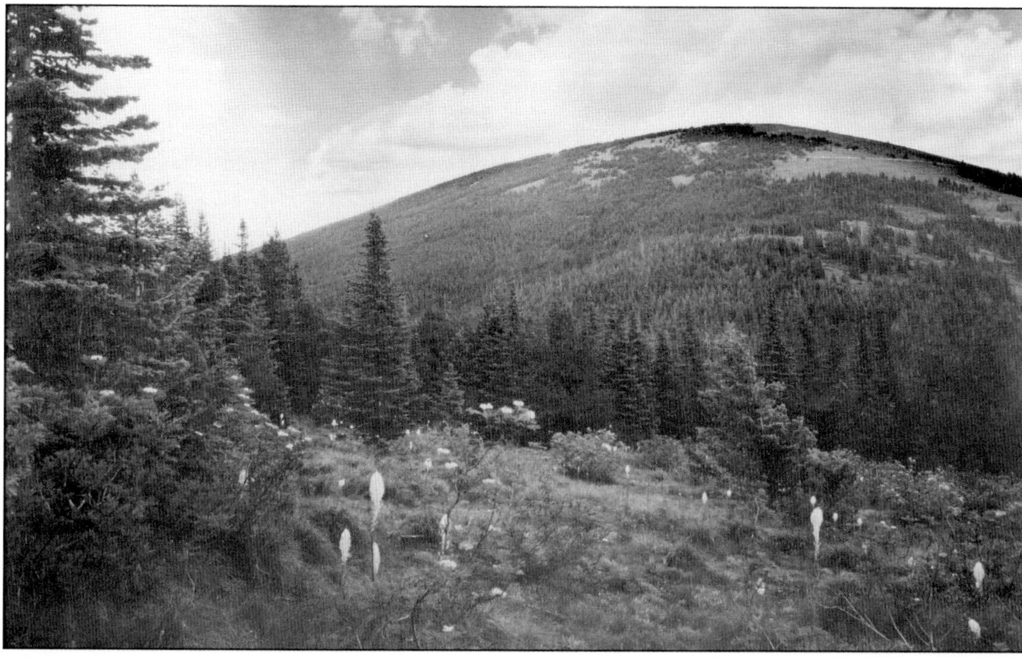

There are many photographs taken from Mount Kit Carson showing Mount Spokane with wildflowers. This is one of the best photographs among all of them. The vegetation and flowers have adapted to the short growing season at these elevations. Snow can remain on the ground through June, with only a brief summer before snow returns in October. (NWR-SPL.)

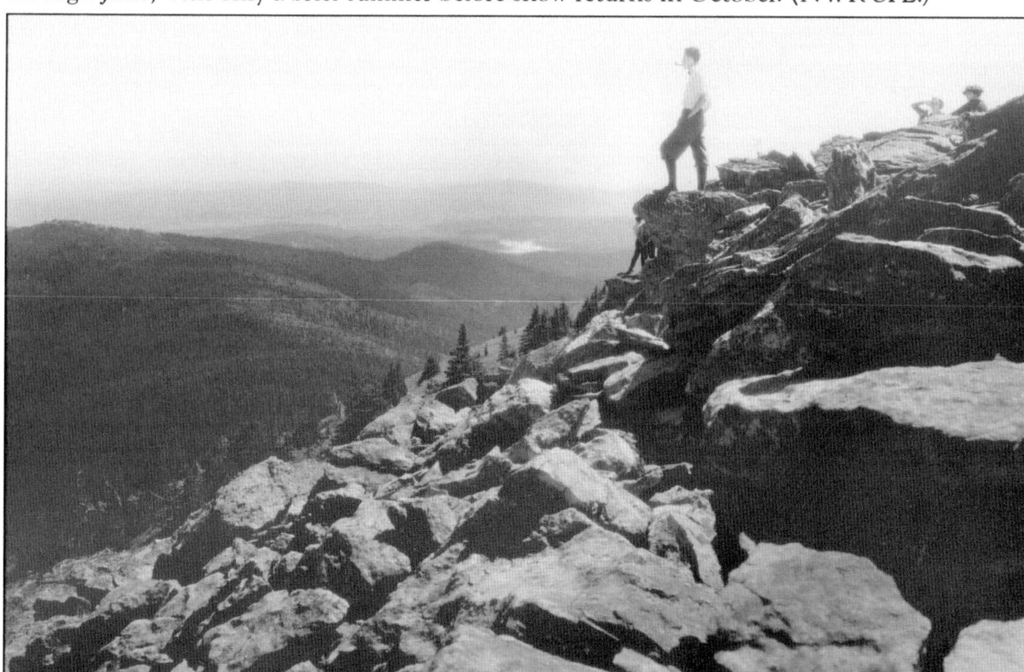

The rocks at the summit of Mount Spokane are very noticeable here. Some are as large as small cars, while others are smaller and loose. Several early pioneers who made the journey to the summit at the turn of the 20th century wrote of the rocks and boulders in their journals. (WSDA.)

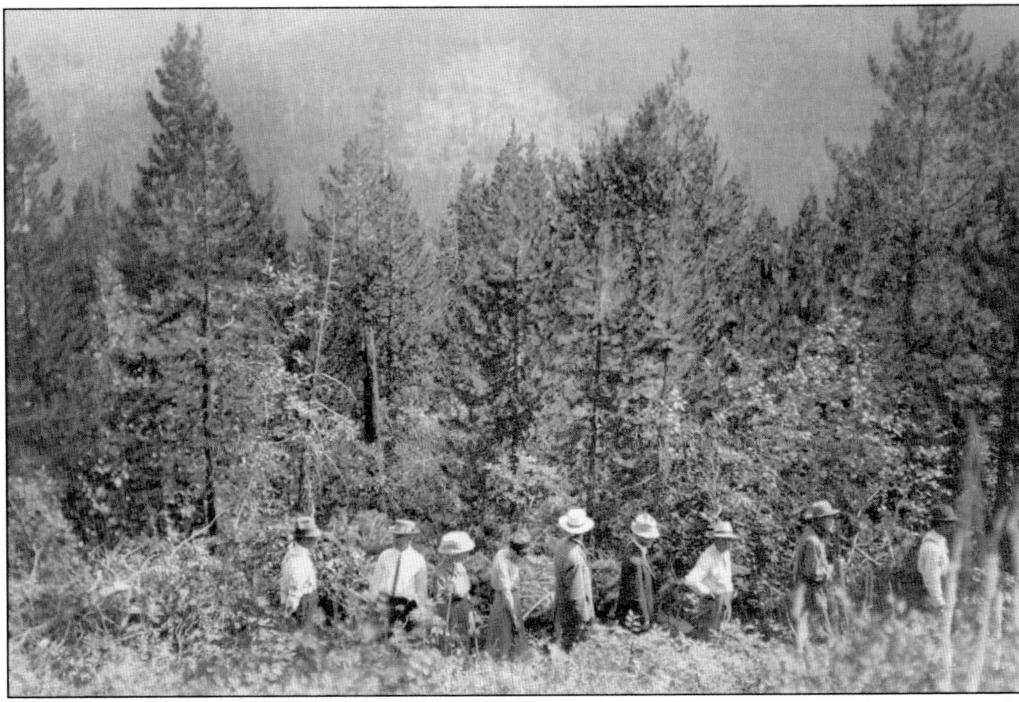

Hiking has always been a major activity at Mount Spokane. This group is out for a day on the mountain in the 1920s. Unlike today, they are dressed in suits and ties. Included are two women dressed up for the hiking occasion, as well. This was common in the 1920s and 1930s. (TSB.)

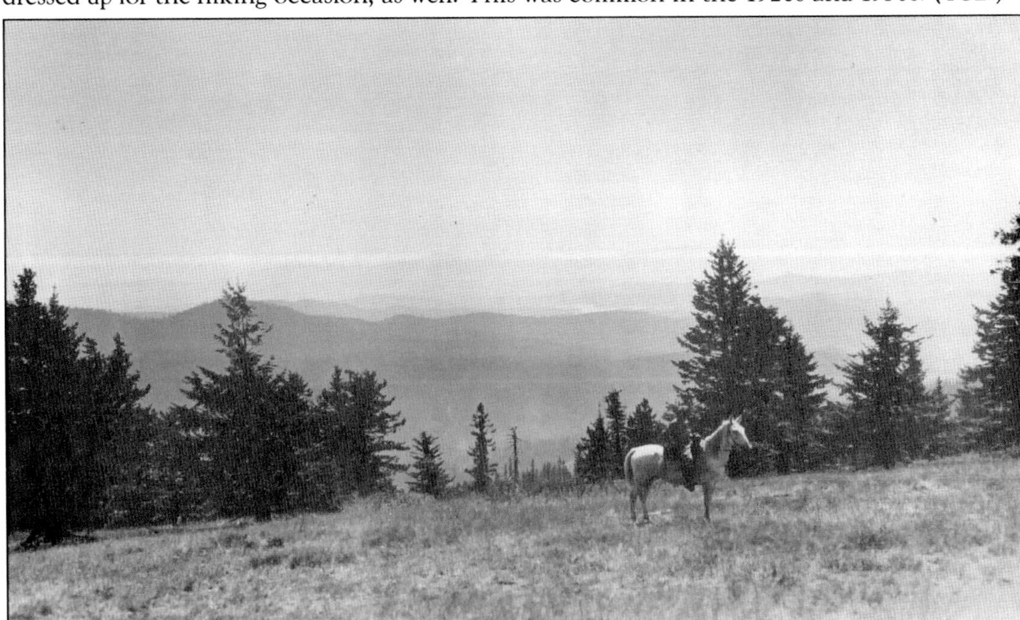

Horseback riding has always been popular, and this is one of the very few photographs of early-day horseback riding at Mount Spokane. Today, riding continues to be a popular activity at Mount Spokane. Horses also played a major role in road construction and farming around the area during the early days. (NWR-SPL.)

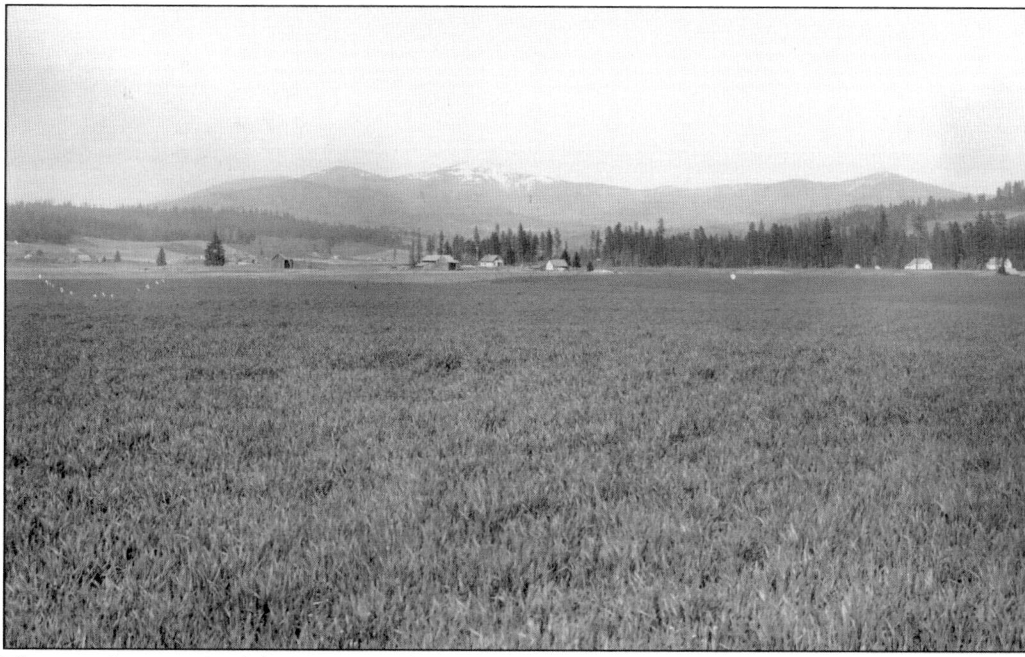

This is a photograph of the Mount Spokane country with the Mount Spokane chain of mountains in the background. This early photograph, taken in the Green Bluff area, located north of Spokane, gives a dramatic view of the mountain in the distance with the open farmland in the foreground. Although this is a vintage photograph, the scene is very much the same today. (NWR-SPL.)

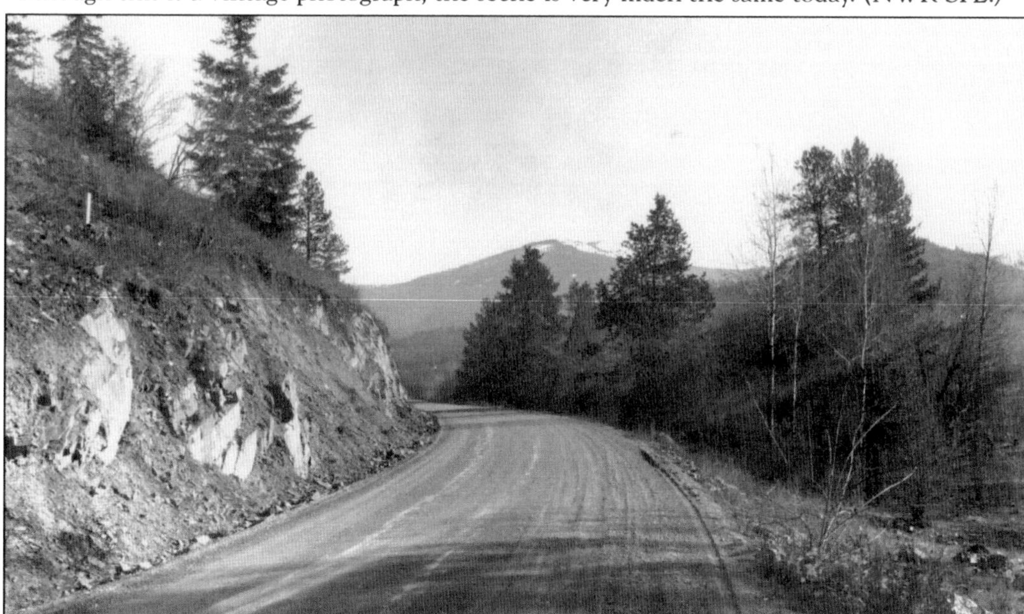

This photograph was taken in the early 1930s from southwest of Mount Spokane. During this time, roads improved because of the work programs initiated by the New Deal, Works Progress Administration (WPA), and the CCC. Road maintenance and new road construction were top priorities for some of these organizations, which helped the nation recover from the Depression. (NWR-SPL.)

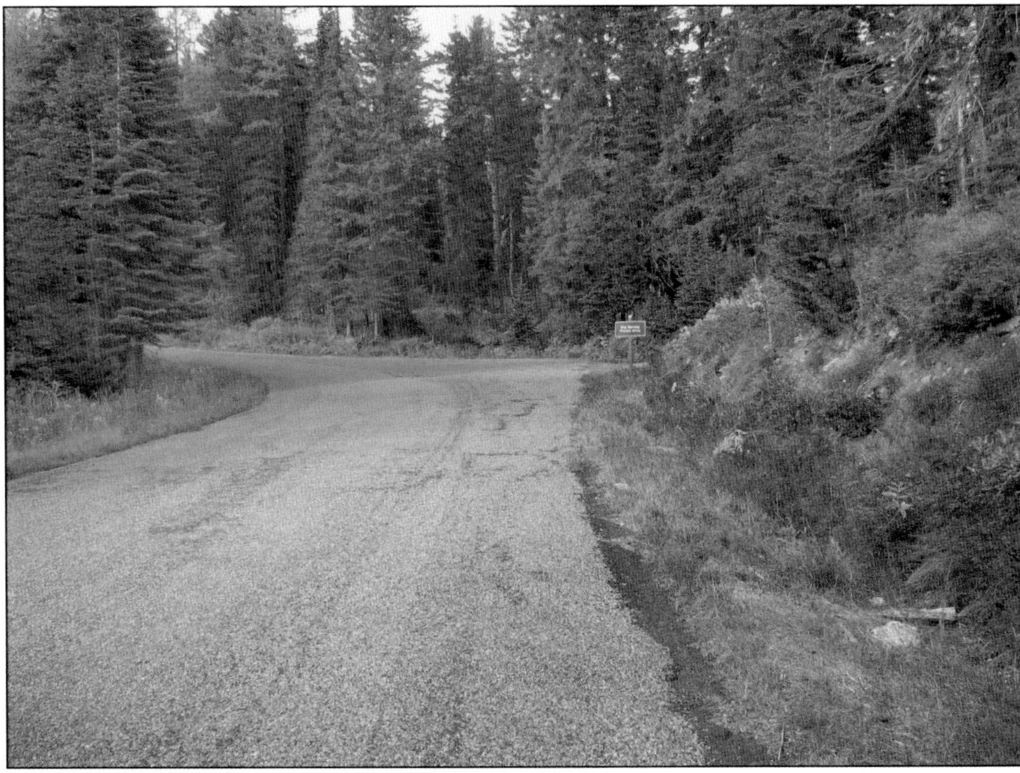

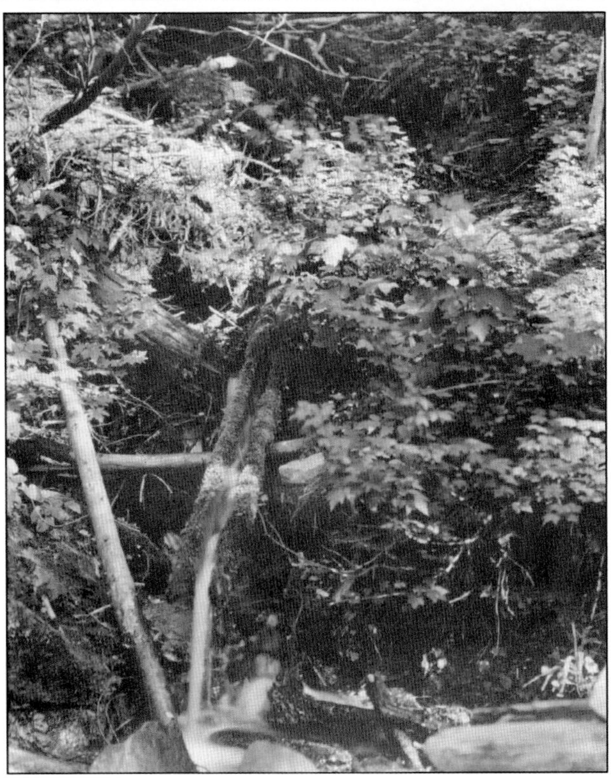

Just below the Bald Knob area is a switchback with a small creek running across the road. During the early years, automobile radiators would overheat going up the mountain grade. This creek location was a perfect spot to stop, let the vehicle cool, and add more water to the radiator. Later, the creek and switchback were called Big Spring. This photograph shows the area and switchback curve. (Terri.)

This early photograph shows the actual Big Spring at the road switchback. Someone stuck a piece of pipe in the creek so that water would flow through it, making it easier to fill water buckets for radiators. This was a constant and needed pit stop for everyone heading up the mountain with an automobile in the early days. (NWR-SPL.)

On Sunday, June 26, 1932, at 3:00 p.m., Mount Spokane State Park received a gift and dedication. At the summit, a 10-foot-tall monument in honor of George Washington's Bicentennial was built, courtesy of the Spokane Federation of Women's Organization. The base was constructed out of granite rock from the summit and had anchored at the top a large four-foot chromium-plated copper ball. When the ball reflected sunlight, many people could see the reflected light in Spokane. Because of vandalism, the monument was removed in 1950. Also pictured is the same sun ball in ice and snow. Many marveled at just what the winter weather did to the sun ball as well as the trees. (Right, DB; below left, Leo; below right, AC.)

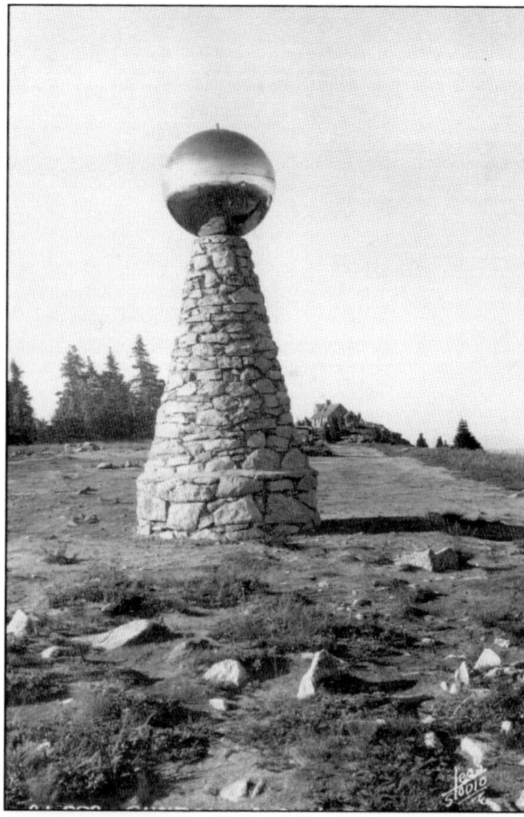

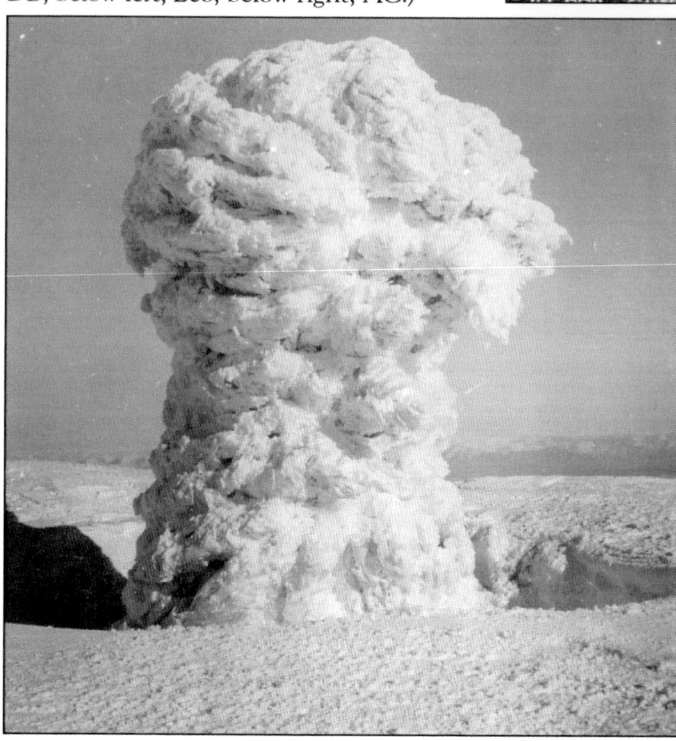

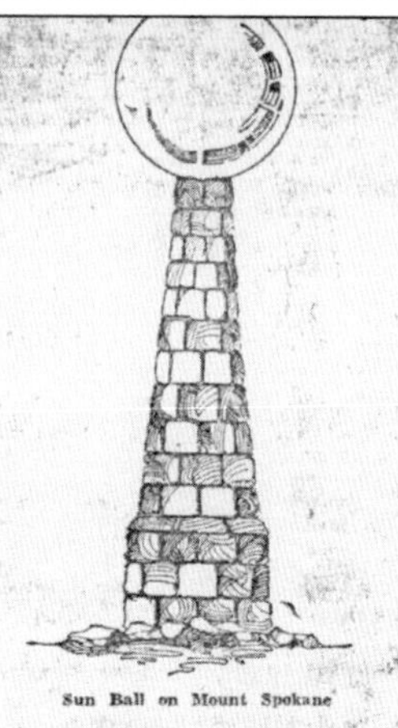

Sun Ball on Mount Spokane

Visit Mt. Spokane

Sunday, June 26, at 3 p. m. 1932

At that time the Spokane Federation of Women's Organizations will dedicate a mammoth copper sun ball on the top of Mount Spokane as a tribute to universal fatherhood and as a part of Spokane clubwomen's celebration of the George Washington Bicentennial.

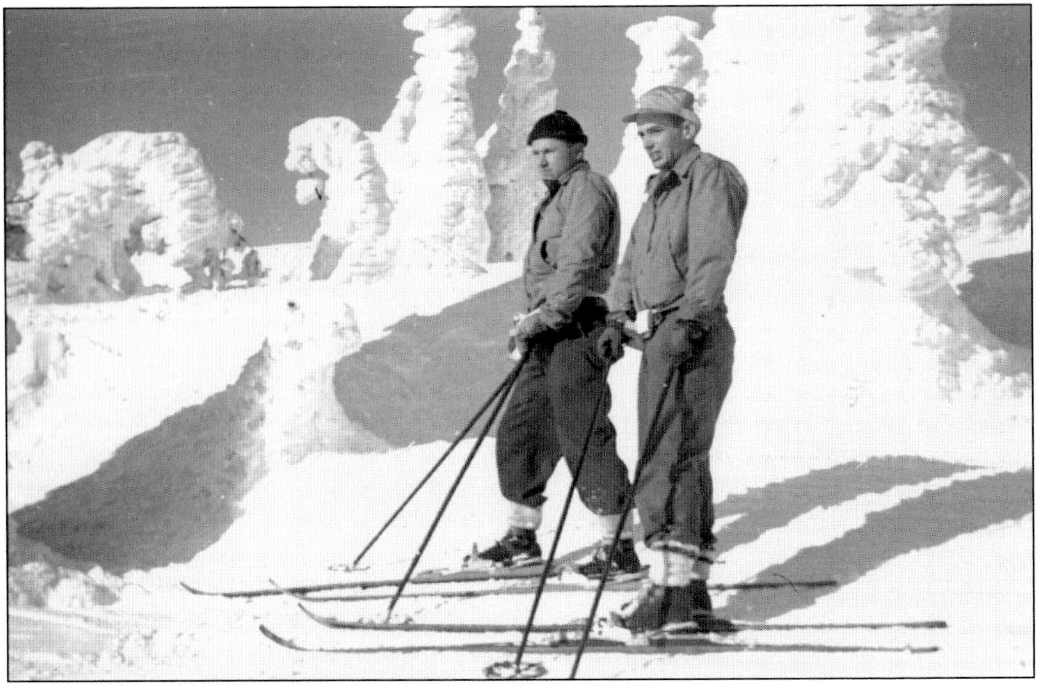

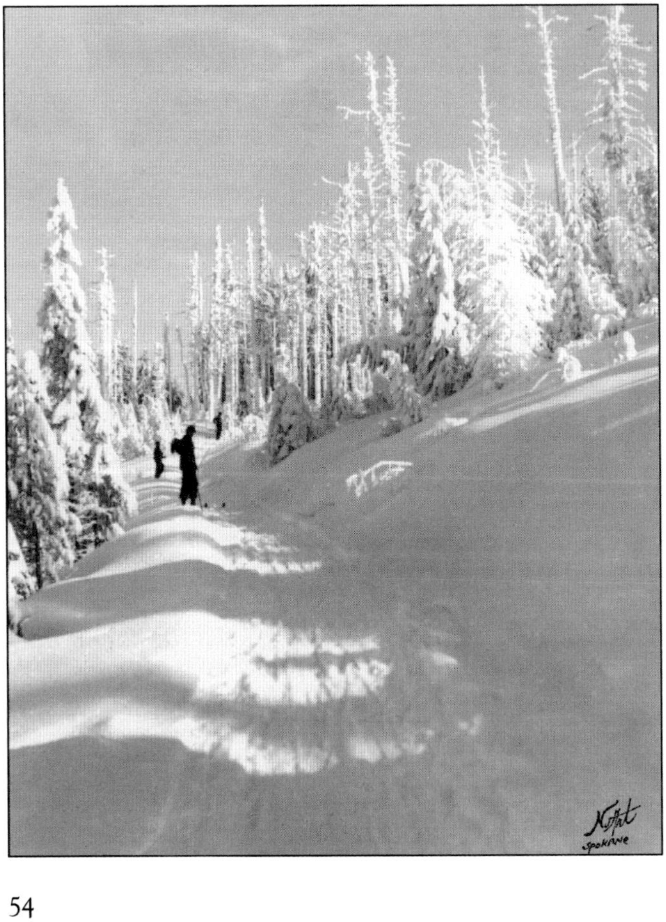

This is a very early photograph showing off the ski apparel. Skiers do not wear this type of ski clothing today, or else, they would get strange looks. Note the skis, bindings, and poles—all a thing of the past. George Stine is on the left, and George Ladd is on right in the photograph above. In the early 1930s, the Mount Spokane Association was formed. With Cheney Cowles as its first president, it raised money to purchase additional land for the park and promoted the mountain. The association was also very active in bidding on tax-delinquent Spokane County property that was near or bordered the mountain, which, in turn, would be bought for a fraction of its value and then given to the State of Washington to be added into the Mount Spokane State Park acreage. (Above, DL; left, NWR-SPL.)

Three

The Skiing Begins

Skiing and jumping have always been popular winter sports for Spokane and the surrounding area. One of the first Spokane ski destinations included the jump and downhill area at Moran Prairie. This location was just east of Fifty-seventh and Custer Streets at Moran on Spokane's south hill and was in operation as early as 1913. Guy Brown, the owner of this area, which was called the Brown farm by locals, also helped with the meets. Browns Mountain, located in the same area, was named after his family. In those early days, if one wanted to ski, then he or she would have jumped on the jumping hill. The few skiers who did not jump were called ski runners. Moran tournaments were held often during the winter and featured some of the best jumpers in the nation, including Olaus Jeldness, Ole Larsen, and E. Engen. Meets were held not only at Moran but also at Leavenworth, Washington, which was one of the largest ski-jump hills. Other meets were held at the Rossland Carnival, British Columbia; Hibbing, Minnesota; and Eau Claire, Wisconsin.

The ski tournaments at Moran Prairie were very popular throughout the 1920s. However, one of the big problems was the short winter season. Skiers wanted a longer skiing season than was available at Moran. By 1930, many began to look for ski areas in the nearby mountains. Although Mount Spokane was always considered a possible location in those days, because of the distance, lack of roads, and transportation, it was not feasible. But with the roads in better shape and reliable transportation, people gave the Mount Spokane area a second look. Skiers began to drive to Mount Spokane to look for suitable downhill and jump areas. The very first spot chosen was not even alongside the Cook's Auto Road but rather to the south and farther down the mountain. Taking local farm and ranch roads, skiers chose a spot and began to clear brush and trees for a downhill area and ski jump. This was located just off the present Mount Spokane Park Drive and just past the state park entrance to the east.

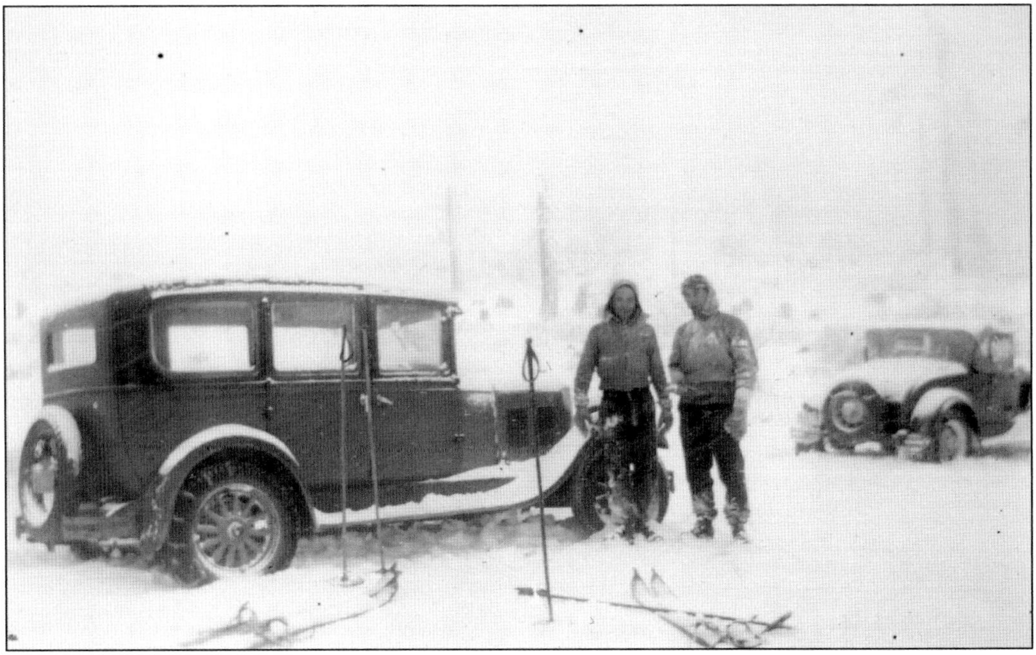

The first skiers at Mount Spokane had no lodge or facilities. They would drive up the unplowed road as far as they could go, park their vehicles, strap on skis, and start skiing. Pictured here are George Ladd (left) and Richard Francis with an automobile. Skiers found that Mount Spokane's snow was deep and that it lingered into late spring. The Mount Spokane Association would invite state legislature, county commissioners, and other state officials to Spokane to lobby for financial support. Often, tours would take guests to the mountain showing them the wonderful views and the skiing developments. The Mount Spokane Association was very successful in obtaining funds from the state legislature and private donations. (Above, DL; below, Leo.)

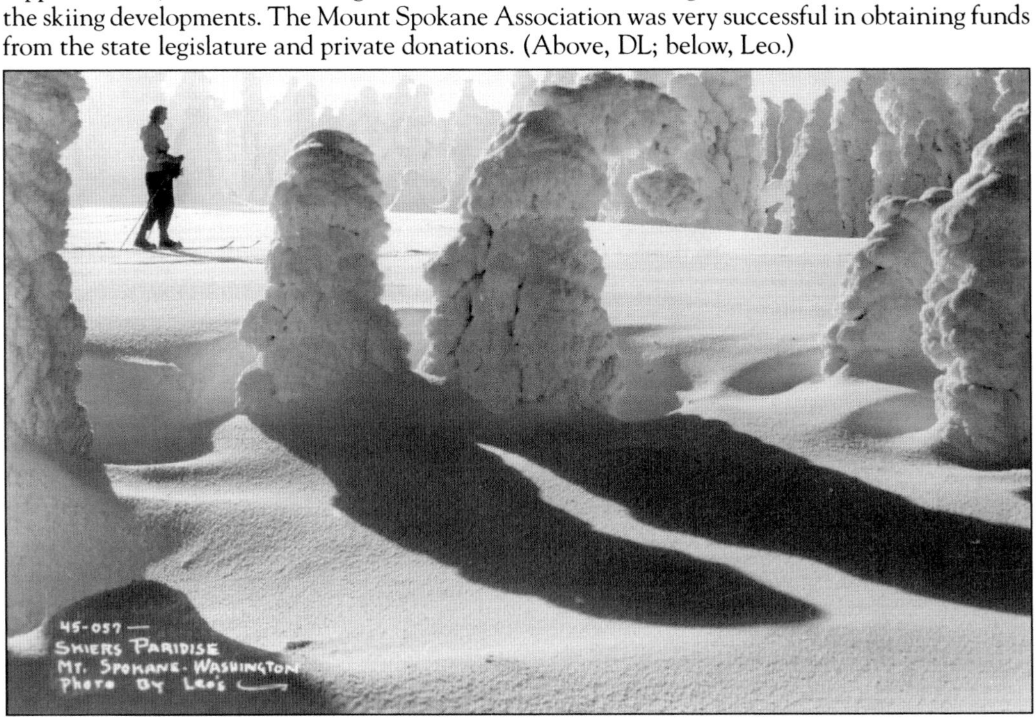

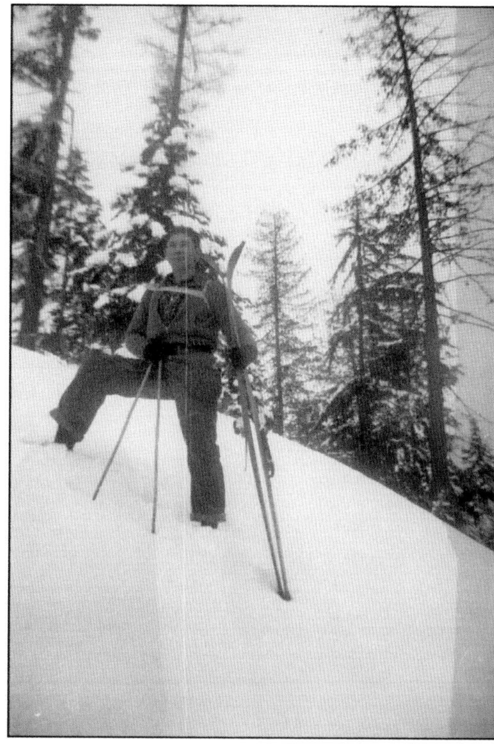

Years ago, one had to be tough when skiing. There were no rope tows, no lifts—nothing. In order to ascend a steep hill or ravine, the skier did one of two things. Some skiers would strap sealskins to the bottom of their skis, which would grip and help with not sliding, and would then walk up the snow-covered hill. Others would walk up the hill sideways, using the ski poles for support. Sometimes it would take two hours to climb the hill just to ski down it in two minutes. Richard Francis is shown in photograph at right. Skiers were overwhelmed by the scenery on Mount Spokane, and word soon got out that a winter wonderland awaited skiers on Mount Spokane, thus bringing more skiers to the mountain to give it a try. (Right, DL, below, NWR-SPL.)

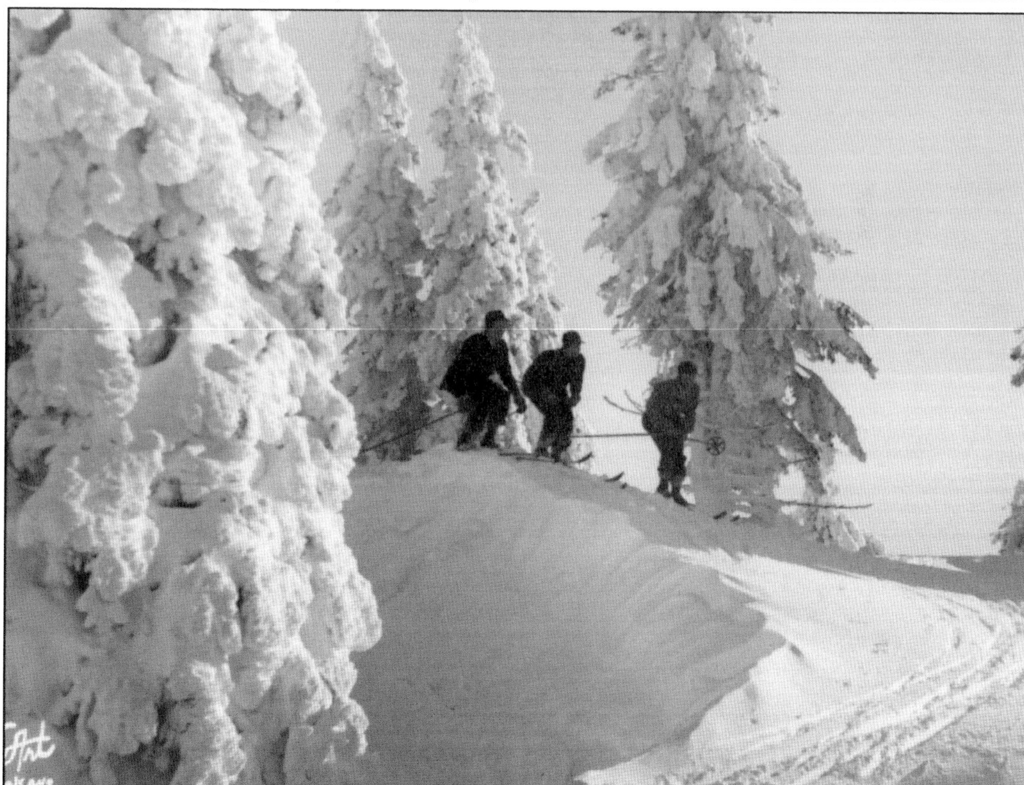

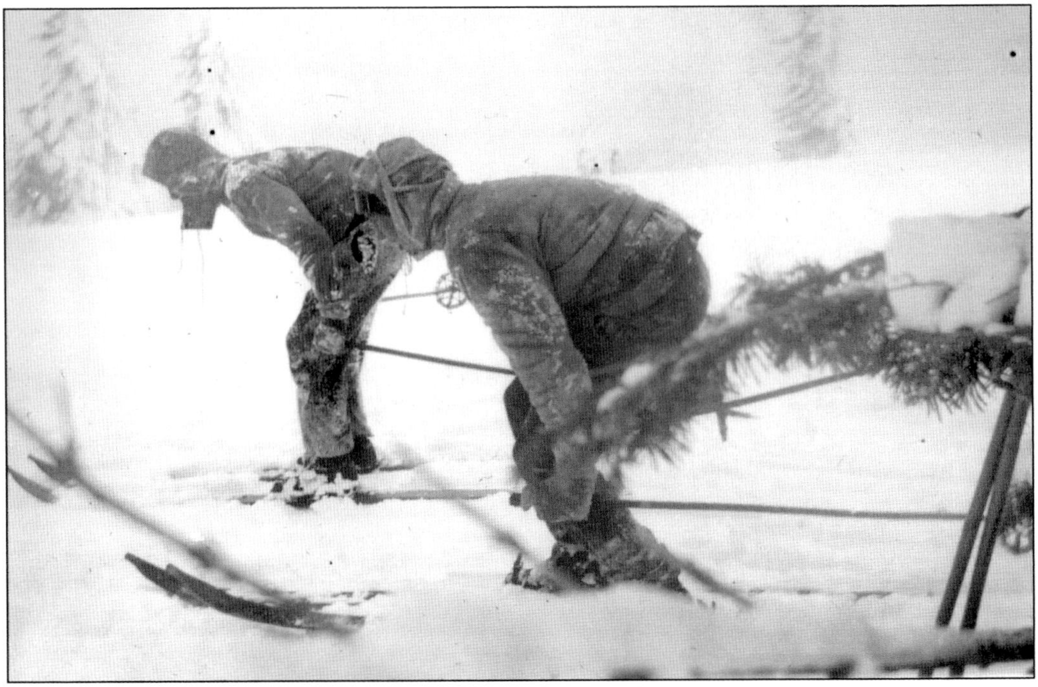

Many skiers would plan multiday or overnight camp/ski outings on Mount Spokane, especially during the 1930s. Pictured here are two unidentified skiers. They used a modified sleigh to carry their overnight camping gear. It is hard to distinguish features in the very old photograph below; however, two skiers huddled in their makeshift overnight shelter can be seen. Many would spend the night this way with a small campfire and then start skiing at first daylight. (Both, DL.)

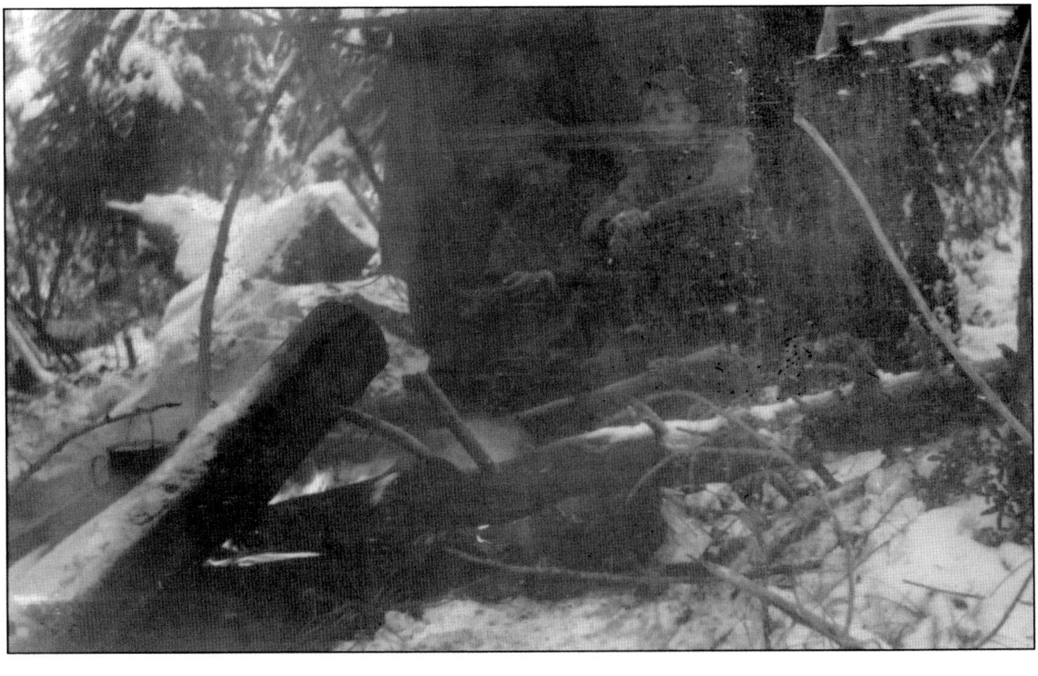

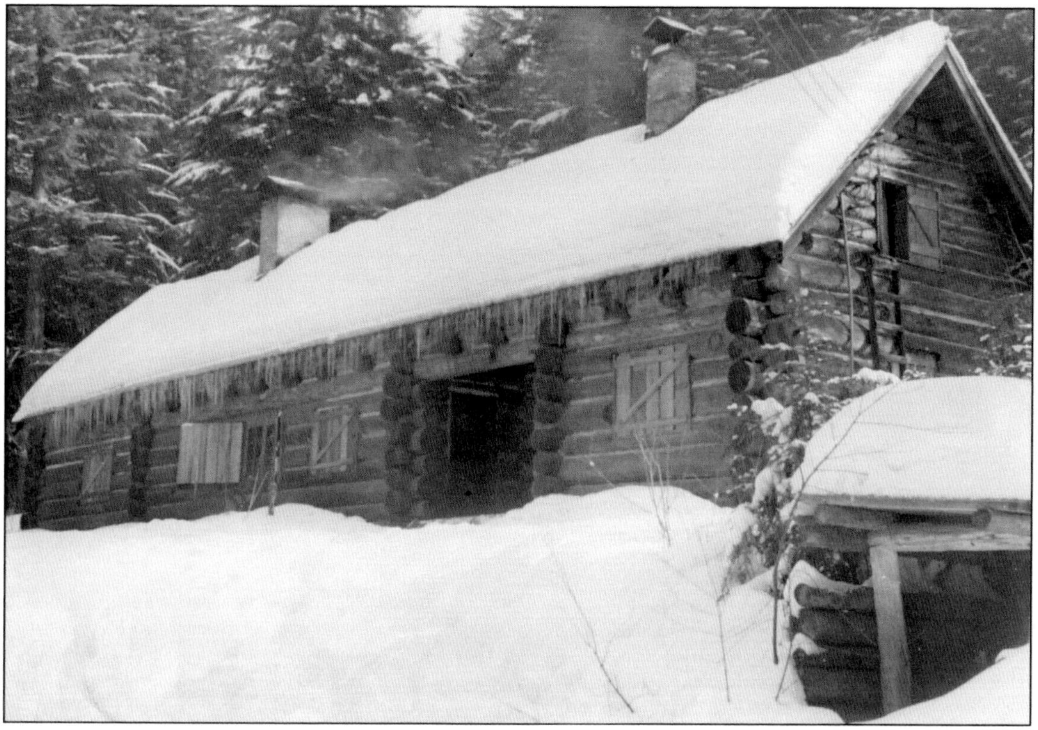

This was the first ski cabin at Mount Spokane. By 1931, the Spokane Ski Club had formed under the leadership of Spokane newspaper publisher Cheney Cowles. In May 1932, volunteers began construction on the log clubhouse and ski areas, including two rope tows and two ski jumps. The grand opening for the cabin was January 1, 1933, with a large crowd from Spokane. The four-foot snow depth blocked the road, forcing people to park their vehicles five miles from the ski cabin. A sleigh pulled by four horses furnished the transportation to the cabin. The ski club first used automobile engines to power the rope tows; however, once power lines were installed, the rope tows were switched over to electric power. Soon other ski clubs, including the Selkirk Club and the Mountaineers, staked out pieces of land for skiing on the slopes of Mount Spokane. Each had their own cabins and ski runs with gas engine–operated rope tows. (Above, BSA; below, NWR-SPL.)

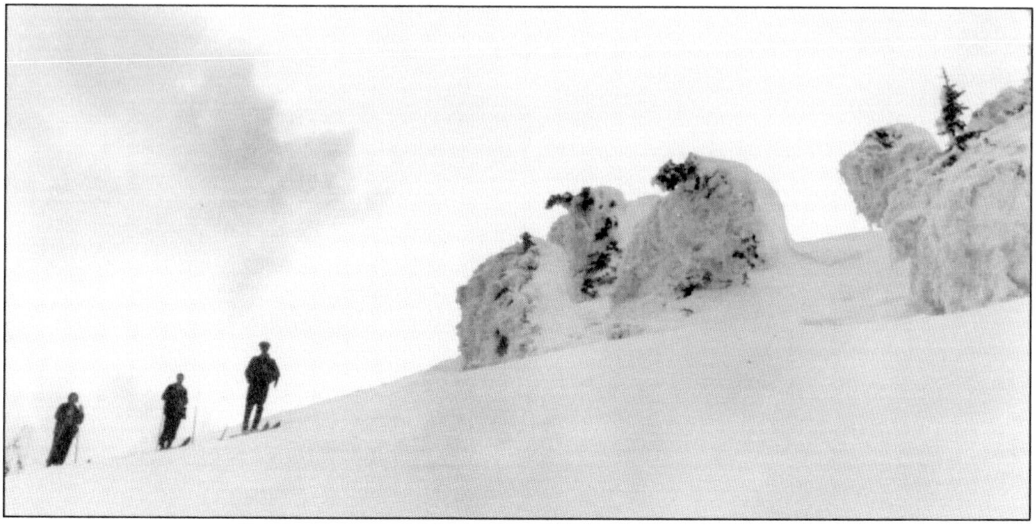

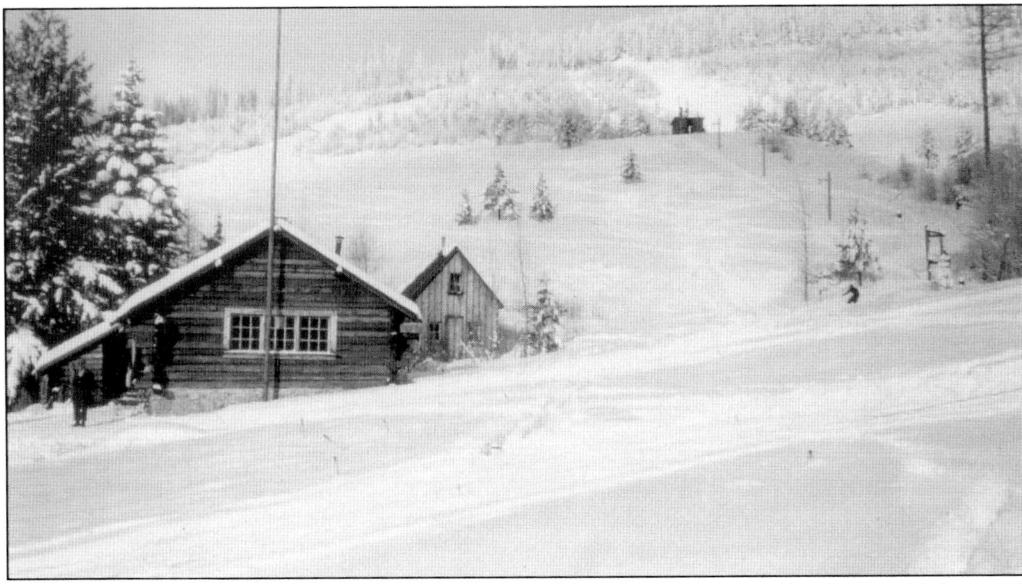

The Selkirk Ski Club was formed in the 1930s and bought acreage on the slopes of Mount Kit Carson. Building a ski clubhouse lodge and a rope tow, the club was very successful. On the right is the rope tow with upper terminal in view. By the end of the 1930s, the club could accommodate up to 25 people in the lodge. Several ski tournaments were held here throughout the 1930s into the 1950s. (SSP.)

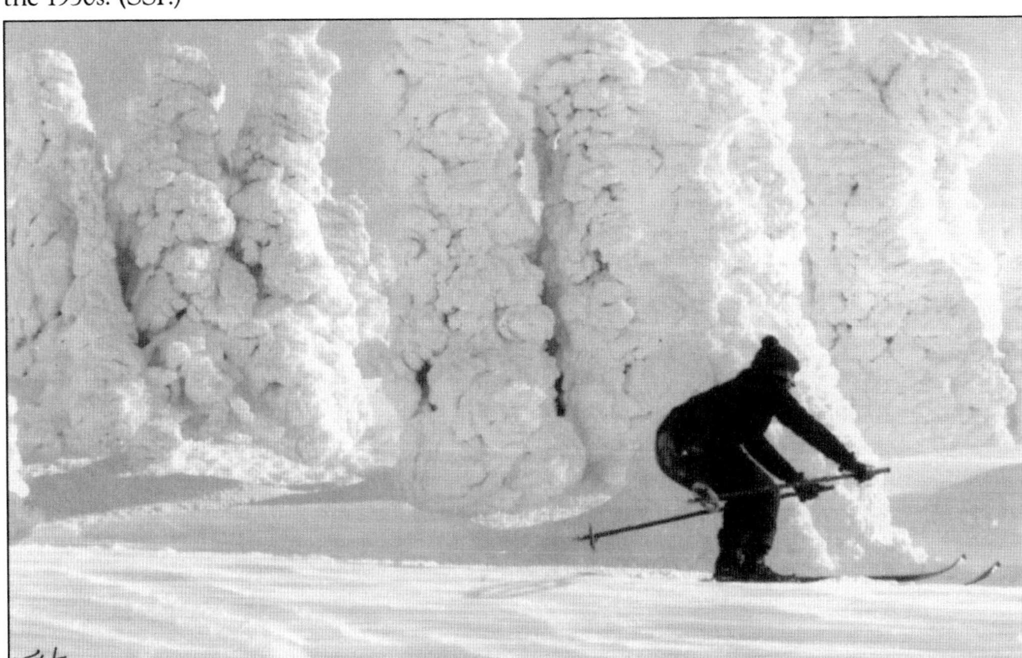

All the ski clubs joined the Mount Spokane Association. With ski clubs joining forces under the leadership of the Mount Spokane Association, cooperation and planning for new ski runs, warming huts, and future developments became very easy. Other clubs in the Inland Empire, including the Kiwanis Club, the Spokane Chamber of Commerce, and the Northwest Conservation League, were association members, as well. (NWR-SPL.)

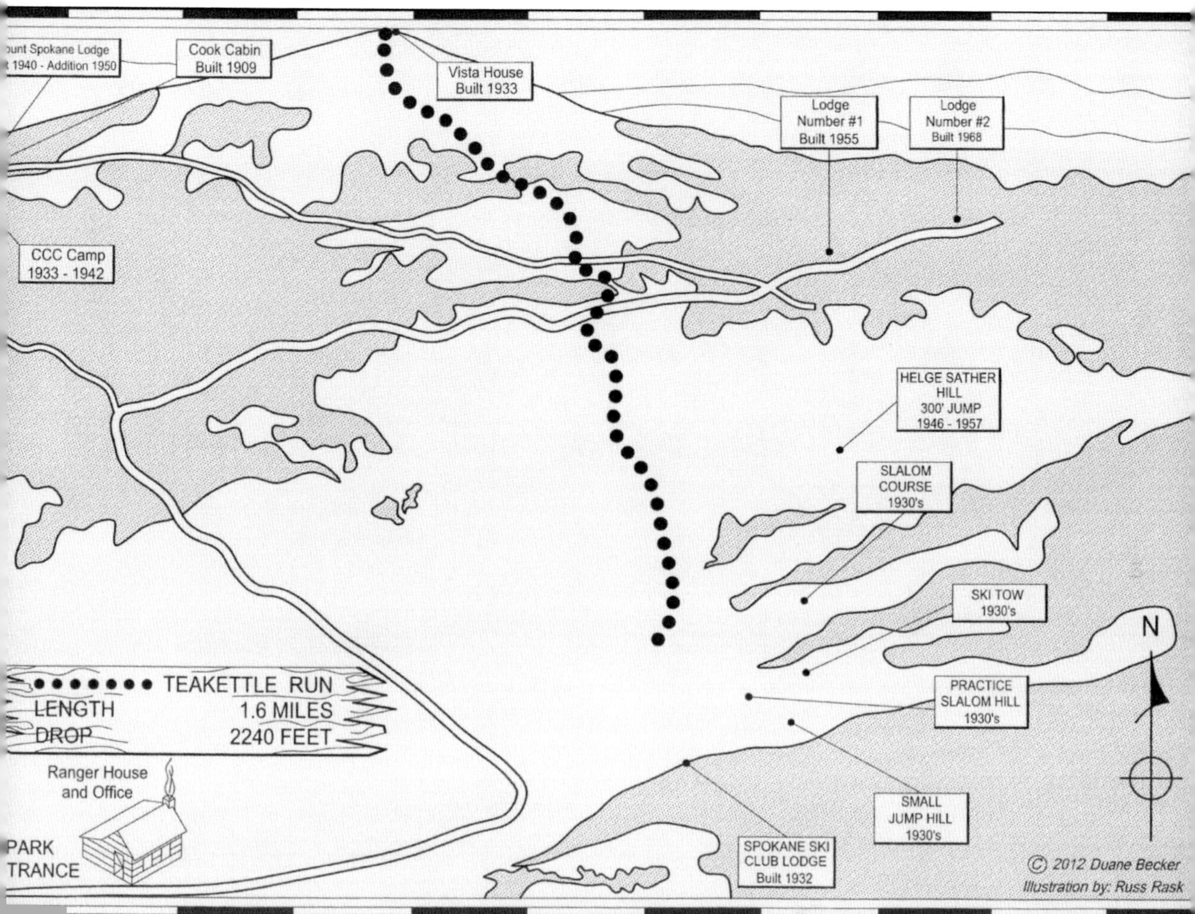

This map shows the location of the first ski cabin, downhill runs, and the ski jumps. The closest road to this ski area in 1932 ended near the present-day state ranger office and entrance. Cook's Auto Road, which headed for the summit, was on the west side of the mountain and could not be used to access this first ski area. Today's current road, Mount Spokane Park Drive, is included for reference but was nonexistent before 1937. Note the locations of the first ski club lodge, jump hill, and downhill runs. One of the very early downhill runs, called the Teakettle, is shown. The Teakettle run was for racers, and recreational skiers did not use it. The Vista House, Cook's Cabin, the CCC camp, and the current Lodge No. 1 and Lodge No. 2 locations are shown for reference. Later on, in the 1950s, there was a larger jump hill named the Helge Sather Hill, and its location is shown on this map, as well. Today, except for the Teakettle, there is no trace of any of these first jump hills and downhill runs; vegetation and trees have covered the area over. The Spokane Ski Club Lodge is gone except for the still standing chimney and portions of the floor. (WK, RR.)

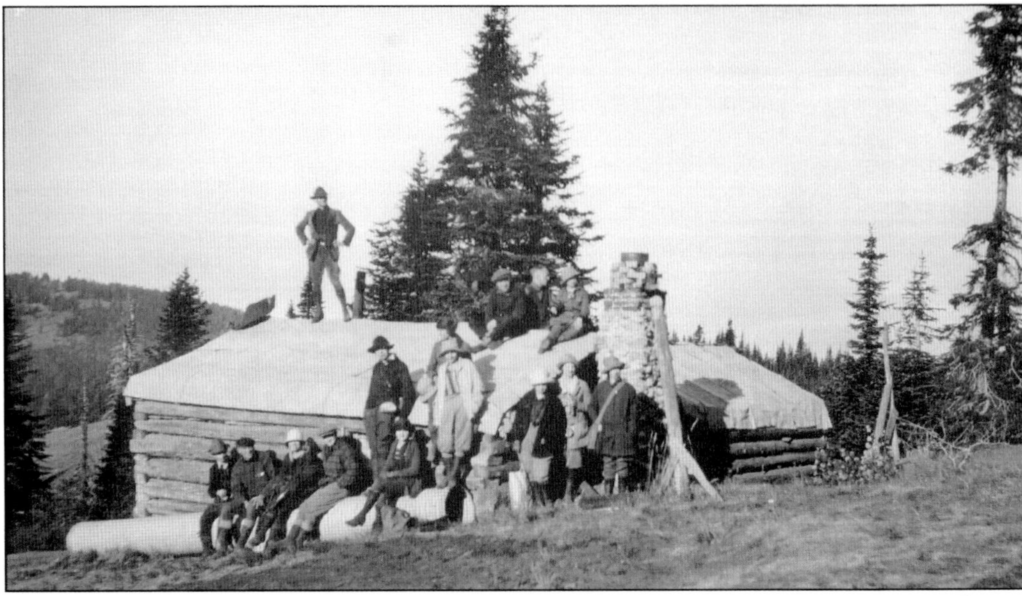

The original Cook's Cabin in the early 1920s is seen here. The cabin had fallen in need of repair with the roof caved in. By 1925, Spokane County engineers reported that most of the old cabin's logs were rotting, and over the last several years, water had been running down the hill into the cabin filling it with mud. (TSB.)

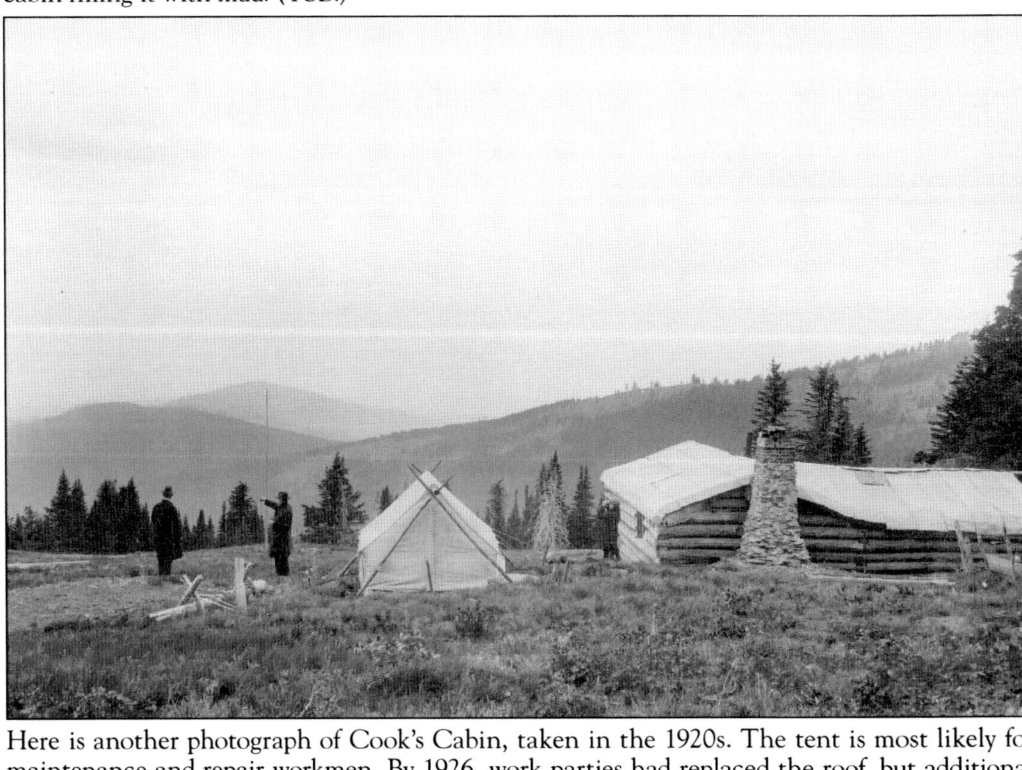

Here is another photograph of Cook's Cabin, taken in the 1920s. The tent is most likely for maintenance and repair workmen. By 1926, work parties had replaced the roof, but additional repair work was also needed. Note the hand-mortared fireplace chimney, a common method of chimney construction in those days. (NWR-SPL.)

Four

Cook's Cabin

By the late 1920s, the original cabin that Francis Cook had built was in a very poor condition, with the roof caved in and the log walls rotting away. In 1933, state officials announced plans to build a public ski building and rope tow at this original cabin site, with work starting that same year. Part of this new building would be home for the park's caretaker. The other section would have a large 17-by-23-foot public room for skiers and hikers to use as a warm-up and resting area. The ski rope tow, called rope tow No. 1, was constructed a short distance from the new building and took skiers to the summit area. Cook's Cabin's ski area became very popular the remainder of the 1930s into the 1940s and would put Mount Spokane on the skiing map.

On July 24, 1952, the state parks and recreation commission announced two new construction projects for Cook's Cabin, a 20-by-40-foot addition to Cook's and a new rope tow; both were to be completed before the coming snow that year. Plans called for the tow to be operated daily if skiers were there to use it. The 20-by-40-foot addition to the west side of Cook's Cabin would provide ample space for skiers.

Up until 1952, the park superintendent's living quarters were located in a portion of Cook's Cabin. But plans now called for the living quarters to be moved near the park entrance. Within the addition on Cook's Cabin, there would be a small lunch counter that served sandwiches and coffee. Also planned for the summer of 1952 was a logging operation to widen the ski area near Cook's. The logging was completed by the end of that summer. Cook's Cabin continued to be the public ski area until it was closed at the end of the 1954–1955 skiing season, with all ski facilities being moved to the present location on the east side of the mountain.

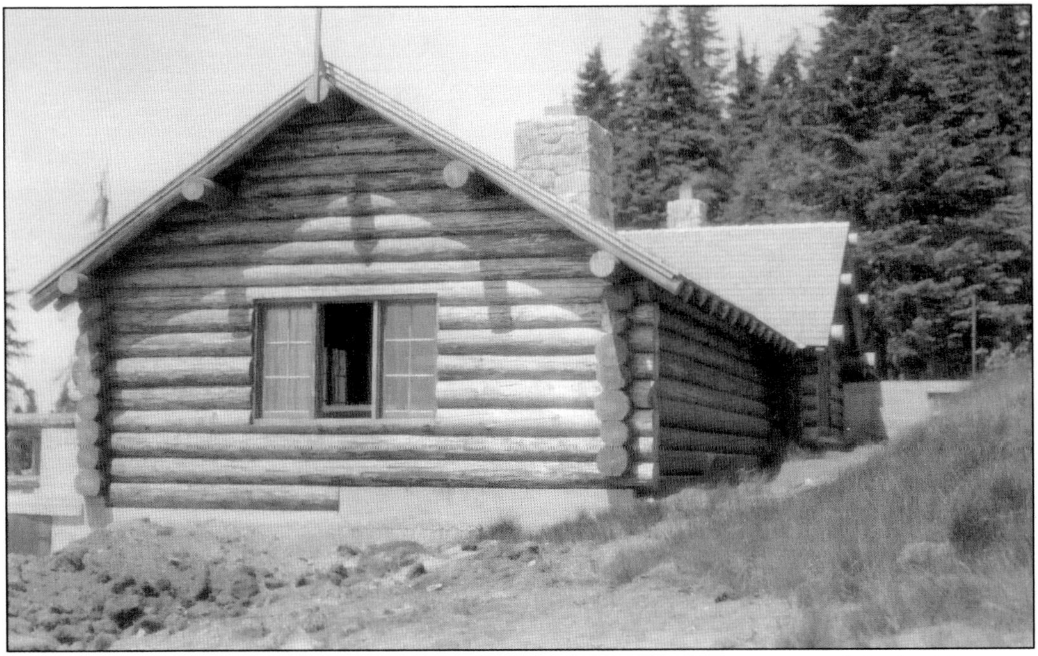

Newly constructed Cook's Cabin was completed around 1935. One section of the building was home for the park's caretaker. The other section would have a large 17-by-23-foot public room for skiers and hikers to use as a warm-up and resting area. The public rope tow was built and in use by this time at Cook's, taking skiers to the summit area. (NWR-SPL.)

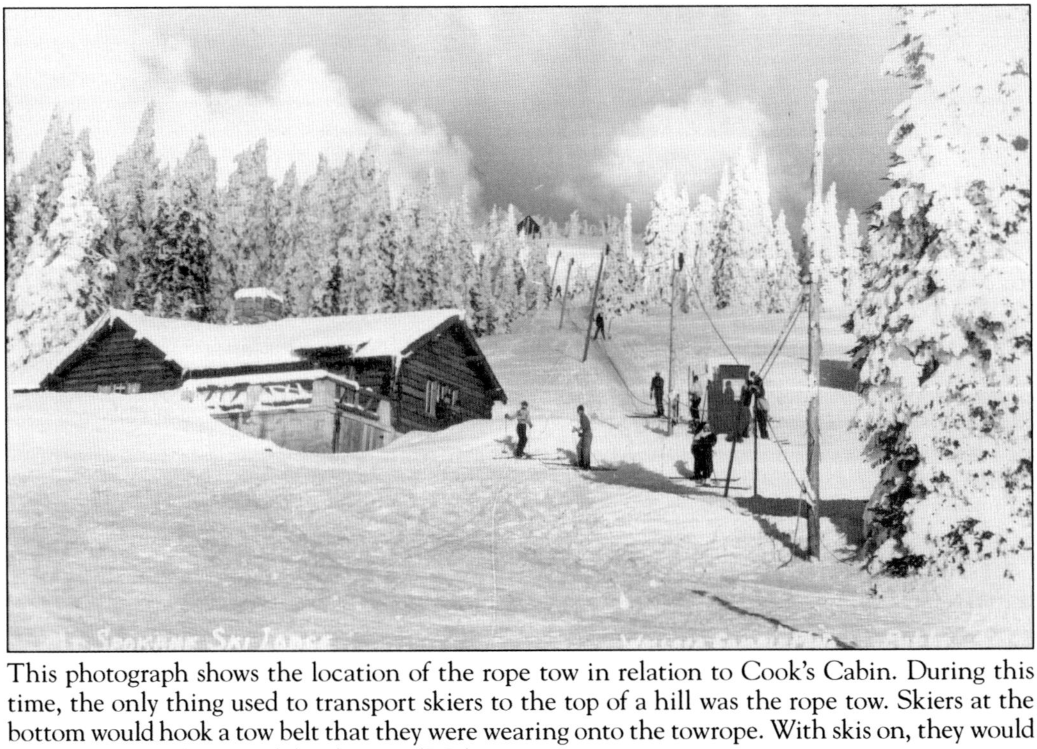

This photograph shows the location of the rope tow in relation to Cook's Cabin. During this time, the only thing used to transport skiers to the top of a hill was the rope tow. Skiers at the bottom would hook a tow belt that they were wearing onto the towrope. With skis on, they would be pulled up to the top of the ski run. (DB.)

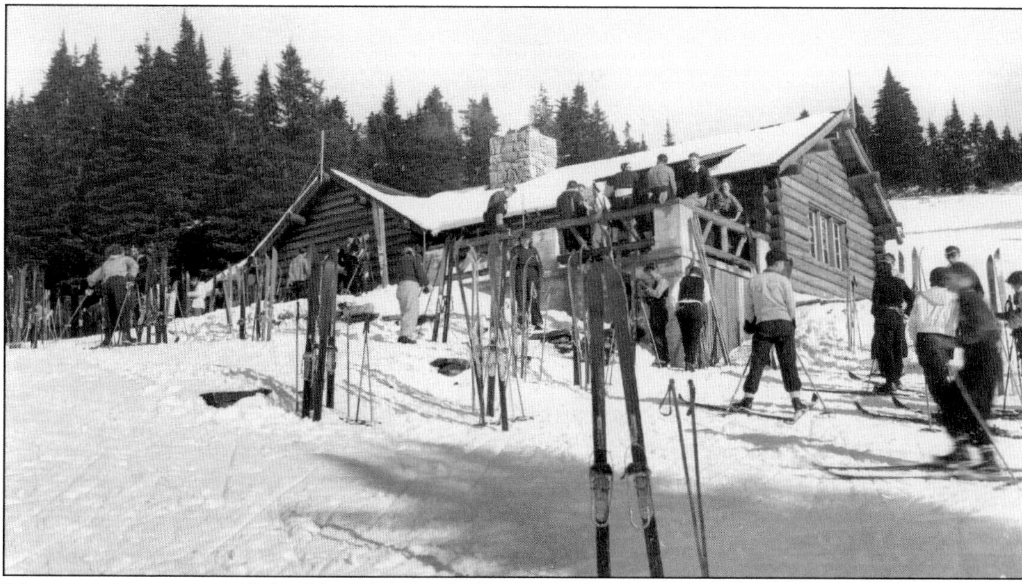

This is a closer view of Cook's Cabin with skiers on the front deck, which was used frequently. During the 1930s, skiing attendance hit an all-time high. With every weekend of the season open, Cook's was crowded with skiers. Many people from Spokane learned how to ski at Cook's. It was during this time that Mount Spokane skiing became very popular. (DB.)

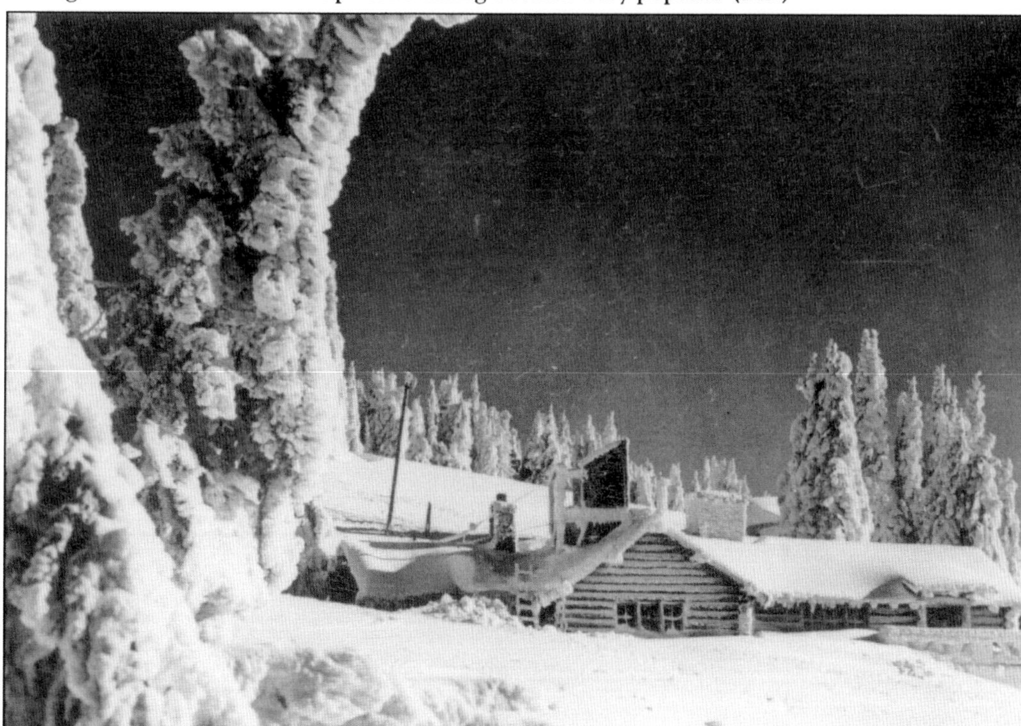

Here is one of the earliest photographs that could be found of Cook's Cabin covered with snow. Note the rope tow pole in the back and the ladder propped against the roof for shoveling snow. From time to time, the roof would be shoveled off after major snowstorms. (DB.)

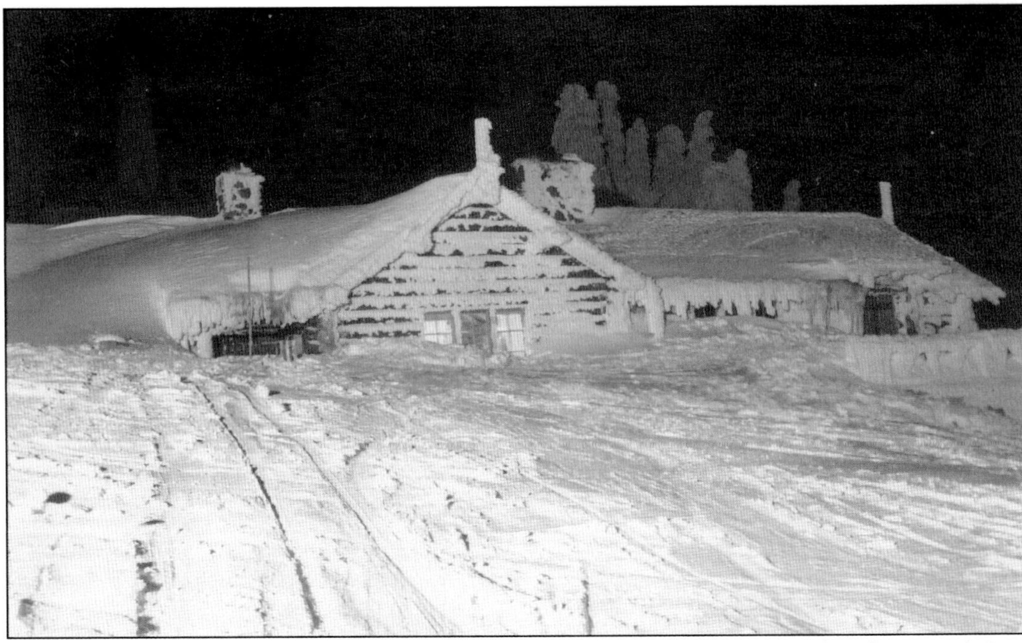

This photograph and the one below show Cook's Cabin in the same view. The photograph here suggests that it was shot at night with either a floodlight burning or a large flash on the camera because of the dark background. Winter snows are setting in and almost cover the roof. (NWR-SPL.)

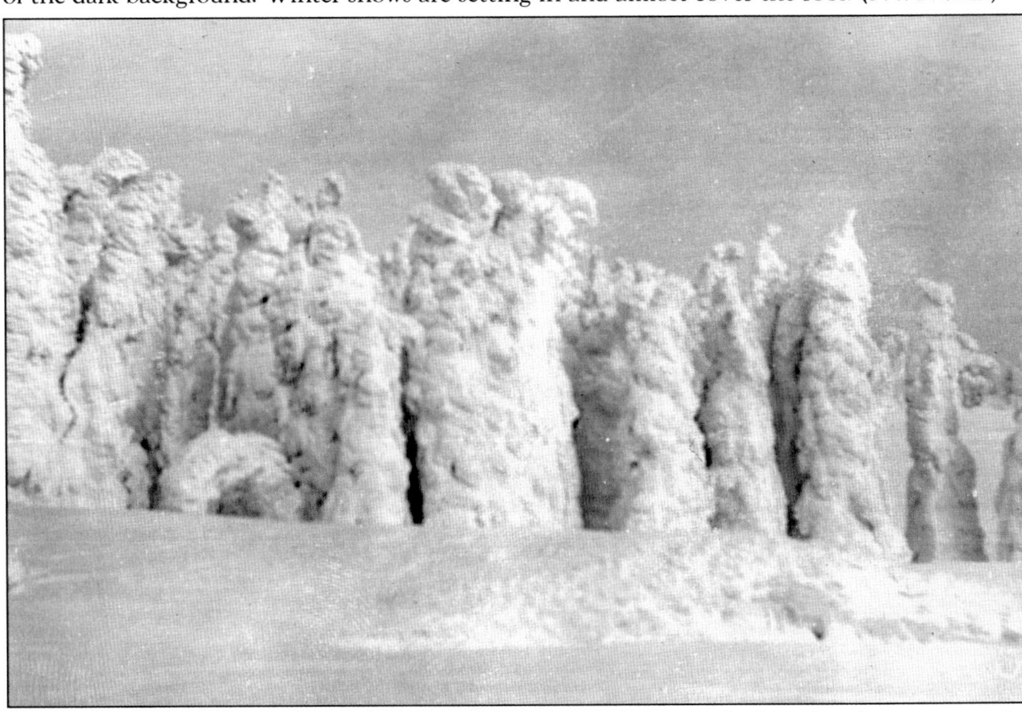

This is Cook's Cabin after a heavy snowfall. It is in there, tucked under the snow in the lower-right corner. Thanks to the dedication of the skiers and park staff, there were never any reports of roof collapse with the large amounts of snowfall on the cabin throughout the 1930s and 1940s. (Leo.)

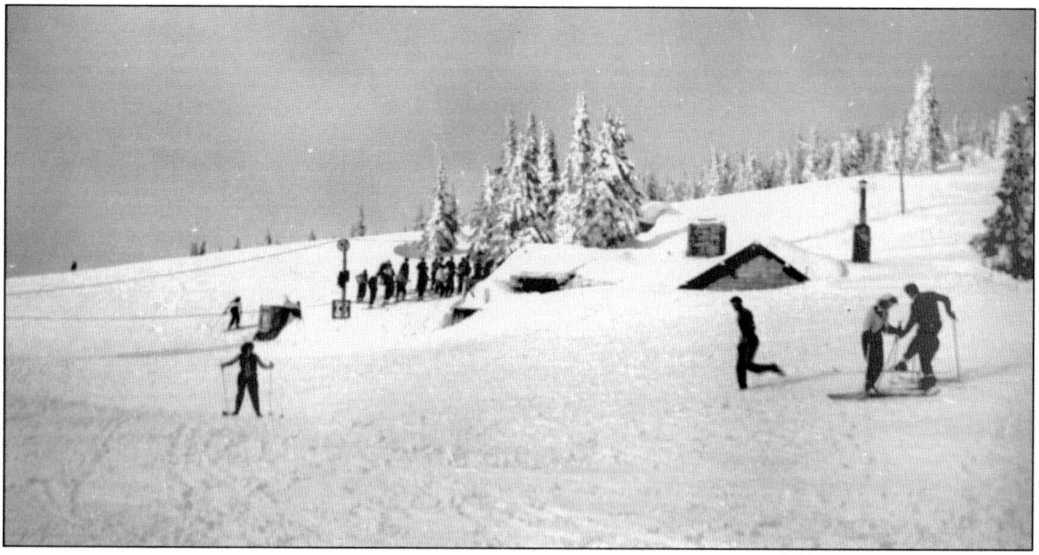

Above is a rare photograph of Cook's Cabin buried in snow during a great ski day in the 1930s. Shown below is Cook's Cabin from the back. Cook's in the center is gone today. Note the power lines to the right of Cook's. Power was installed to the mountain in 1940 by Inland Power and Light Company. Crews beginning at Hillyard, just northeast of Spokane, cut a right-of-way and began to install power poles and lines across the countryside and up the southwest slope of Mount Spokane to Cook's Cabin's location. Working in rain and fog, the Inland crews hacked their way through brush that was 20 feet tall; the brush was so thick that workers could not see from one pole to the other. In the winter, freezing fog would hamper the workers. (Above, DL; below, Leo.)

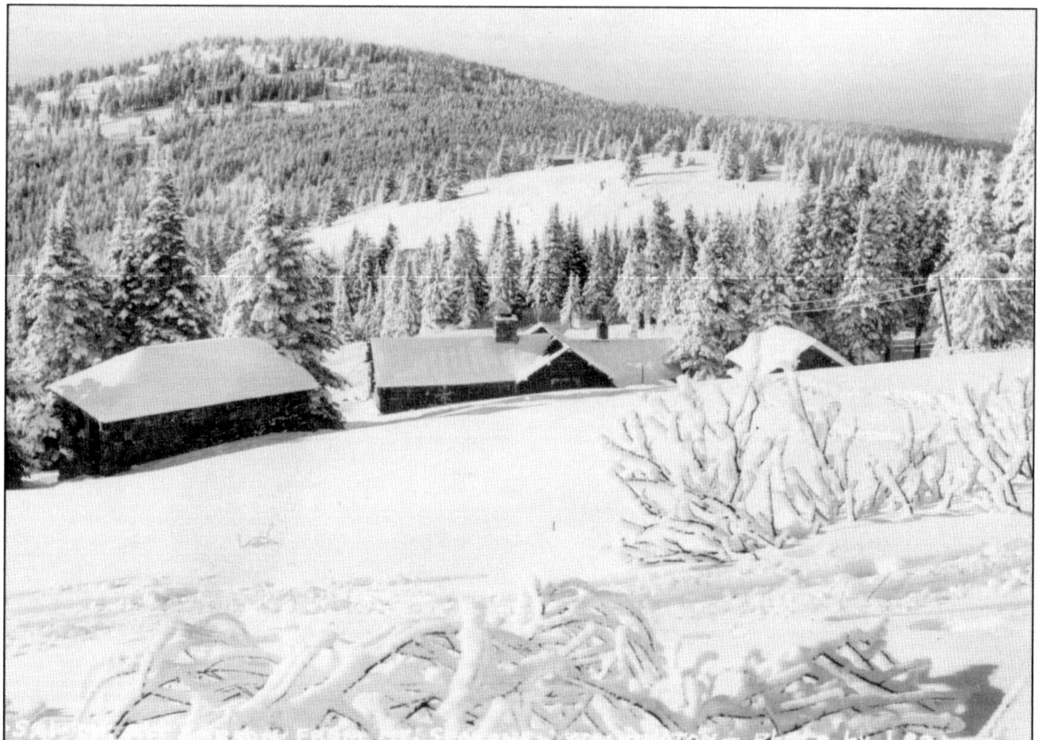

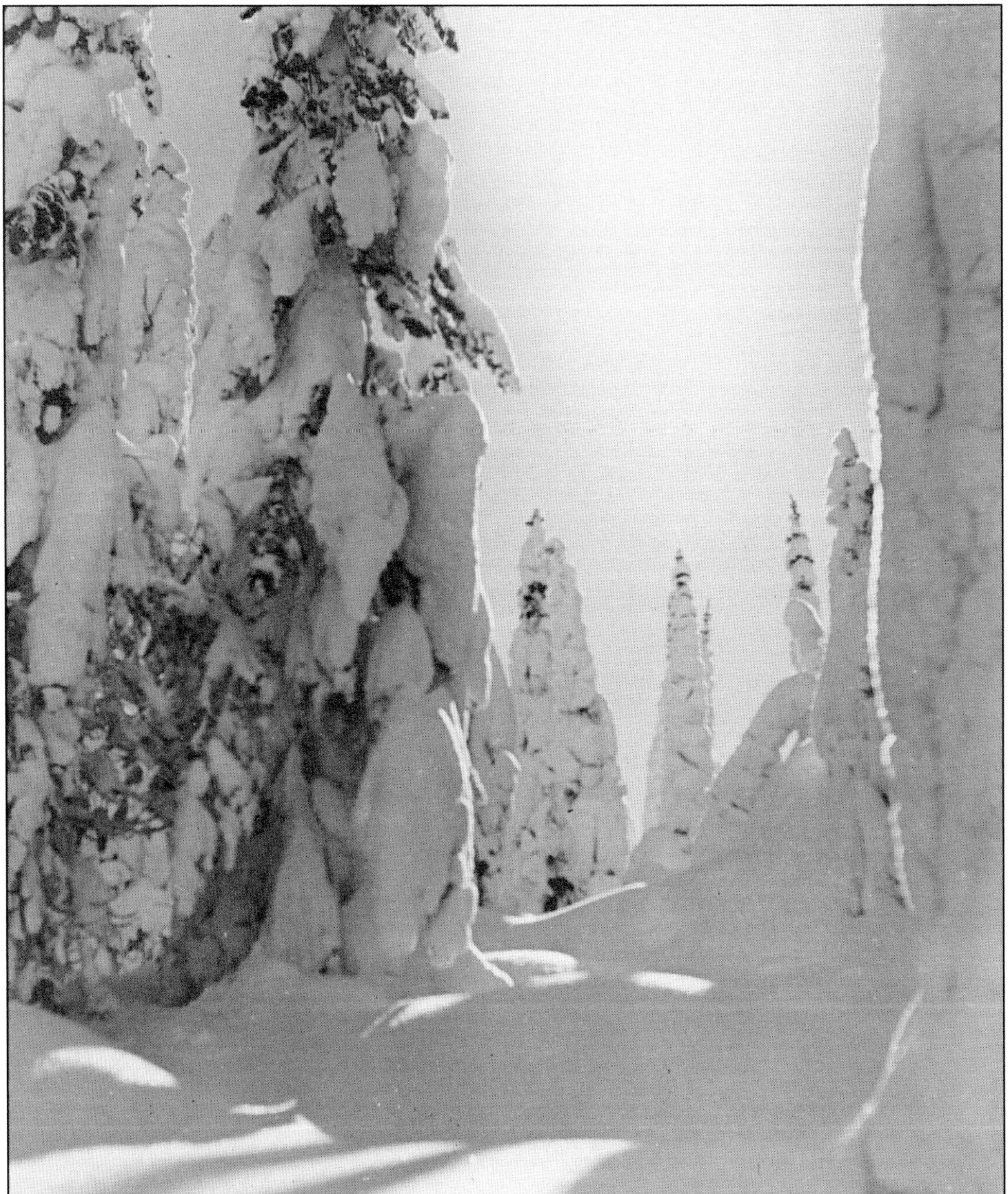

In addition to the Spokane Ski Club and the Selkirk Ski Club, the Spokane Mountaineers staked out a spot for skiing at Mount Spokane. In addition to the success at the public ski area of Cook's Cabin, the three ski clubs had many accomplishments throughout the remainder of the 1930s well into the 1950s. The Spokane Mountaineers purchased 40 acres of land on the south slope of Mount Spokane to the east of Linder Ridge. A cabin and ski rope tow were constructed and opened in 1939 with four downhill ski runs. The Mountaineers' cabin was large enough to sleep 10 people and had a small public area with cook stove. Although the Spokane Mountaineers was an outdoors club and not exclusively a ski club, almost a third of its members were skiers. Club officials believed that a ski facility would benefit the members in their club. Ski meets and tournaments were held at the club's location through the years. (NWR-SPL.)

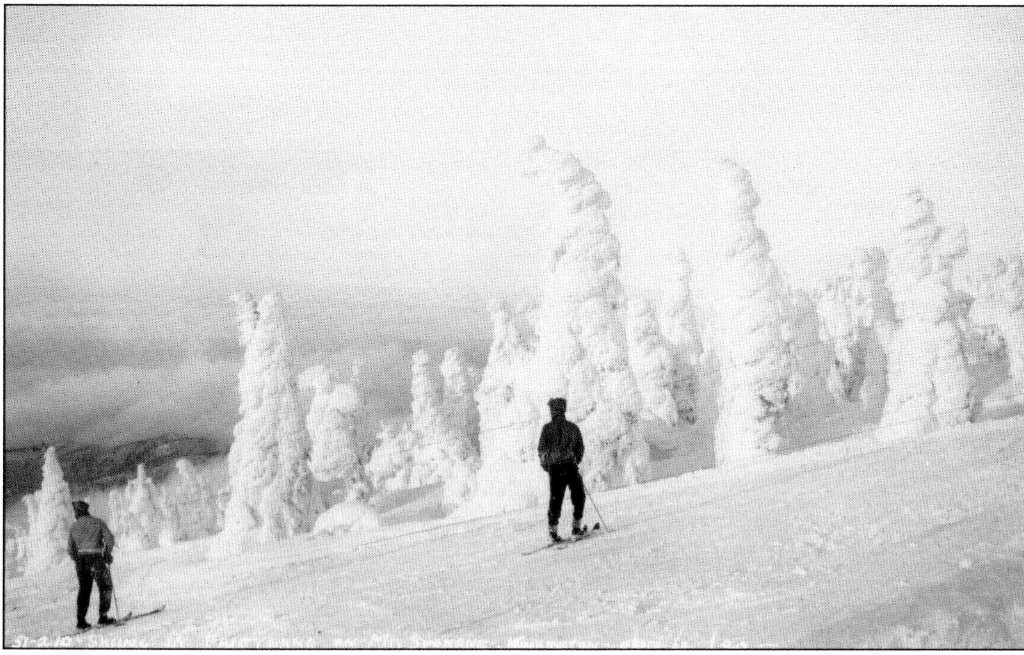

On the slope above Cook's Cabin, two lines of the rope tow can be seen at the center of the photograph. Shown below is the area above Cook's Cabin, including the upper terminal house for the rope tow. This area included the natural, open meadows of the Mount Spokane's southern face, which skiers loved. Although weather was a factor at times, especially the high winds, this area was used until the mid-1950s. (Above, Leo; below, DL.)

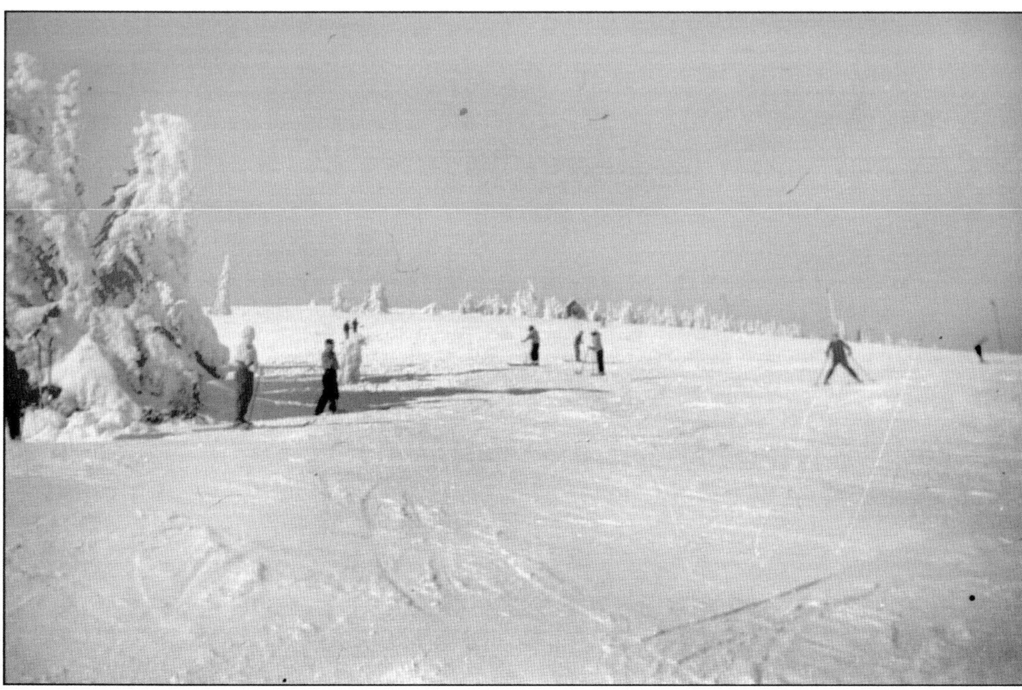

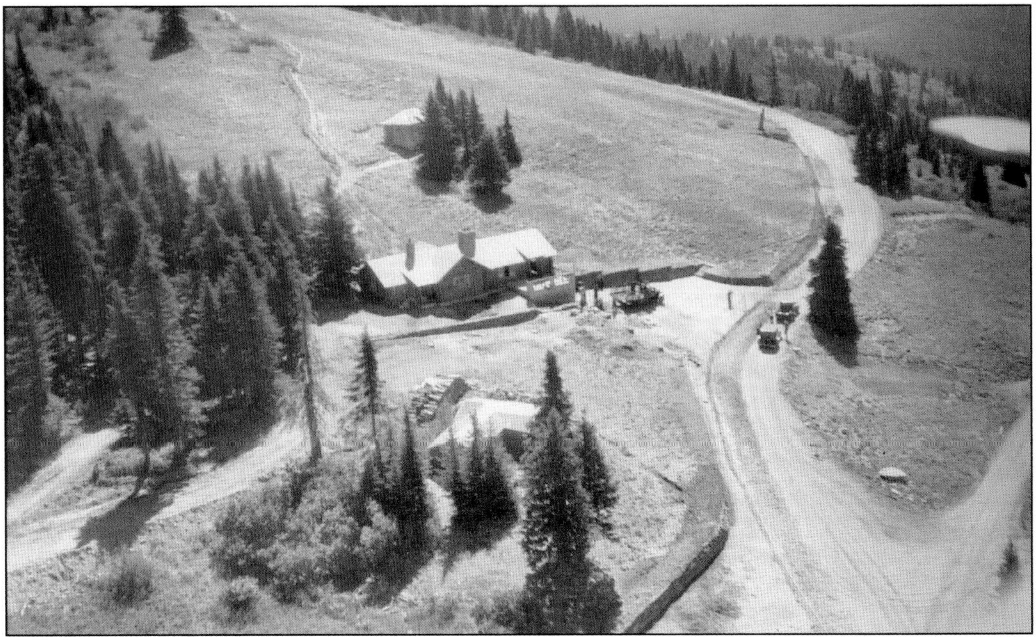

This aerial photograph of Cook's Cabin was possibly taken in the 1940s; the road to the left leading to the Mount Spokane Lodge was in existence from October 1940 until January 1952. Note the tail wing of the airplane in the upper right of the photograph. (MNI, Leo.)

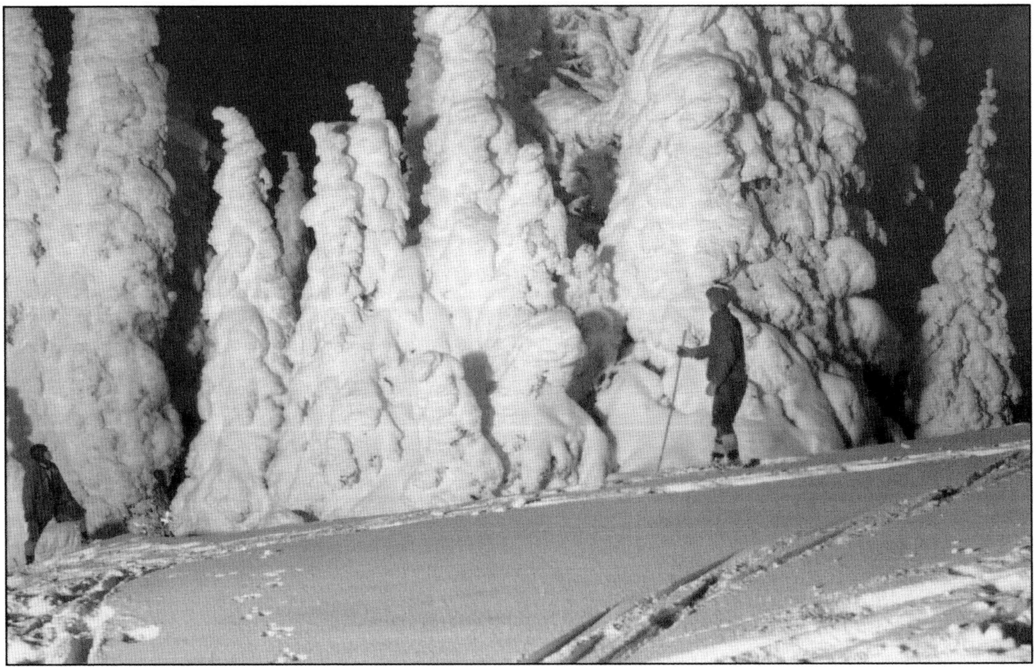

Titled "In the Garden of Snow," this photograph shows a the skier looking at the snow-covered trees. During the early 1930s, the Mount Spokane Ski Lift Association was formed to help raise money to purchase additional land for the park, as well as to improve the mountain's summer and winter recreation activities. The Mount Spokane Ski Lift Association would eventually install the first chairlift at Mount Spokane. (NWR-SPL.)

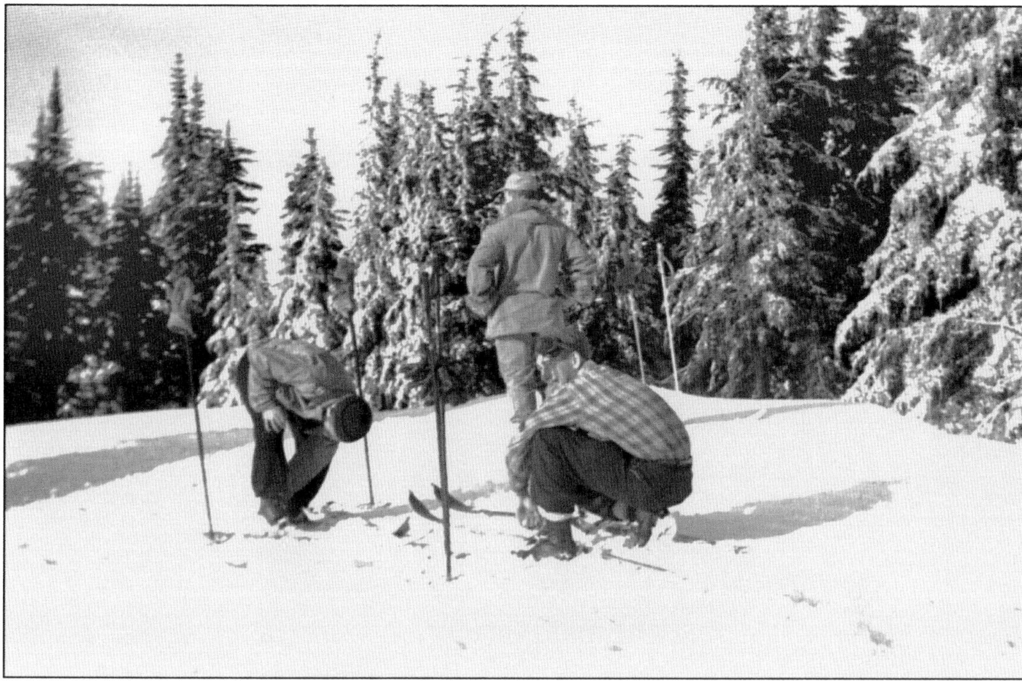

In this vintage photograph, a glimpse of the early ski clothing can be seen. Richard Francis is on the far right kneeling, and the other two men are unidentified. The Simchuk Sporting Goods store was very popular starting in the 1940s and operated for many years. From its retail store in Spokane as well as a shop at Mount Spokane, ski apparel, skis, bindings, and sponsored ski school classes at Mount Spokane were offered. The Simchuk family actively supported Mount Spokane and the ski facilities. During the early years, there were several other ski shops and retail stores in Spokane, including Bill Hatch Sporting Goods Company and Evergreen Sportland, both in downtown Spokane. Nor-Ski-Shop at Northtown and Al Corvi's Sport Shop, located in the Bon Marche, were also in downtown Spokane. (Above, DL; below, NWR-SPL.)

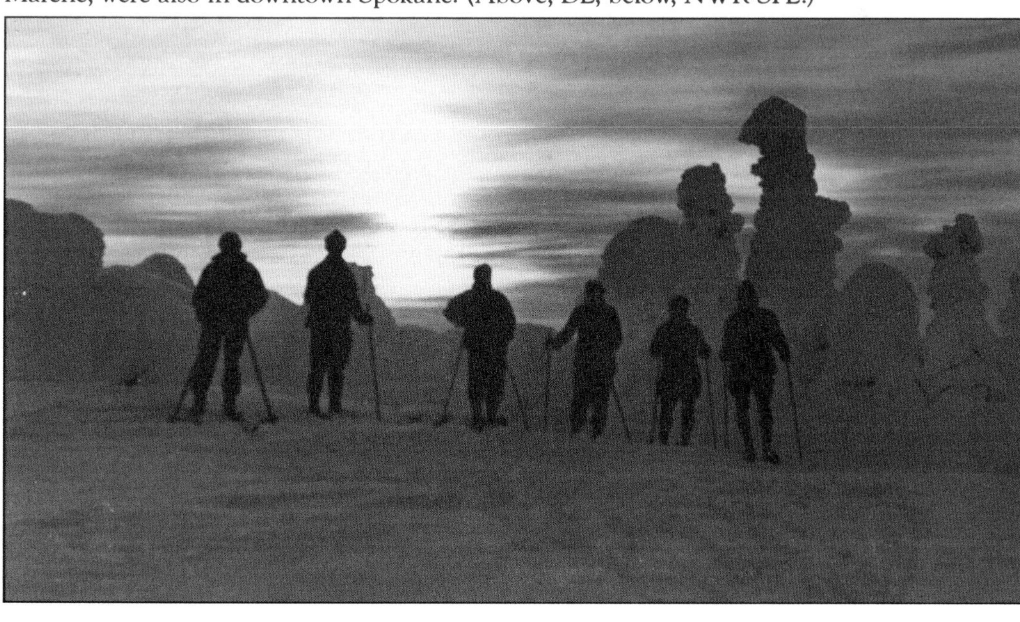

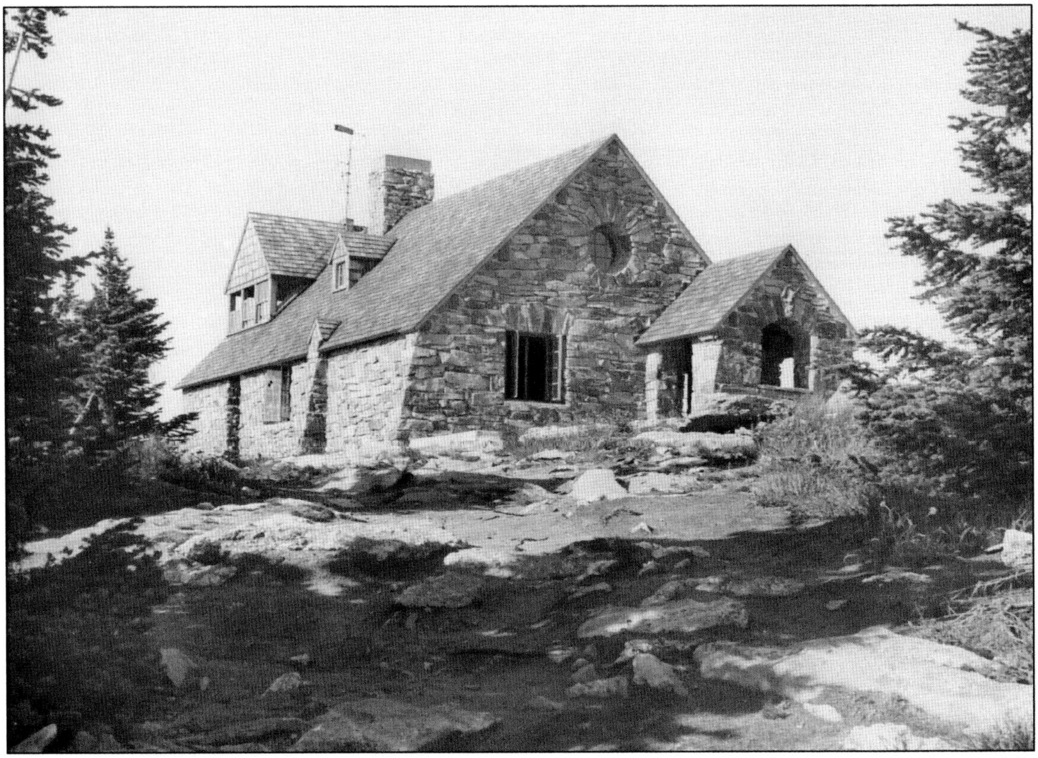

Here is the newly completed Vista House on the summit of Mount Spokane in 1934. (WSDA.)

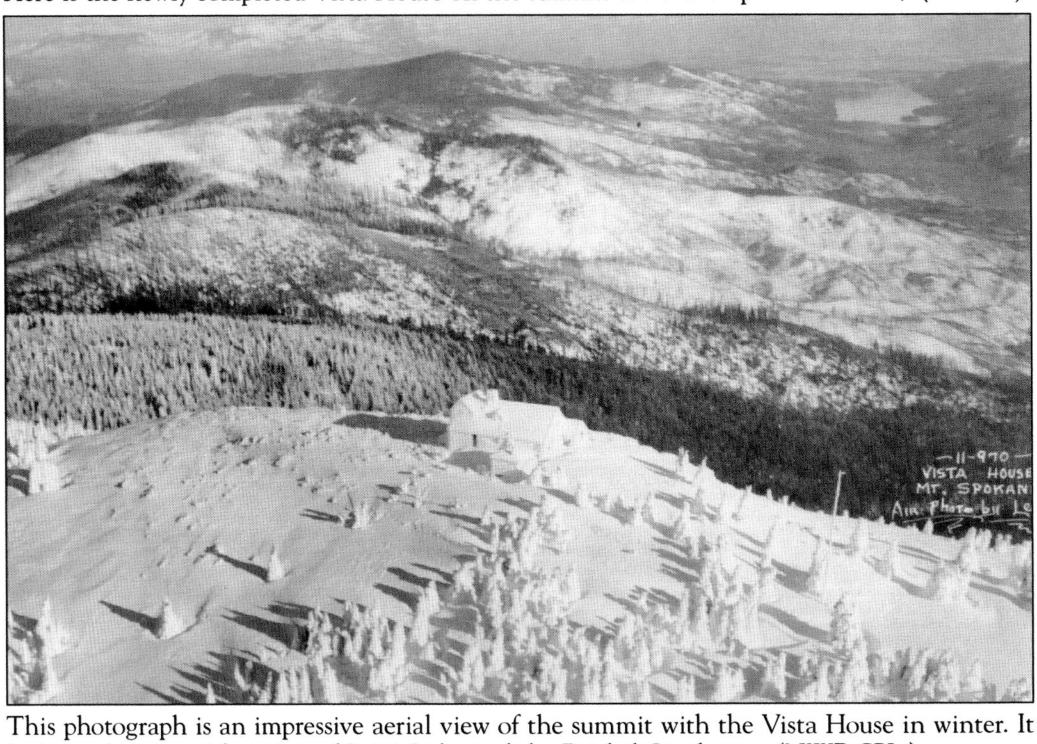

This photograph is an impressive aerial view of the summit with the Vista House in winter. It looks to the east with a view of Spirit Lake and the Brickel Creek area. (NWR-SPL.)

Five

Vista House

The Vista House had original plans that included a forest fire lookout and weather station. Designed by Spokane architect Henry C. Bertelsen, construction was started in 1933 and used native granite rock from the summit for the walls. It is generally accepted by everyone that the CCC crews built the Vista House; however, there are several newspaper articles from that time that suggest a private contractor helped with the work. By October 1933, the granite stone walls of the Vista House had been completed, and the roof rafters were being put in place as quickly as possible before the winter snow set in. The Division of Forestry, later the Washington State Department of Natural Resources, quickly set up a forest fire lookout on the second floor. This was used every summer from 1934 to 1948.

The Vista House was and still is the most photographed spot on the mountain. Throughout the years, the state parks have performed several maintenance projects on the Vista House to keep it structurally sound. From time to time, it has been opened and made available to skiers at the summit for a warming center. Recently in 2002, the state officials authorized a $151,000 restoration project to restore the second floor of the Vista House back to a fire lookout.

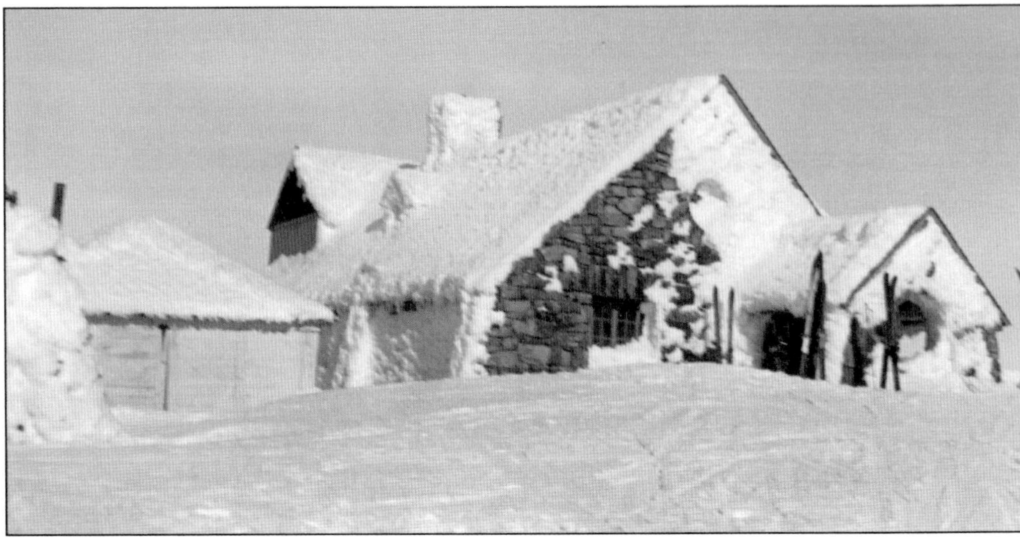

This photograph of the Vista House was taken on January 19, 1934, at the time of completion of the building. It is interesting to note the small building to the left of the Vista House. Whether this was used for construction supplies as the Vista House was being built or for something else cannot be confirmed. (NWR-SPL.)

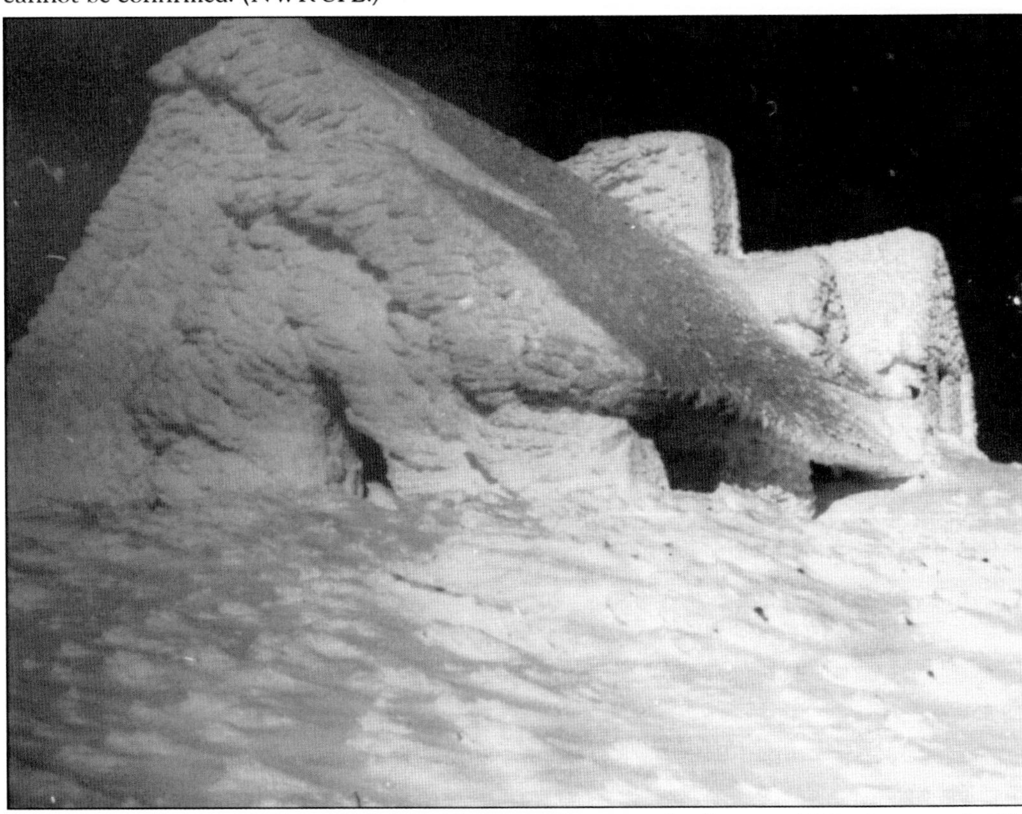

Layer upon layer of ice and snow cling to the Vista House in this January 1968 photograph. The design, workmanship, and periodic maintenance have kept the building in great shape over the years, in spite of the winter ice and snow loads to the building and roof. (RK.)

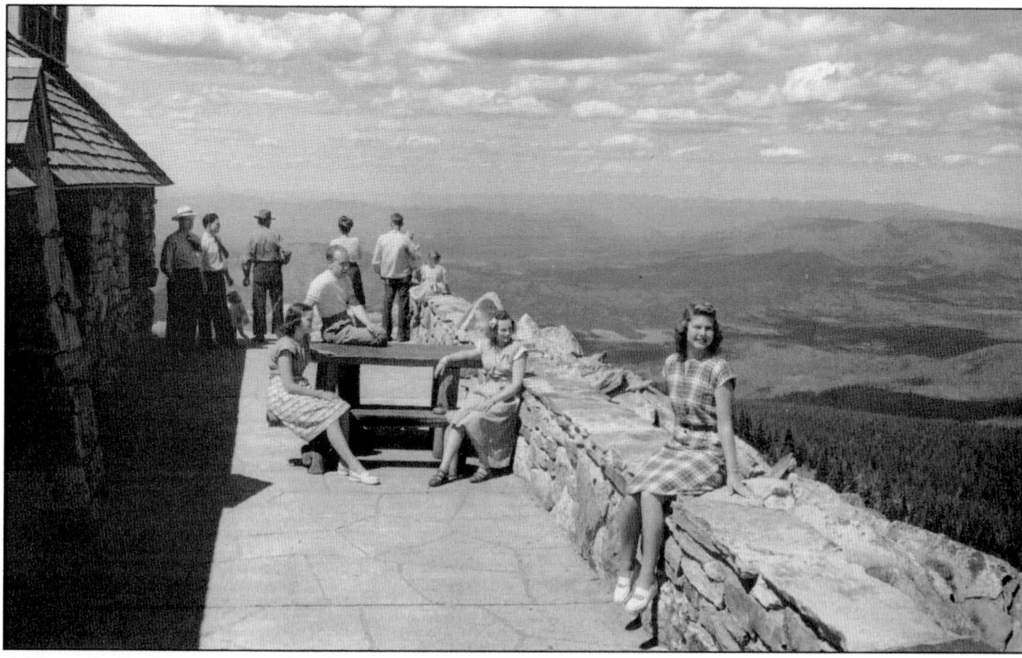

Although the Vista House has been used by skiers as a warming center over the years, summertime is perfect for a visit to the Vista House. The rock walls and wooden beamed roof are all original from the day the construction was completed in 1934. With upkeep by the state parks, the Vista House continues to be very accessible for the public to enjoy. Over the years, picnics have been a common occurrence during the summer. Weddings have also taken place at the Vista House. The Vista House remains a popular place to visit in summer. (Both, WSDA.)

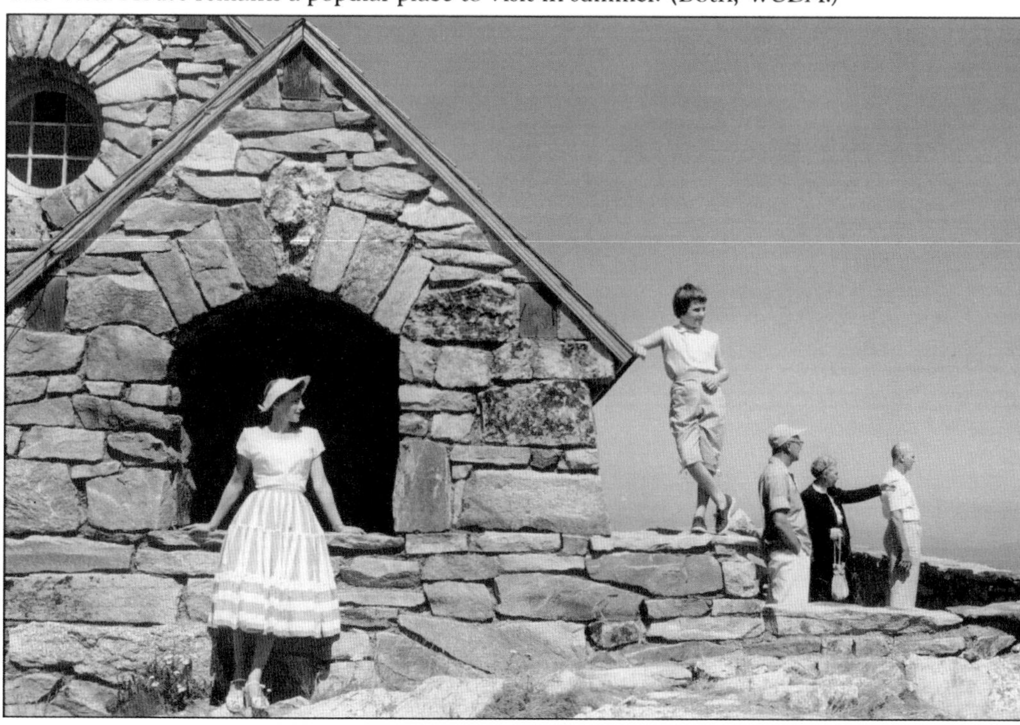

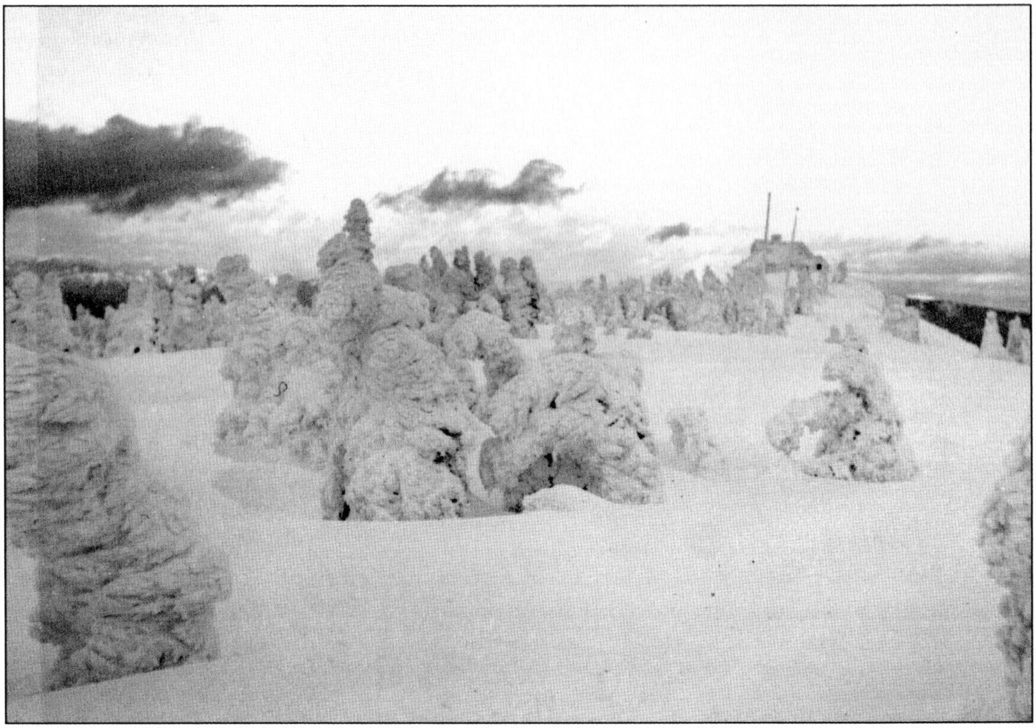

With the Vista House in the distance, this winter scene from the 1940s is paired with a view from the same angle taken during the summer. In the photograph below, note the vehicle at the base of the rocks. As this photograph shows, the Vista House was built on a natural rock bench, which was a little higher than the broad flat area of the mountaintop. The summit area is generally level, with two separate locations being higher. The Vista House is located on the north summit, and the elevation is listed as 5,883 feet. The other section of the summit area, called the south summit, is listed as 5,867 feet. (Above, NWR-SPL; below, DB.)

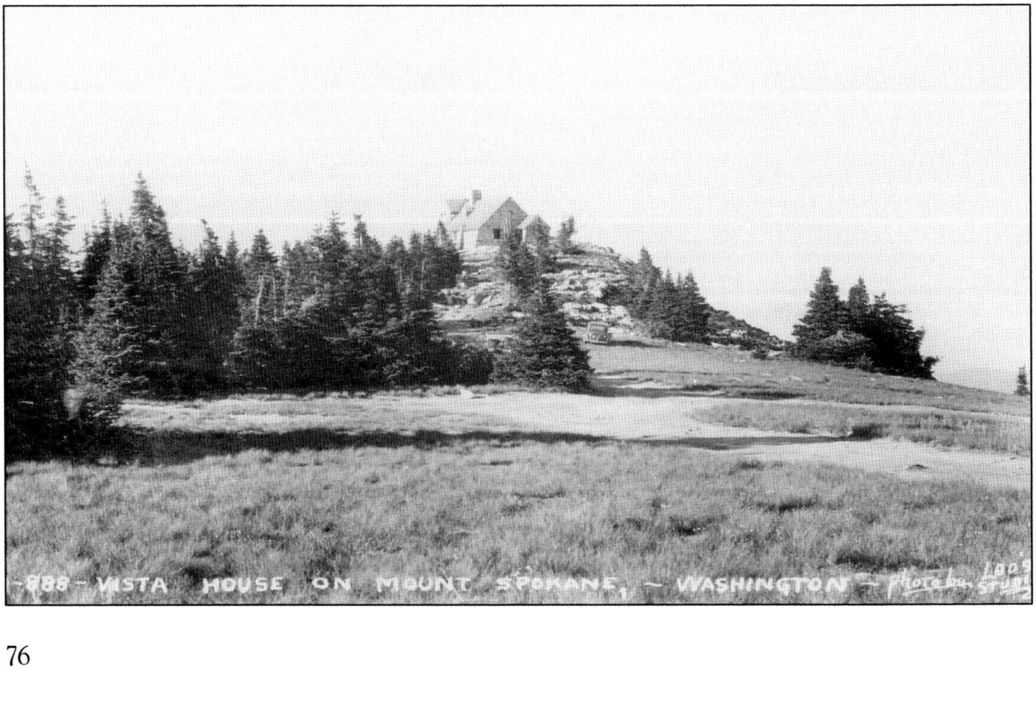

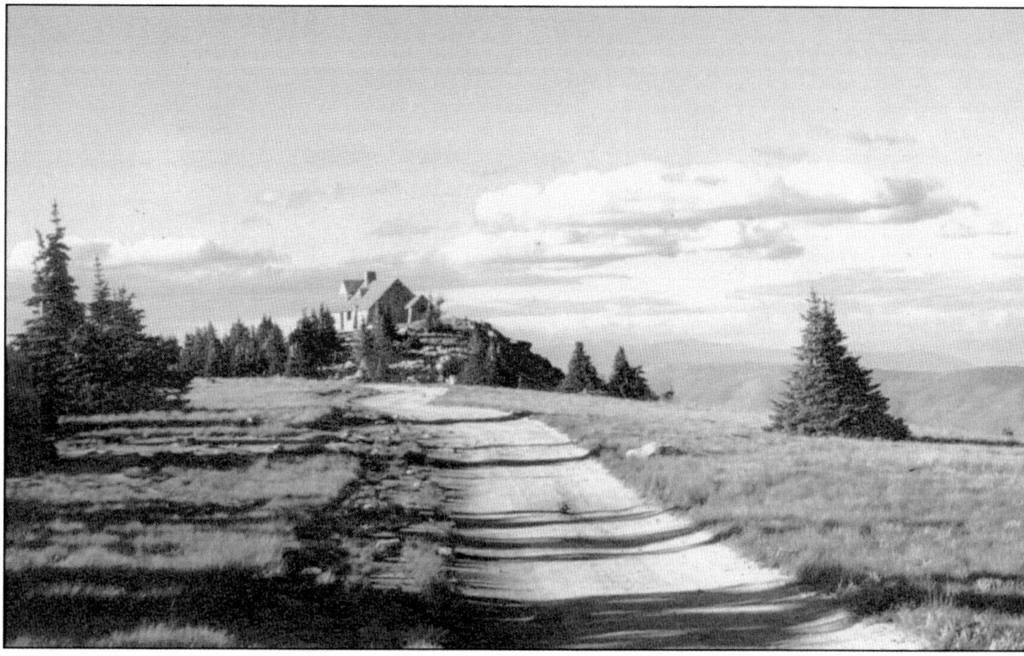

In the 1920s and 1930s, Spokane County and the State of Washington continued summer improvement work on the road up the mountain. By the late 1930s, the summit road had been completed, and vehicles could make the trip to the top. The road improved even more in 1974 when it was paved to the summit. (TSB.)

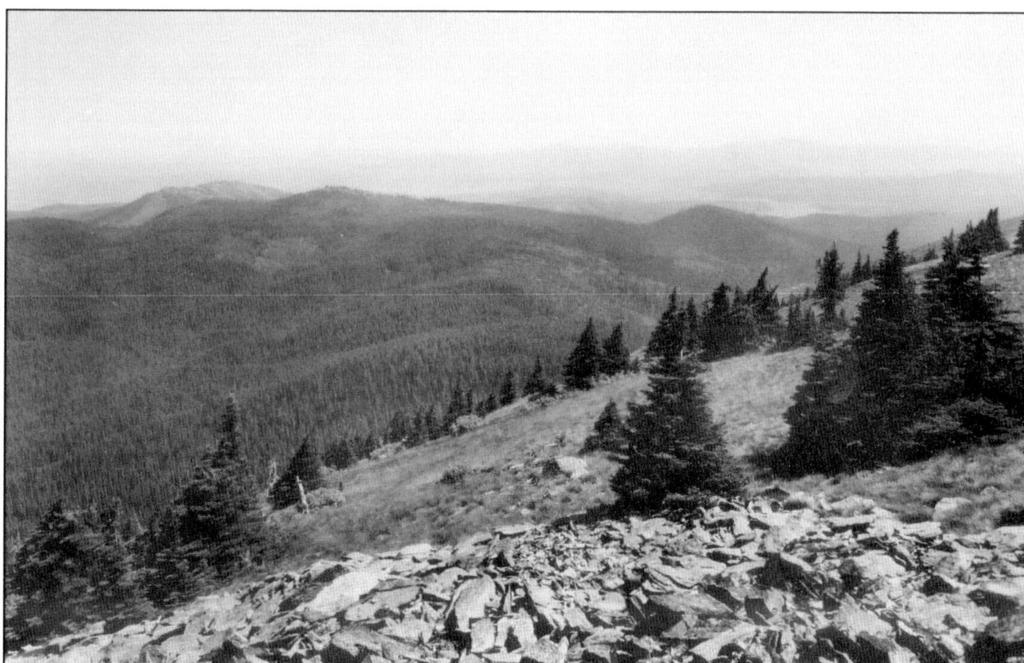

Tons of small, loose granite rocks are scattered about the northeast side of the summit. For hundreds of years, the Indians made rock carrions at the summit. Later, the Civilian Conservation Corps used the granite to build the walls of the Vista House. (NWR-SPL.)

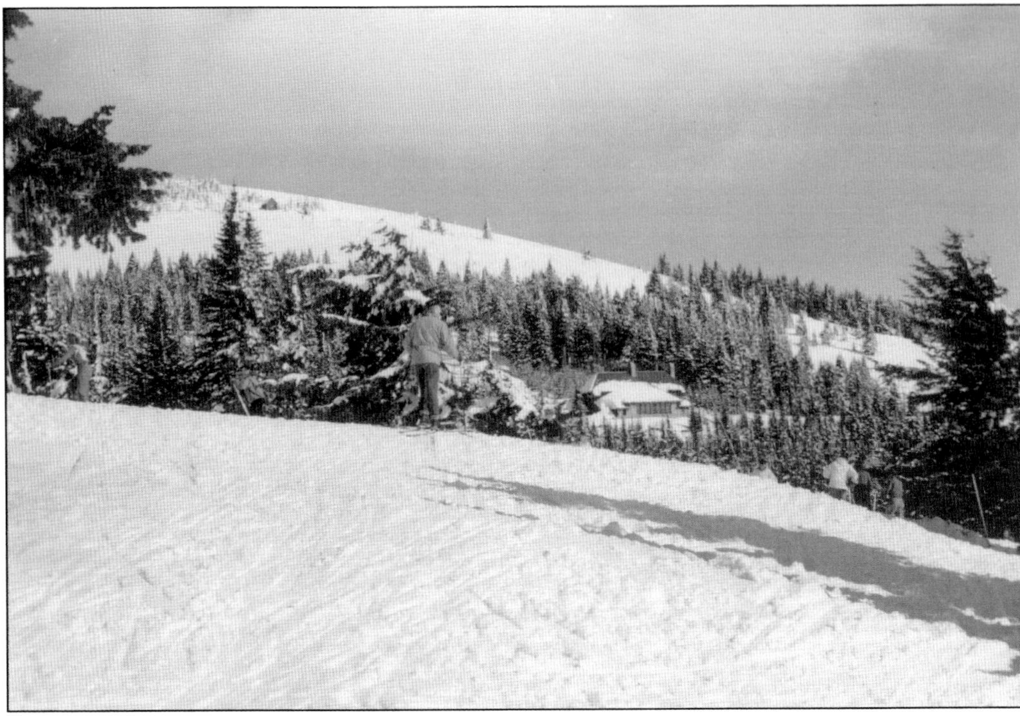

As seen from the Mount Kit Carson area during the 1940s is Mount Spokane Lodge. Note the rope tow's upper terminal near the summit of Mount Spokane. Although Cook's Cabin had a rope tow at the time of the construction of the lodge, officials planned on installing a new rope tow for the lodge. (Leo.)

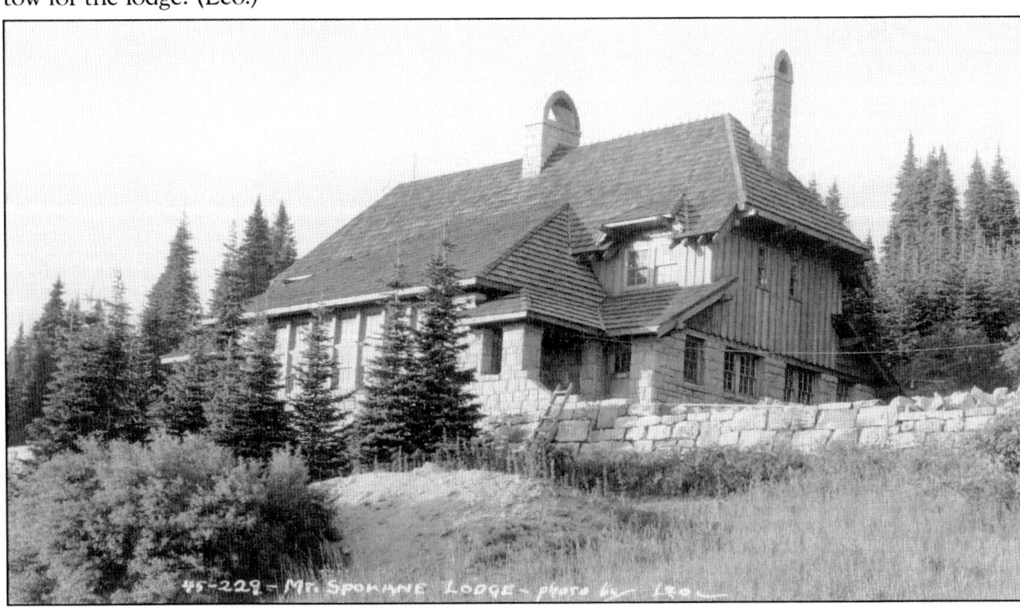

Here is the completed Mount Spokane Lodge shortly after it opened in 1940. The lodge featured cut native granite stonework on the exterior and plenty of large viewing windows. The lodge and its later addition burned in a disastrous fire on January 23, 1952. Parts of the cut stone wall as well as the foundation are still in place today. (DB.)

Six

Mount Spokane Lodge

During the late 1930s, skiing attendance at Mount Spokane hit an all-time high. Park officials began planning the construction of a spacious lodge to be built several hundred feet from Cook's Cabin. Using a federal grant of $58,000, CCC work crews constructed the lodge with work beginning in 1939. The lodge included a lounge, dining room, ski-waxing room, and rooms for 32 people.

The completed Mount Spokane Lodge opened to the public on October 21, 1940. Over 1,000 people attended the open house that day. This would be the first time that actual overnight accommodations and a café would be open for business on Mount Spokane. There were small overnight cabins and warming huts that the ski clubs had used for many years, but nothing was like the service the lodge would be offering.

Over the next several years, the lodge operated at capacity, and people were being turned away. With the help of the Mount Spokane Association, the state approved a plan for a three-story addition to the lodge. With estimates at $100,000 to build, it would be 29 feet by 119 feet. Work was started on the addition in June 1950. By September 1951, work was completed except for some interior work and outdoor landscaping. Opening date for the addition was set for February 1952.

On January 23, 1952, the weather was overcast and foggy with snow showers. During that evening, two employees were working at the lodge. David McMullen and electrician Rulon Downard were both in the lodge around 6:00 p.m. when they smelled gas fumes. Immediately after, an explosion ripped through the area, and Downard was instantly killed. McMullen ran out of the exploding building to call for help. Flames were shooting up 50 to 60 feet, and the whole structure was in flames within minutes. Fire crews arrived on the scene around an hour after the first alarm was called in, but it was too late. Within an hour and a half, the fire completely destroyed the original lodge and its new addition.

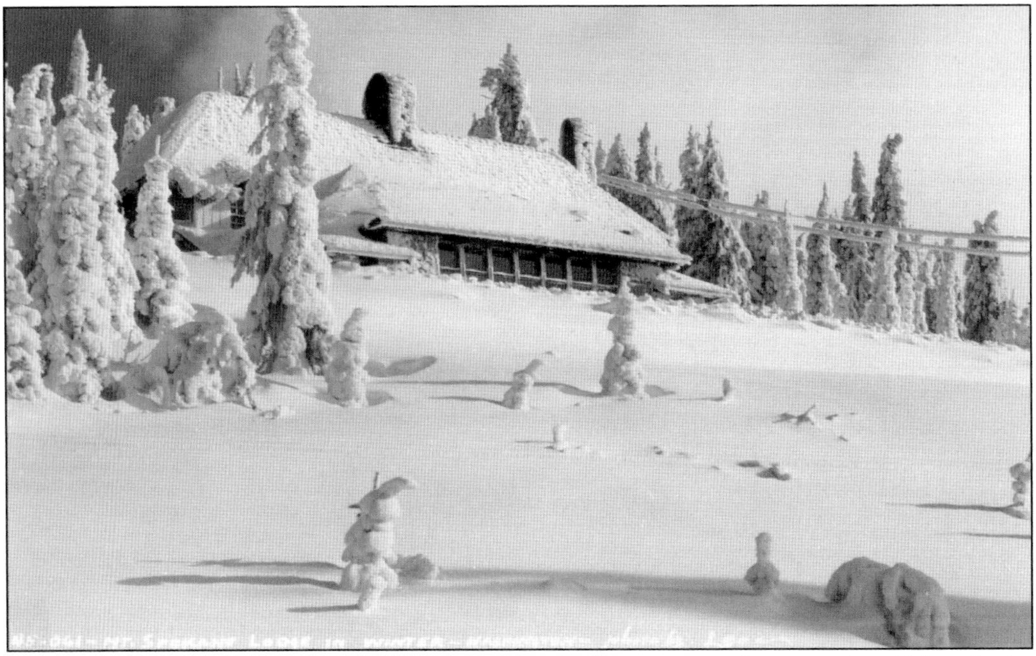

Mount Spokane Lodge is pictured in the winter with electric power line at right. Although the lodge was being built close to Cook's Cabin, Cook's would still be used for skiers. Next to Cook's Cabin was a ski tow that skiers used to access the summit. (DB.)

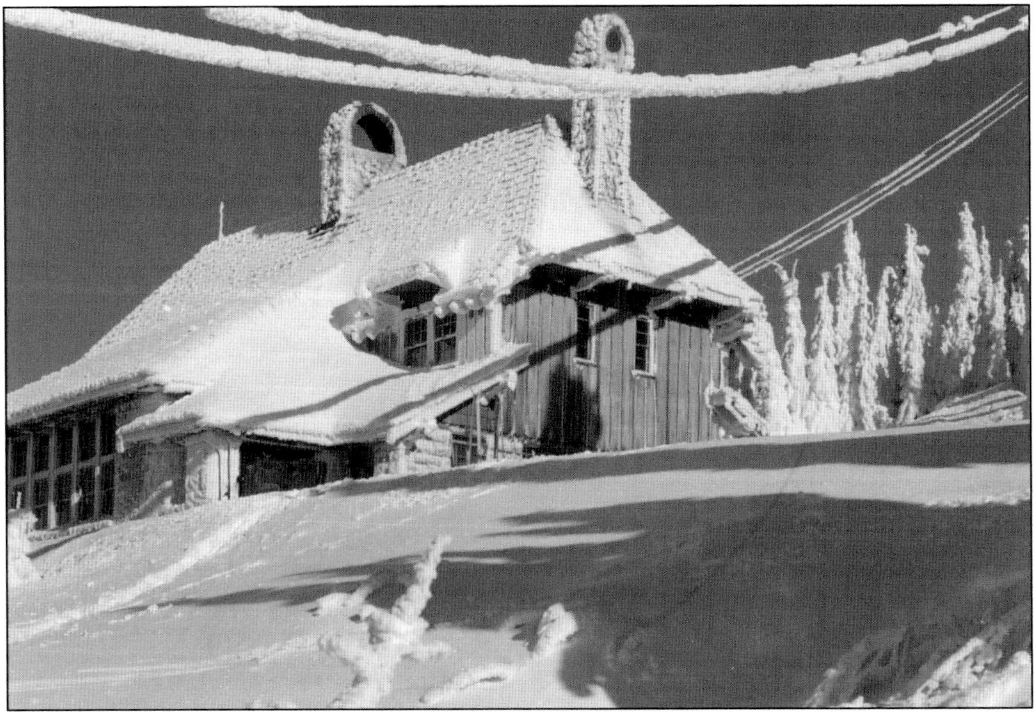

Here is another nice shot of the Mount Spokane Lodge. The lodge was an instant hit. Everyone was very pleased with the big spacious meeting room and natural granite fireplace, which was the focal point of the lodge. (Leo.)

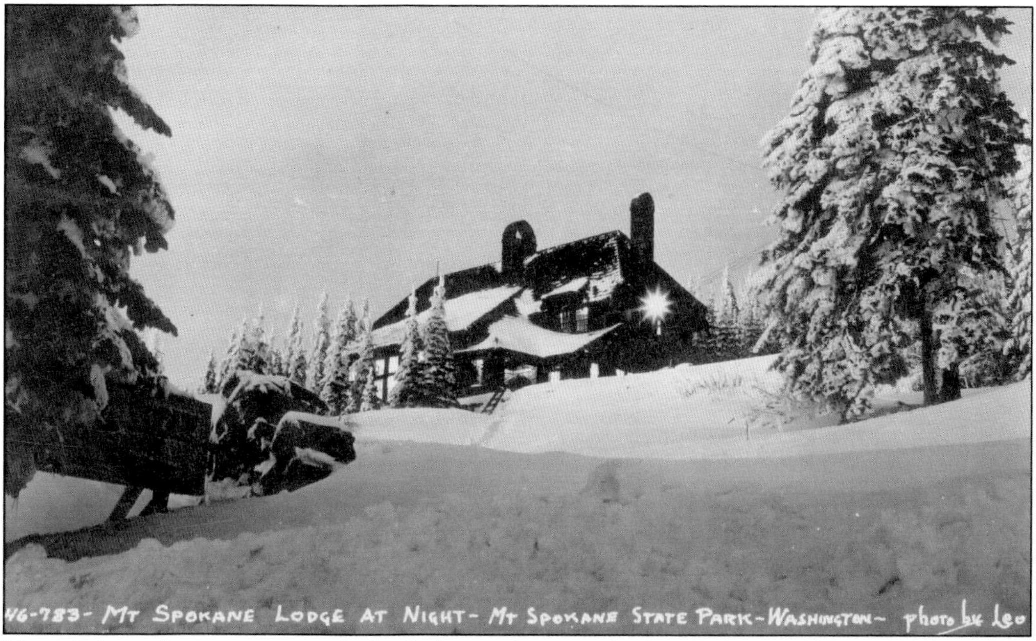

Viewed from the entrance road, the lodge is photographed at night, possibly with the help of moonlight. Note the Mount Spokane Lodge sign to the left. The lodge beckons visitors to its warm, comfortable interior. (DB.)

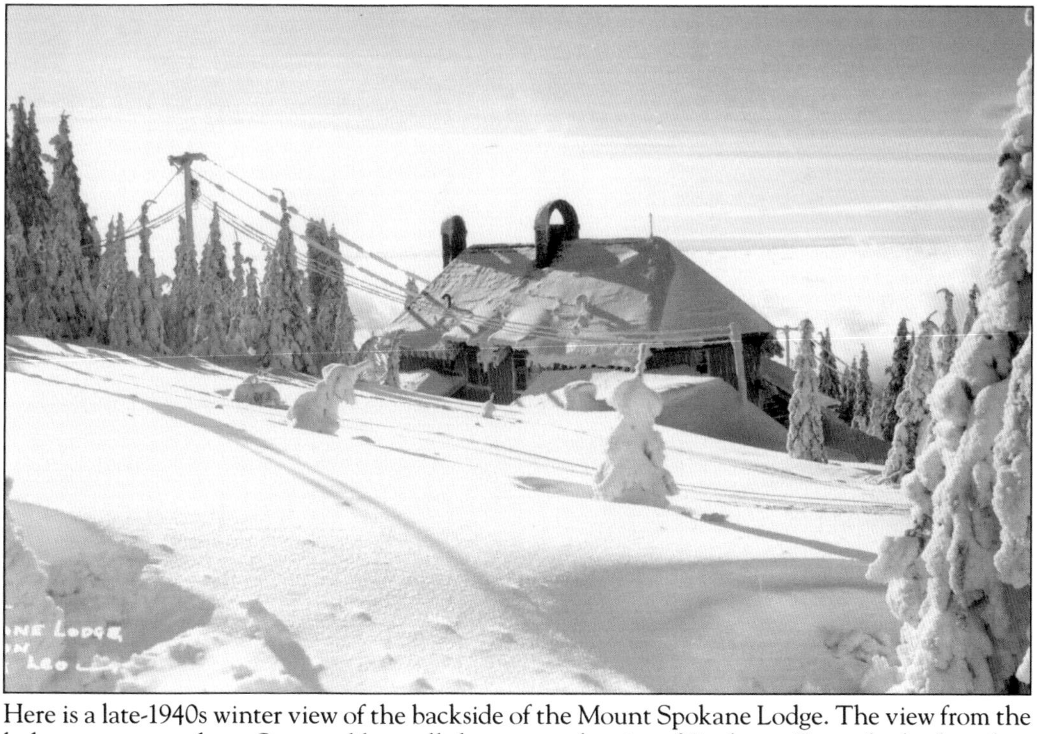

Here is a late-1940s winter view of the backside of the Mount Spokane Lodge. The view from the lodge was tremendous. One could see all the way to the city of Spokane. From the back and up the mountain to the left, skiers had their choice to ski on any part of the open treeless summit as well as the backcountry. (Leo.)

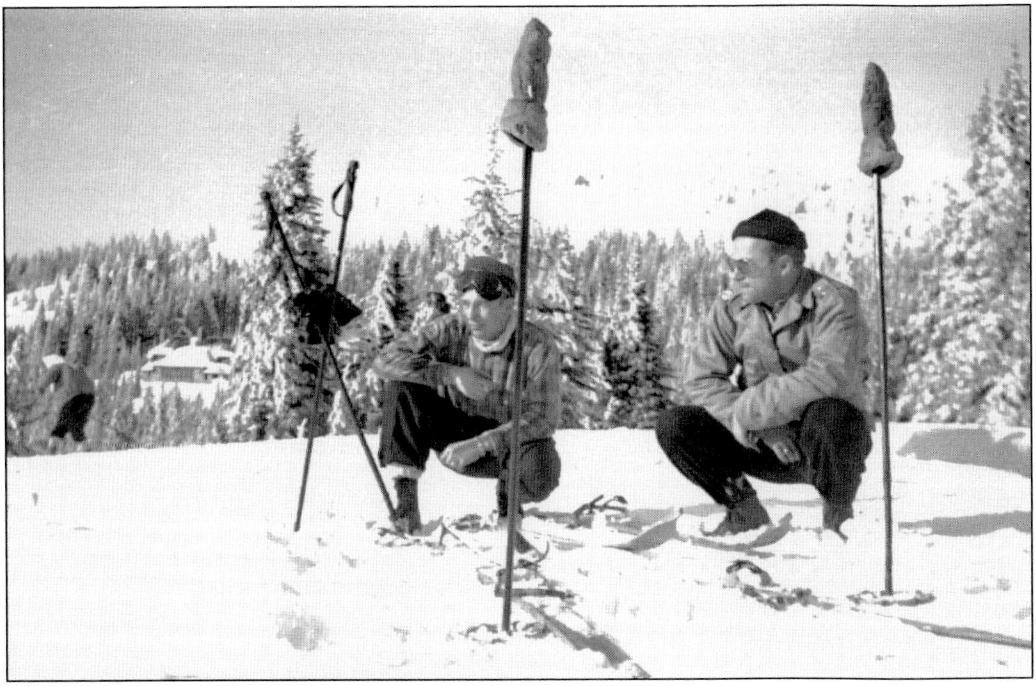

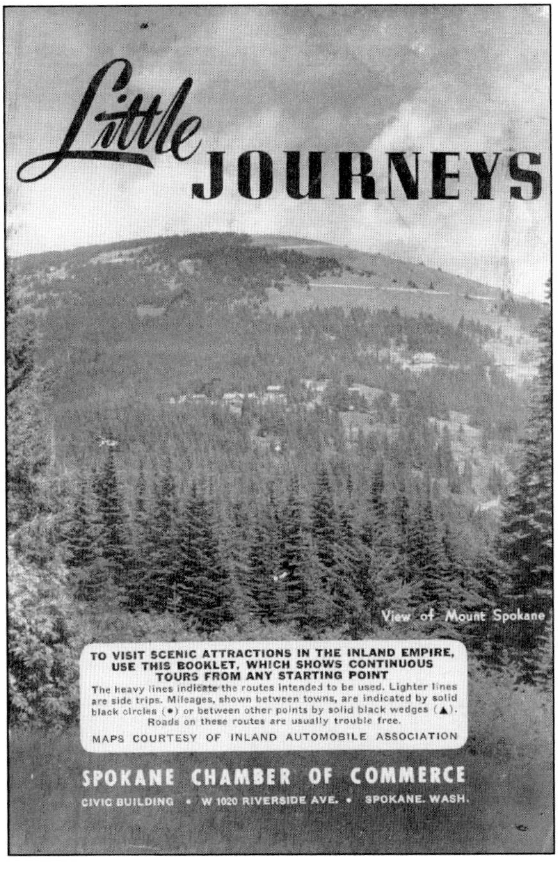

The Mount Spokane Lodge can be seen in the distance to the left, with the rope tow's upper terminal in the top center. Richard Francis is on the left, and George Stien is on the right. In 1951, the *Spokesman Review* newspaper sponsored a ski school at Mount Spokane. Interrupted briefly because of the lodge fire, the school reopened shortly after and was very successful for many years well into the 1970s. (DL.)

In the early 1950s, the Spokane Chamber of Commerce produced this booklet detailing several road trips for automobiles around the Spokane area. On the cover is Mount Spokane, with Cook's Cabin at far right. Moving left is the lodge, and near the center is the CCC camp. The summit road can be seen etched in the mountain headed toward the top. (GSI.)

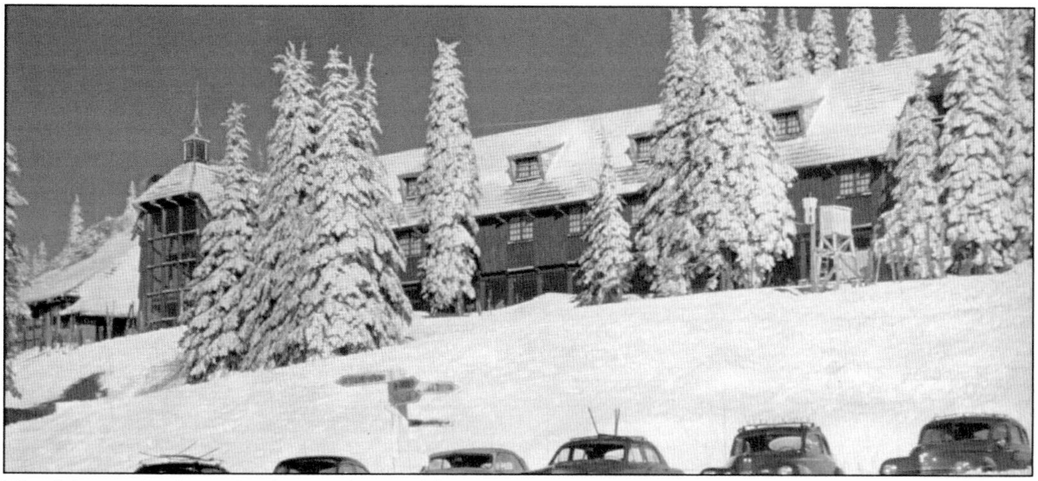

The Mount Spokane Lodge, with its addition, is shown in the late fall of 1951. The Washington State Parks and Recreation Commission was created in 1947 to oversee the state parks. Shortly after this, funding was approved for a $100,000 addition to the lodge. The Loveland Construction Company of Spokane was awarded the addition contract from the state parks commission. Work was started on the addition in June 1950. (AC.)

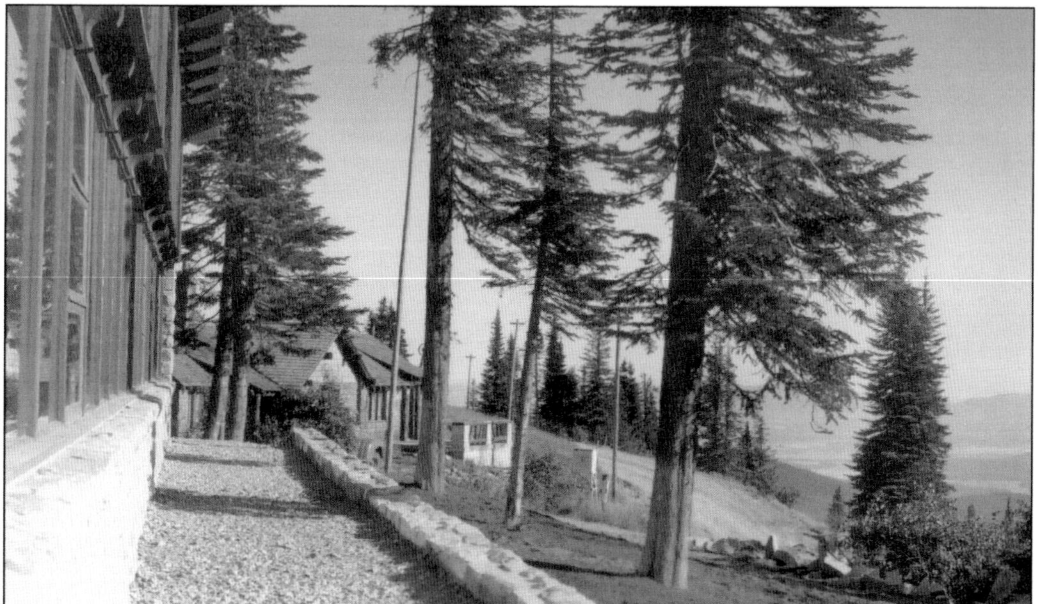

This photograph was taken in the fall of 1951, looking east toward Cook's Cabin from the front walkway of the new addition. The road leading to the summit is off to the right. The addition would greatly increase the overnight lodging capacity as well as provide a new dining and kitchen area. (Leo.)

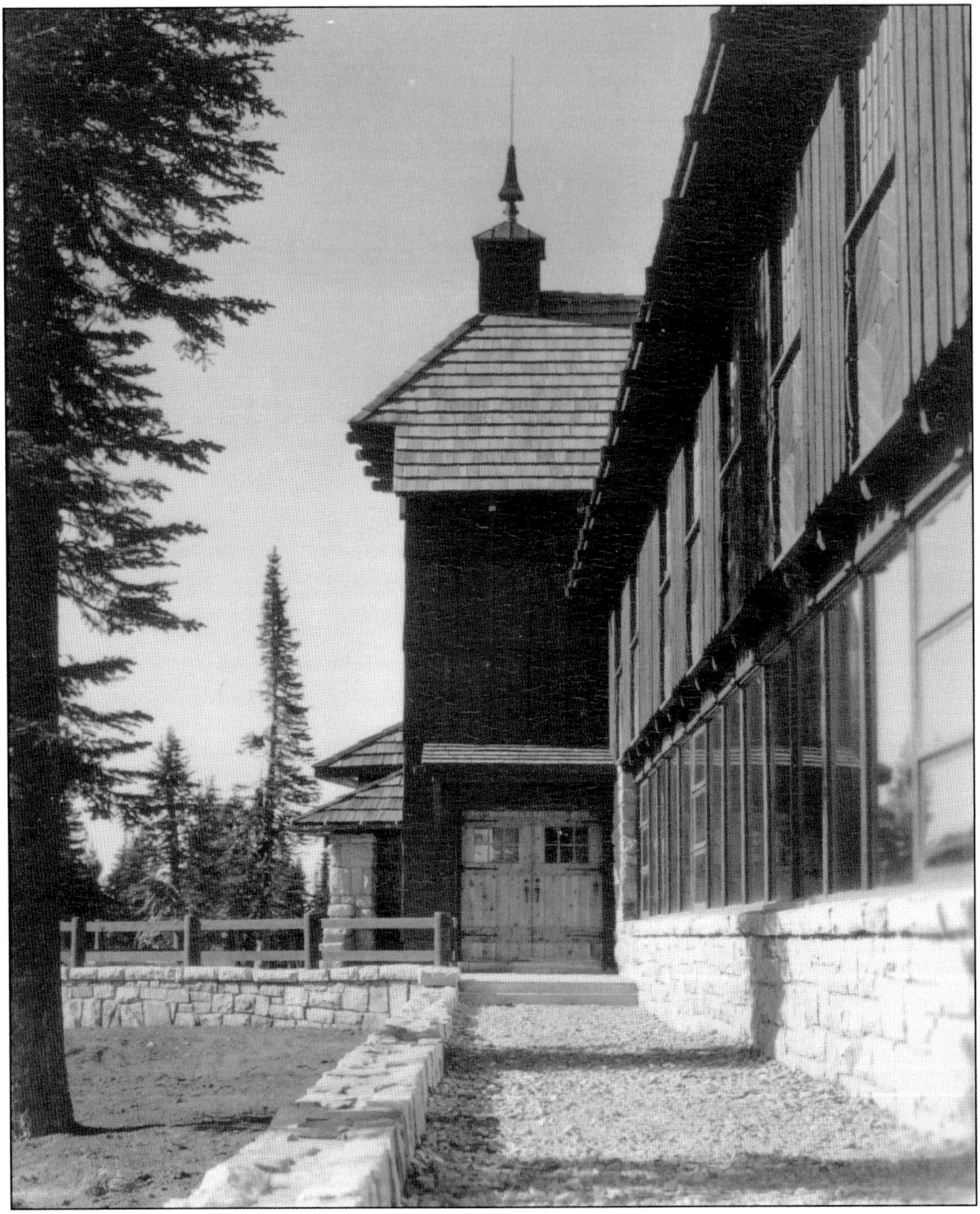

The new entrance on the lodge addition showcases its stonework and large windows. The original lodge can be seen in the background. The main floor of the original lodge was remodeled into a lounge with a rock fireplace. Across a hallway, a staircase climbed through the glass tower to the guest rooms upstairs. The interior was finished in knotty, rough-hewn cedar, and ski shops and a wax room were located in the basement. Attention at Mount Spokane was centered on the new lodge addition. Excitement was high with a "cannot wait for it to be completed" attitude. Also during this time, A.E. (Al) Mettler, operator of the Ridpath Hotel's coffee shop in Spokane, was accepted by the state as the new concessionaire for the lodge and ski facilities. This began a long-term association with Mettler and Mount Spokane. (Leo.)

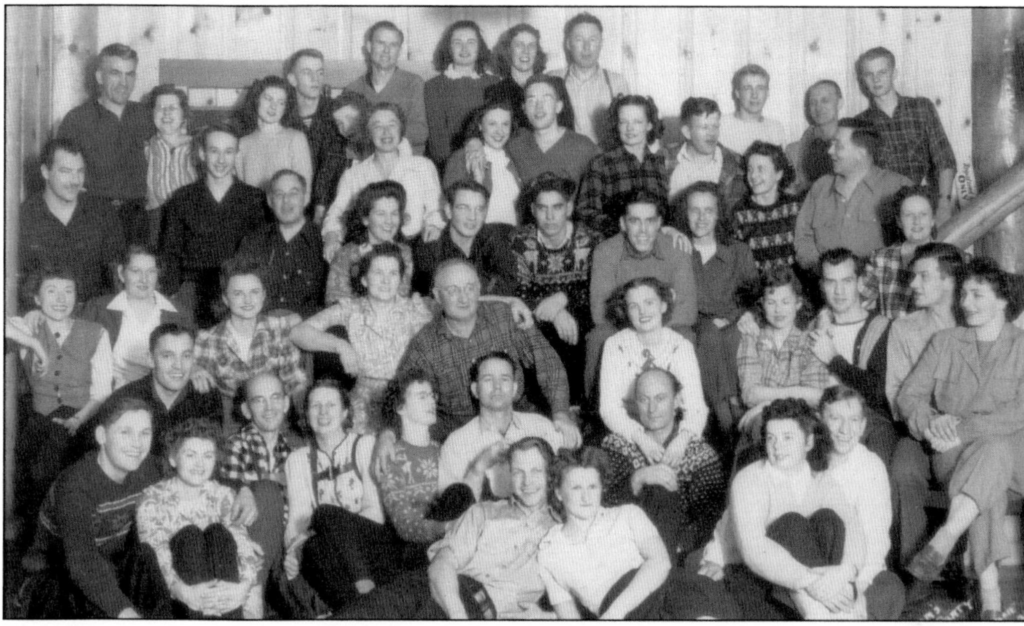

This photograph is of a New Year's Eve watch party at the Mount Spokane Lodge on December 31, 1945. Interior photographs of the lodge are rare. A portion of the wall and stair railing can be seen. New Year's Eve watch parties at Mount Spokane were very popular in the 1940s. (SSP.)

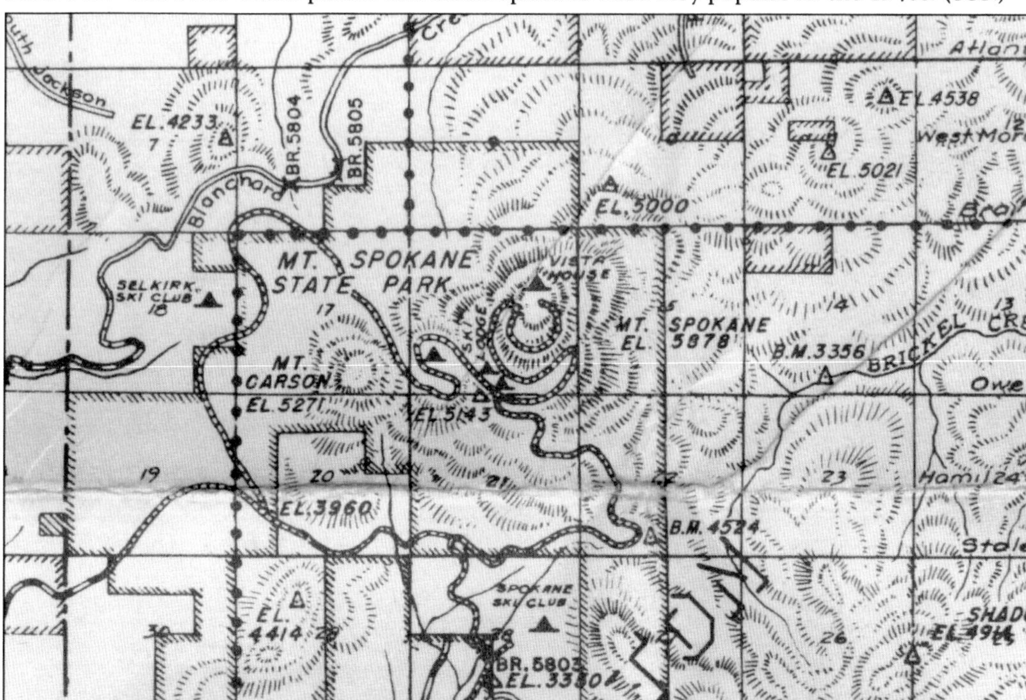

This 1953 map was produced by AAA of Spokane. The Spokane Ski Club cabin is shown at lower center. The Selkirk Ski Club cabin is at left center with Cook's Auto Road on the left. From the location of the Spokane Ski Club cabin, the Deadman Creek Road was extended to the Cook's Auto Road by the CCC work crews and opened in 1937. (AAA.)

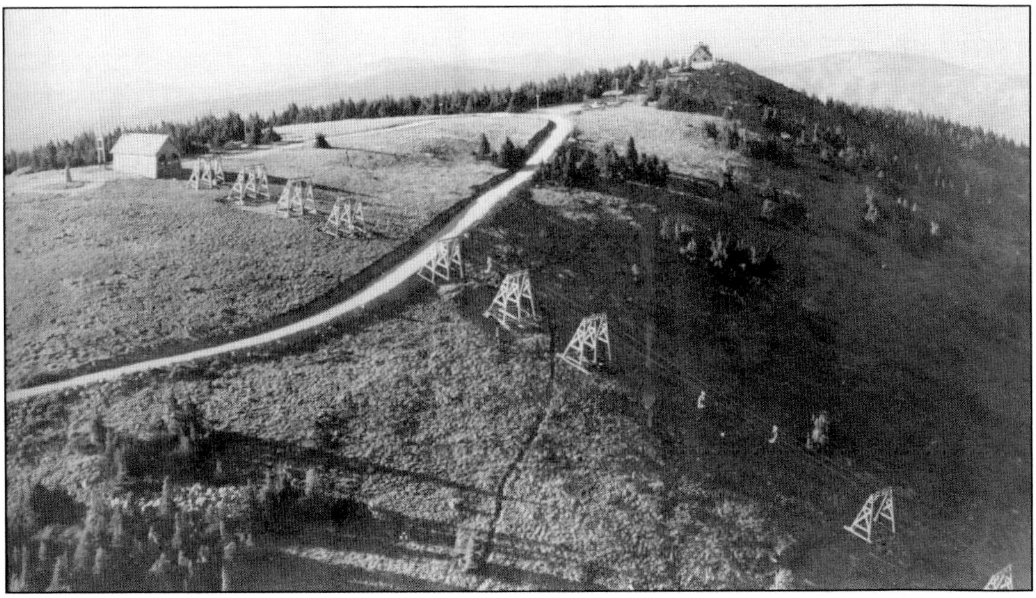

In the early 1940s, the ski clubs began discussion on the need of a chairlift. The Mount Spokane Ski Lift Association and the Spokane Ski Club took direct leadership in the installation of the first chairlift at Mount Spokane. Designed and constructed by Riblet Tramway of Spokane, the length was 3,300 feet with a vertical gain of 1,200 feet. The initial cost was $40,000. The lift opened for the winter season of 1946–1947. Today, the location of the KXLY-TV transmitter is very close to where the upper terminal of the chairlift was located. The lower terminal was not accessible by automobile but rather by skiing to it. People preferred the less-expensive rope tow near the lodge. Winter snowstorms and high winds would damage the chairlift, and so constant maintenance was needed. The chairlift was in operation for just a few years, closing at the end of the 1948–1949 season. It was dismantled in the fall of 1954 by state park crews. (Above, AC; below, SSP.)

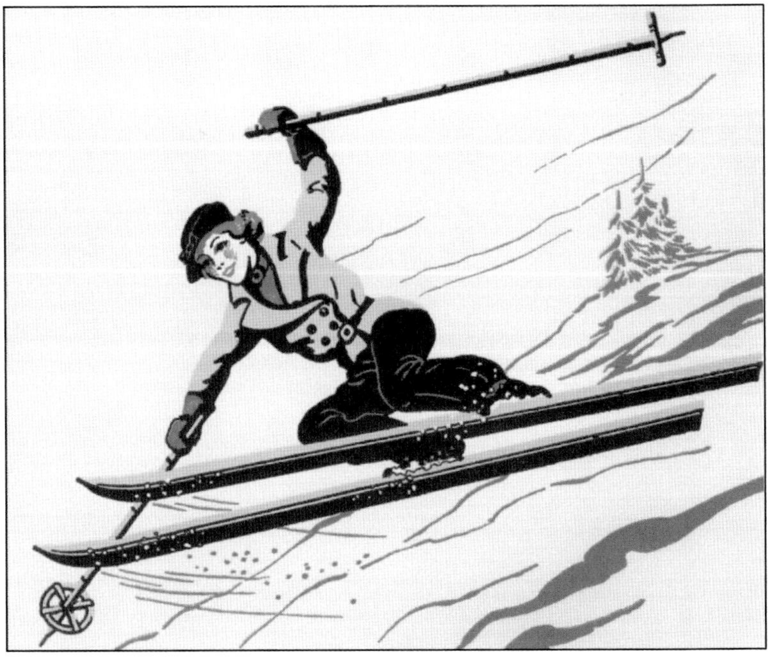

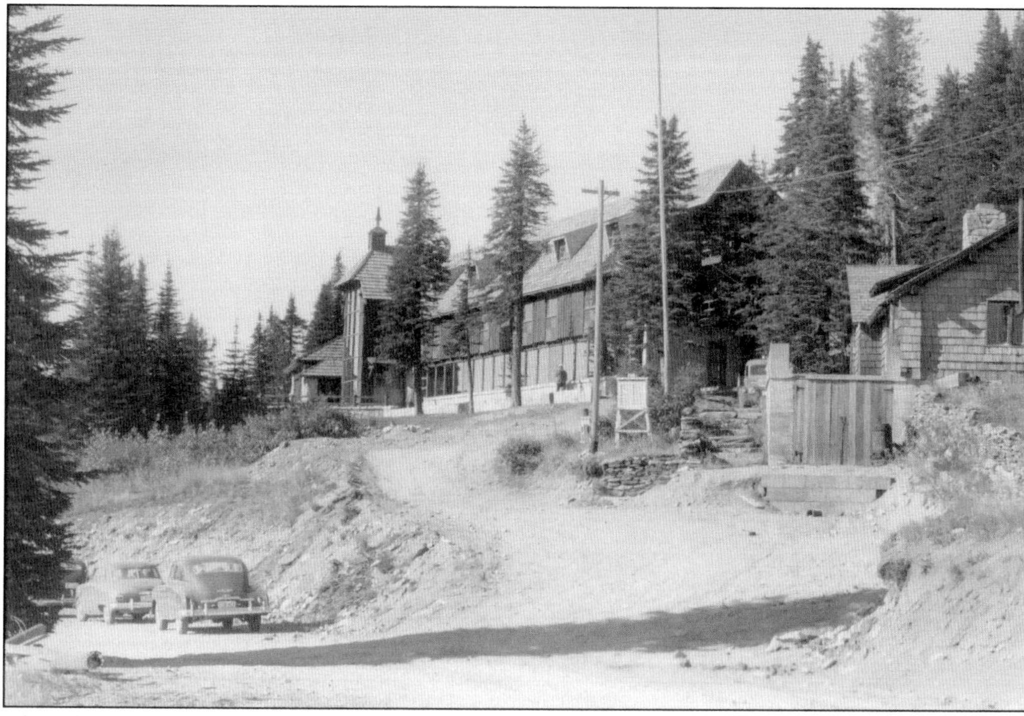

This photograph of the completed exterior of the lodge was taken in the fall of 1951. Note the weather-instrument shelter in the center of the photograph and Cook's Cabin at far right. This photograph shows just how large the lodge with its new addition was. One can only imagine the size of the fire. There was nothing that could have been done to stop it. The heat was terrific, as balls of flame shot in the air with sparks exploding in every direction. Snowmelt and water from the heat of the fire ran down the mountain, flooding the road and parking lot. (Leo.)

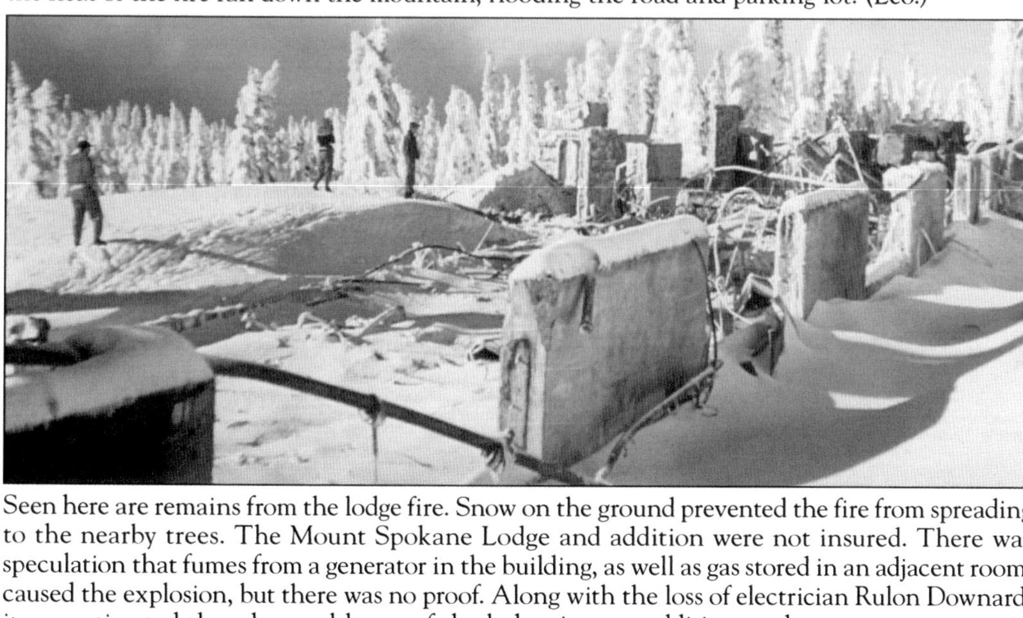

Seen here are remains from the lodge fire. Snow on the ground prevented the fire from spreading to the nearby trees. The Mount Spokane Lodge and addition were not insured. There was speculation that fumes from a generator in the building, as well as gas stored in an adjacent room, caused the explosion, but there was no proof. Along with the loss of electrician Rulon Downard, it was estimated that the total losses of the lodge, its new addition, and contents were around $250,000. (AC.)

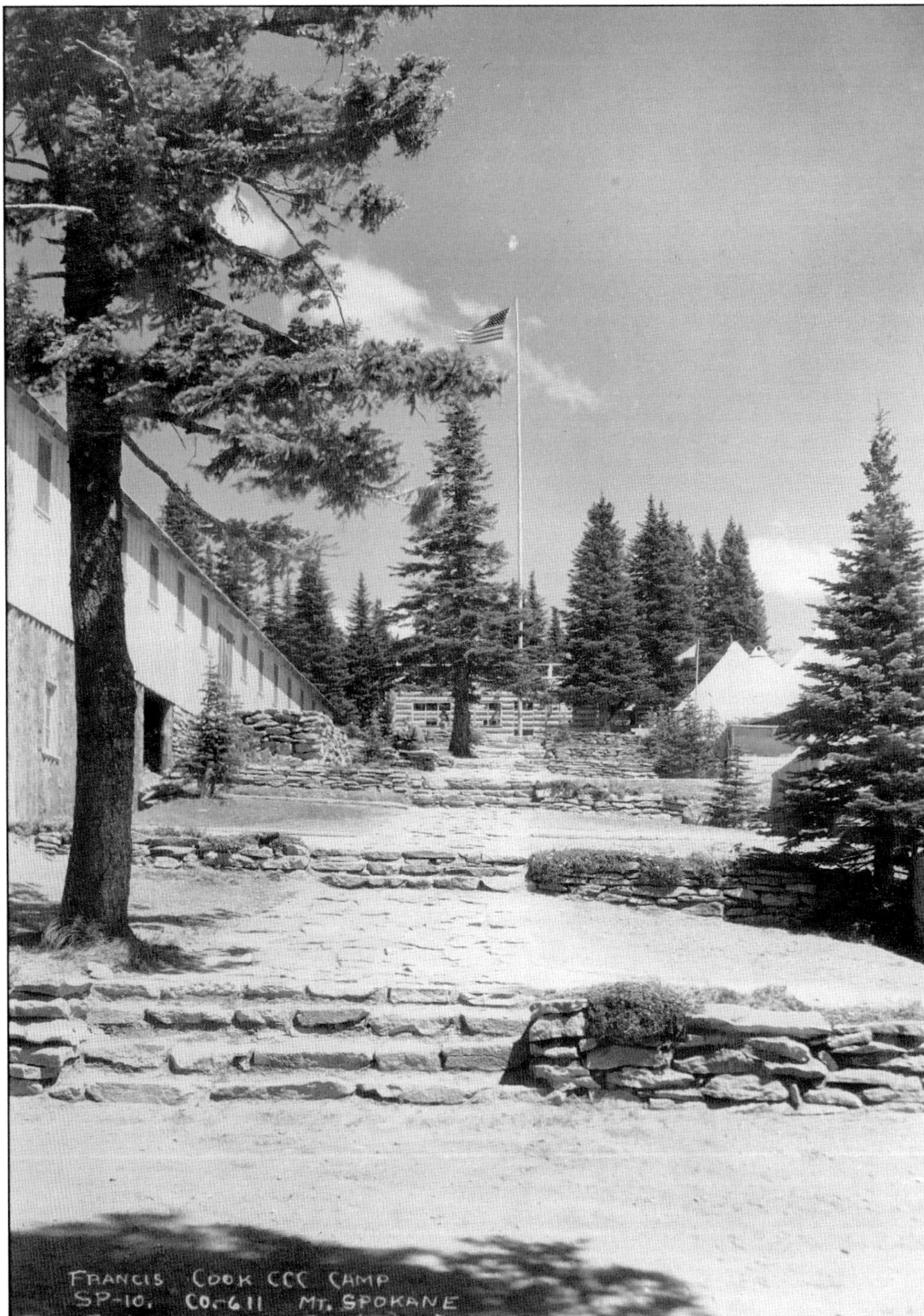

Seen here is the Francis H. Cook CCC camp at Mount Spokane. Several large buildings were built, including an administration building (center). The mess hall with a recreation room is seen to the left, with sleeping quarters on the right. The area around the buildings was improved by planting grass and providing picnic areas complete with tables and stone-lined walking paths. The camp won the Civilian Conservation Corps district first place award, competing with 70 camps throughout the area. Robert Fechtner, head of the Civilian Conservation Corps, stated that the Mount Spokane camp was the finest he had seen in his travels over the country. (MNI, Leo.)

Seven

The CCC Camp

In 1932, during the height of the Depression, Pres. Franklin Roosevelt announced the "Reforestation Initiative." Within this initiative was the Civilian Conservation Corps or simply the CCC. The president proposed the initiative to Congress on March 21, 1932. The bill was approved and signed 10 days later. The CCC was born.

By late 1935, the CCC had 500,000 enrollees in 2,600 camps across the country. The program was a great success and lasted until 1942, when World War II demanded priority.

In 1933, the CCC arrived on Mount Spokane. The CCC began by building a camp area between Mount Spokane and Mount Kit Carson. The camp housed approximately 200 men. Employed by the CCC, they were under the direction of camp superintendent Oscar Kuckenbecher. On June 17, 1934, Camp Company No. 611 was dedicated and named the Francis H. Cook camp.

Over the next couple of years, work continued on the camp, and by 1937 piped water was available. Additional picnic areas were constructed, and fire pits were placed around the area for outdoor camp cooking.

Throughout much of 1934 and 1935, the CCC crews worked on the original Cook's Auto Road. Work was done to widen, regravel, and shore up the road with rock where streams crossed. Besides building the Vista House and Mount Spokane Lodge, the CCC also constructed a new road from the south side of the mountain. This was the same road used by the early skiers to get to the Spokane Ski Club cabin. Plans were to extend the road following Deadman Creek to meet up with the Cook's Auto Road. By the late fall of 1934, the clearing and leveling had been finished, and the new Deadman Creek Road opened in the summer of 1937 and is now the main route to Mount Spokane, called Mount Spokane Park Drive.

Today, snowmobilers are using the CCC area. Most of the original stonework from the camp remains.

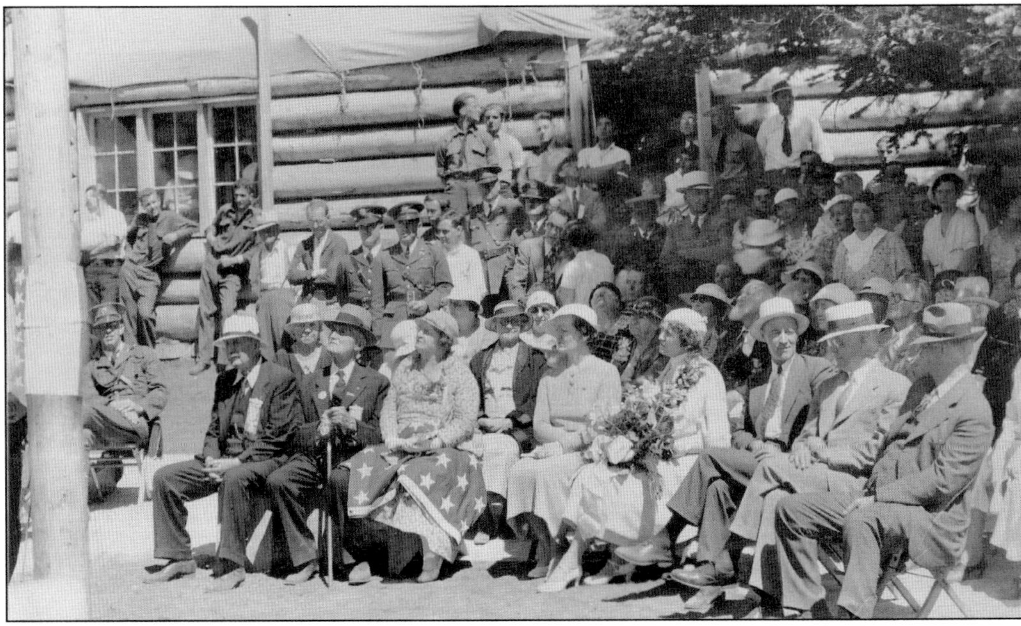

This was dedication day at the Francis H. Cook CCC camp on June 17, 1934. It was estimated that 1,000 people attended the dedication. Members of the US Army, state officials, patriotic groups, and citizens all took part in the ceremony. A large 20-by-38-foot American flag was raised to the beat of the American Legions Drum and Bugle Corps. The 4th Infantry Division Band from Fort George Wright was featured. (MNI, Leo.)

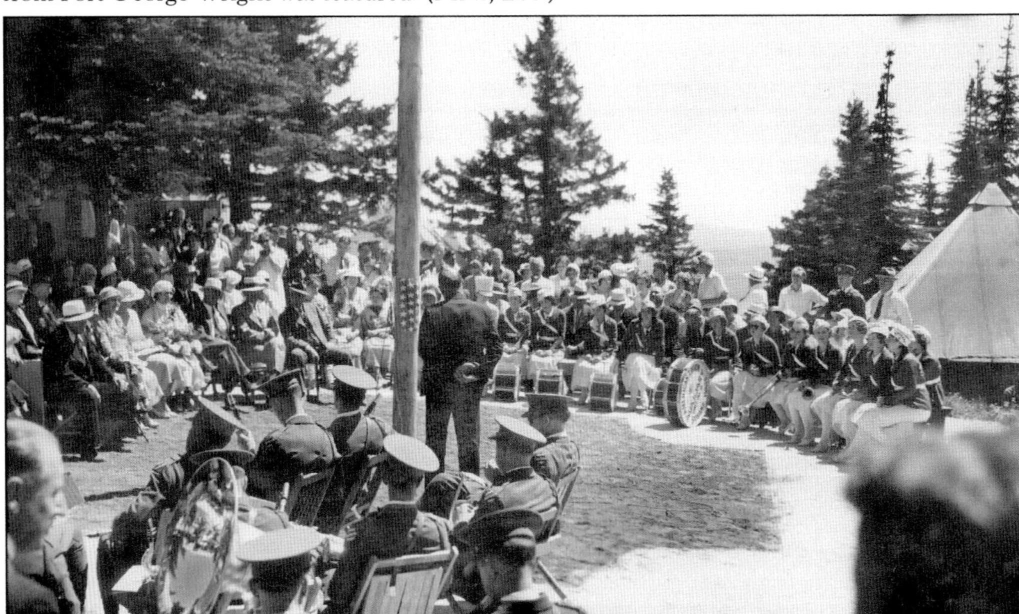

Several US flags, a bronze tablet, and multiple photographs and drawings, including photographs of Francis Cook and Abraham Lincoln, were all presented for display in the camp. An airplane flyby was also incorporated into the dedication. Cook family members were introduced, and Silas Cook gave a short speech about his father. Speakers from the ski clubs, state land commissioner, national parks, and Sonora Smart Dodd, the founder of Father's Day, spoke briefly. (MNI, Leo.)

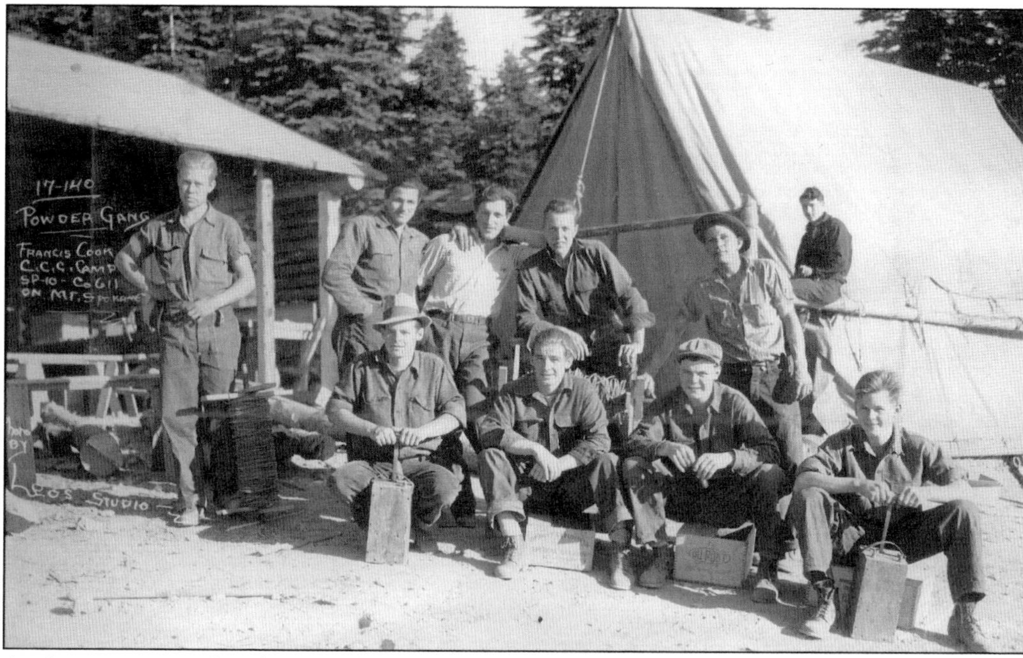

As the caption in the photograph says, this was the "powder gang" or the explosive unit of the CCC. It was their job to set dynamite charges used in road building. Dynamite charges were readily available in those days and used at will. This photograph was most likely taken in 1934 or shortly after the dedication of the camp. (MNI, Leo.)

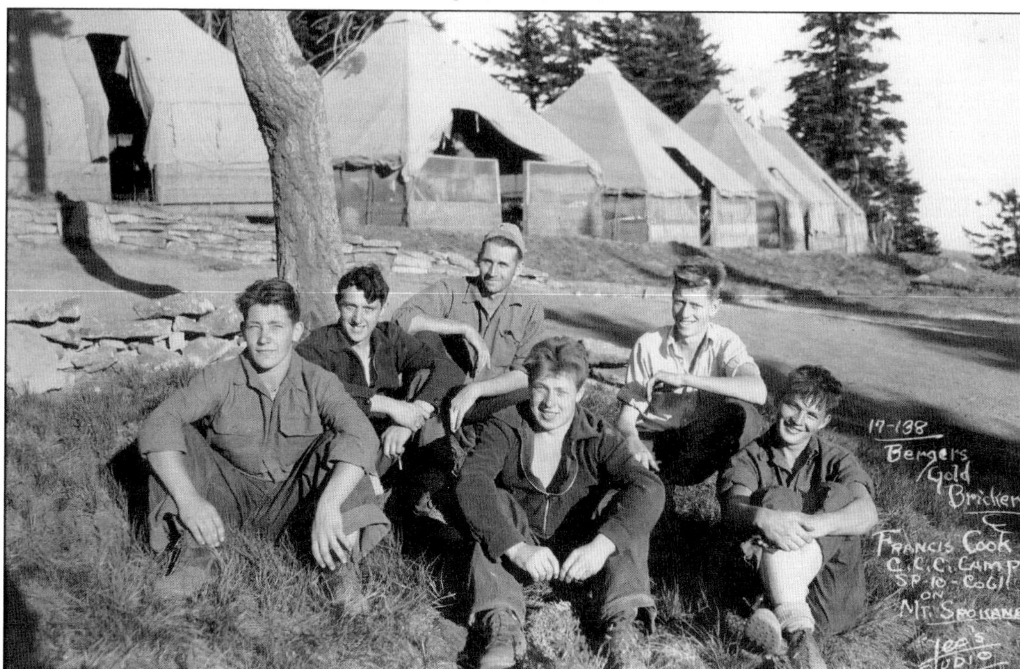

A group of young men at the CCC camp on Mount Spokane is pictured. Note the sleeping quarters in the background with walls that are half wood and half screen. The tarps used for roofs came down to cover the screened portions of the walls. (MNI, Leo.)

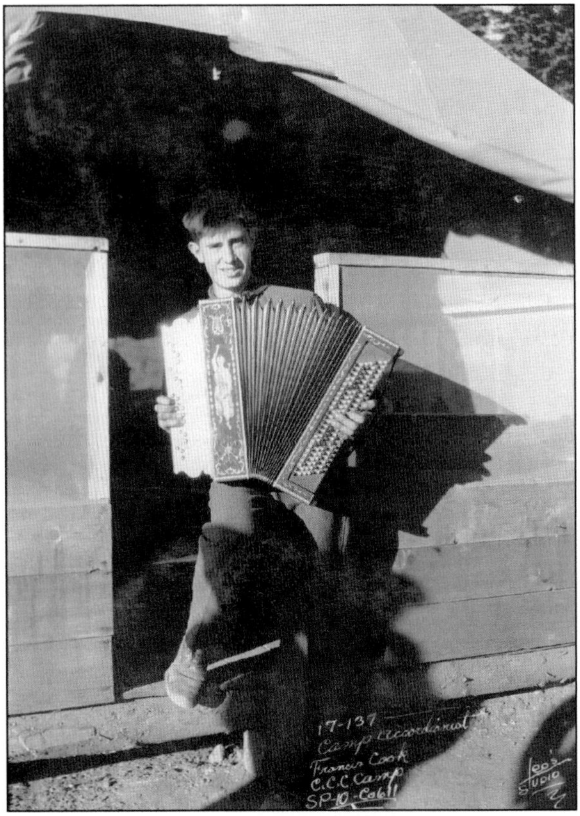

The Francis H. Cook CCC camp accordionist is seen here. Every camp needs an accordionist. Music was very important to the CCC boys. During the evening or on a day off from their work, they would be serenaded with music. (MNI, Leo.)

This aerial view of the CCC camp shows sleeping quarters in the lower left. On the right center of the photograph is what seems to be the firewood pile for cooking and heating. The insignia on the lower right that resembles the Nazi swastika was undoubtedly a signal designation for airplanes. Although Germany's Nazi party was in existence at the time this photograph was taken, it is not believed to have anything to do with the Nazi party. (MNI, Leo.)

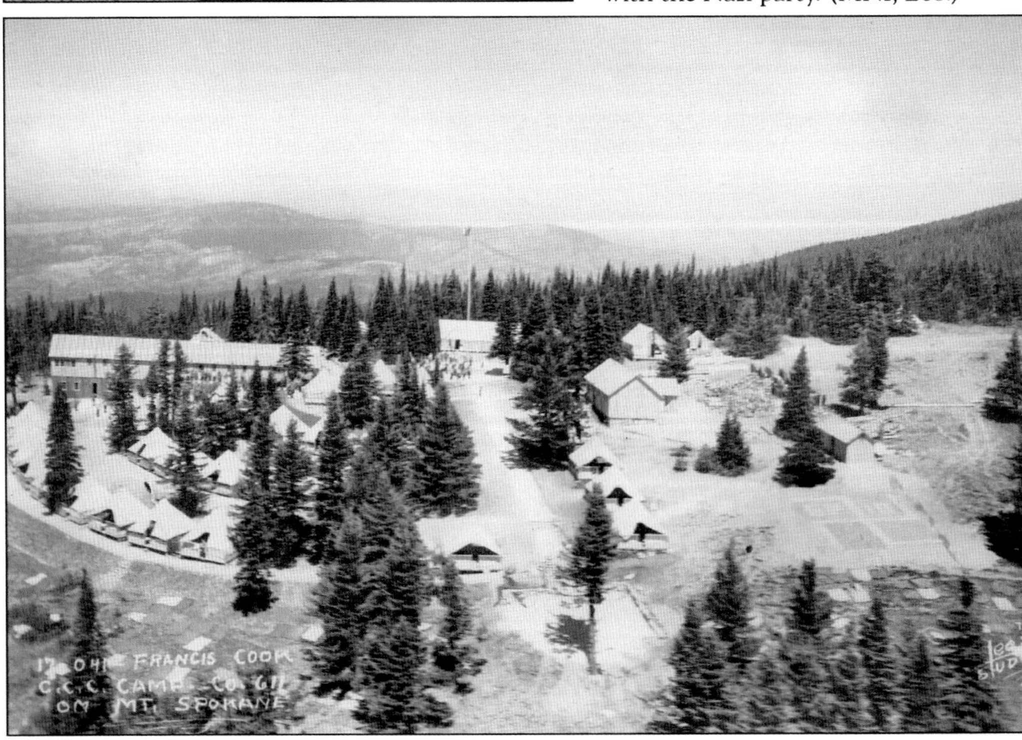

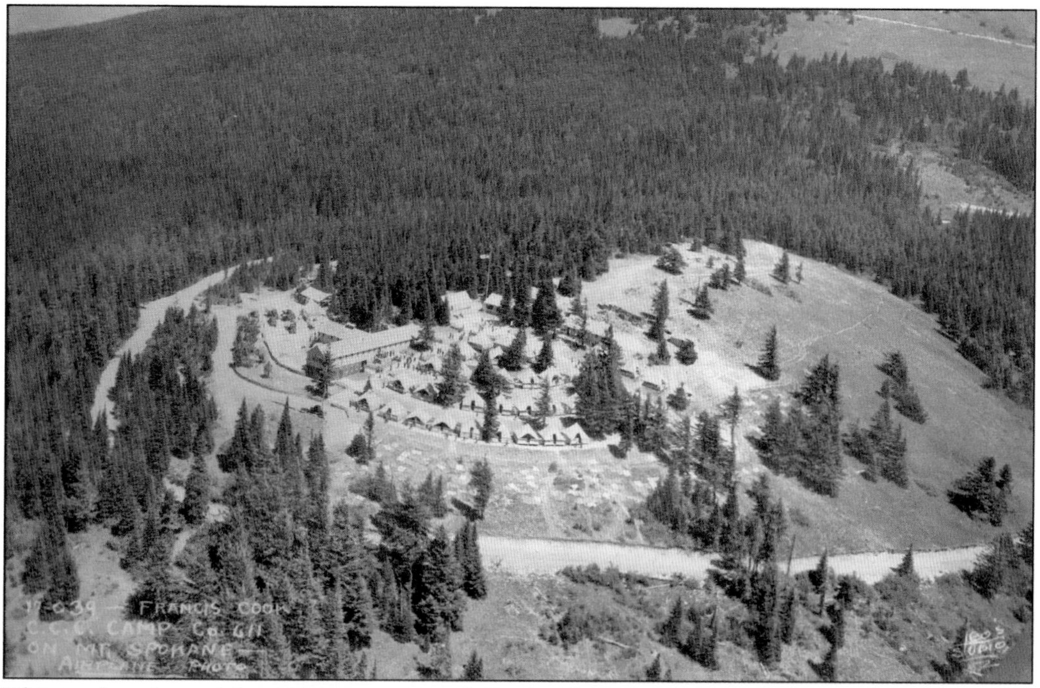

This is the view of the CCC camp in relation to Mount Spokane. The road visible at the bottom of the photograph is the original Cook's Auto Road, which switchbacked up the mountain. (MNI, Leo.)

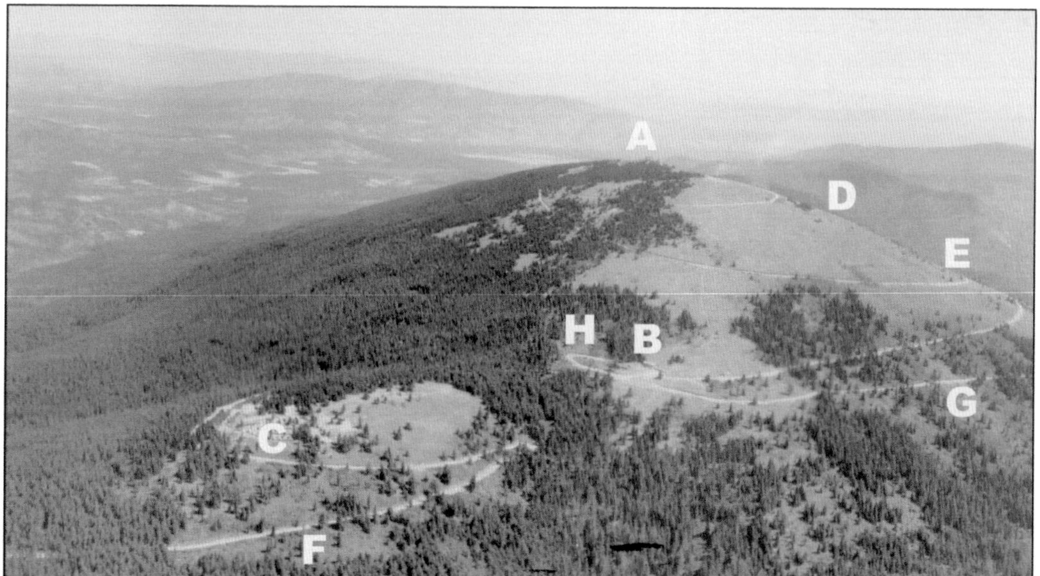

This is an aerial photograph of Mount Spokane's south slope. A is the Vista House, built in 1933. B is the original Cook's Cabin that was built in 1912. The new Cook's Cabin's location was here from 1935 to 1955. C was the site of Civilian Conservation Corps from 1933 to 1942. D was the location of the first double chairlift from 1946 to 1949. E is the current ski facilities after 1955. F was the original 1909 Cook's Auto Road, now Day Mount Spokane Road. G is the Deadman Creek Road addition from 1937. H is Mount Spokane Lodge from 1940 to 1952. (Leo, RR.)

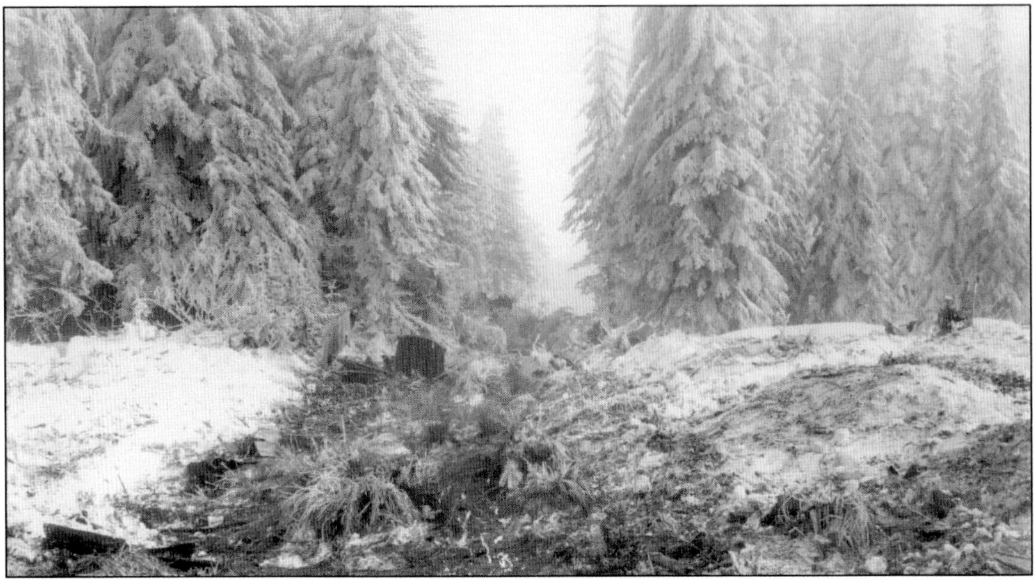

This path through the trees was made from a B-29 Superfortress as it crashed into the side of Mount Spokane on November 13, 1947. The crash claimed the lives of the following five men: 1st Lt. Gordon R. Sundberg, pilot; 1st Lt. Charles C. Kline, copilot; 1st Lt. Robert J. Thomas, copilot; M.Sgt. Carl E. Bushman, radio operator; and M.Sgt. Edwin I. Mann, engineer. The two survivors were Sgt. Truman W. Haley, right scanner, and T.Sgt. Marshall F. Fine, left scanner. Both men recovered from their injuries. (Haley.)

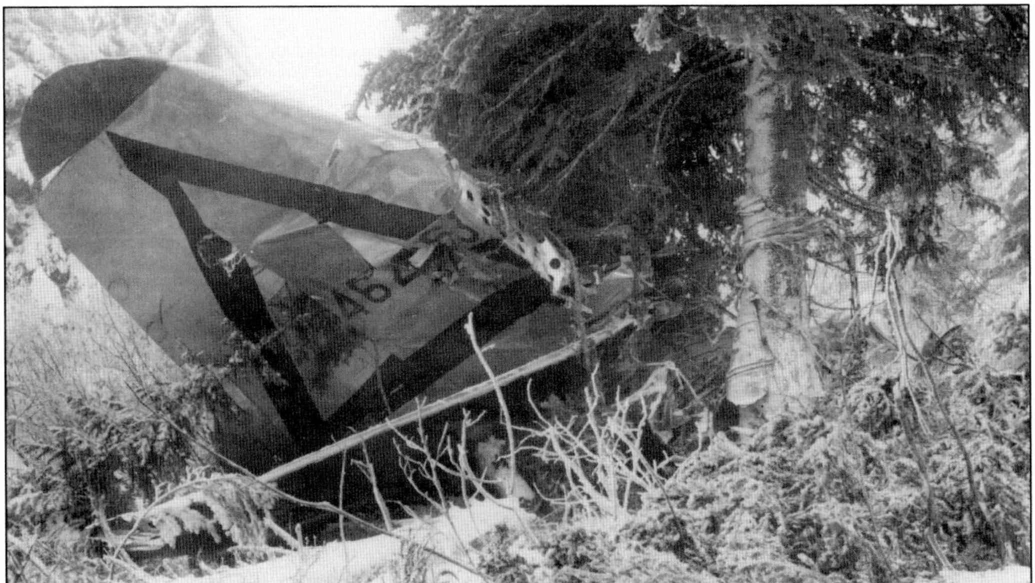

The tail section where the two survivors, Sergeant Haley and Technical Sergeant Fine, were seated was knocked loose and thrown clear before impact. Sergeant Haley reported that the plane encountered turbulence after hitting a snowstorm near Mount Spokane. He remembered sliding around during the crash and coming out of the plane via the bomb bay doors. Technical Sergeant Fine reported he noticed the ground about 100 feet below, and as he picked up the radio microphone to call the pilot, the plane began to clip the trees. (Haley.)

Eight

The B-29 Crash

The Boeing B-29 Superfortress was the aircraft used for dropping the two atomic bombs over Hiroshima on August 6, 1945, and Nagasaki on August 14, 1945, to end World War II. A large strategic bomber, it was used in the Strategic Air Command starting in 1946 and saw action during the Korean War in 1950. On a more local level, a B-29 slammed into the side of Mount Spokane on the night of November 13, 1947. Of the crew on board, five were killed and two were severely injured.

There have been several aircraft crashes at Mount Spokane over the years, but what is unique about this particular crash is the fact that the sons of one of the survivors researched the accident using Air Corps reports and then visited the crash site 63 years later in 2010.

Charles and Larry Haley made the trip to Mount Spokane on September 15, 2010, to visit the B-29 crash site that their father, Sgt. Truman Haley, was involved in. The trip to the crash site was instigated when two volunteers of a ski trail brush-cutting group, Don Etten and Russ Hart, found a piece of the plane several years prior. It was pictured on the Prime Timer ski group's website that Charles found online. The brothers were able to still find parts of this plane while visiting.

On November 13, 1947, the B-29 took off from the Spokane Airfield on a routine training mission. Seven crewmen were aboard, including an instructor pilot and two student pilots. After a couple of hours of flying, plus several landings and takeoffs, the B-29 approached the Mount Spokane area. Frank Denton, superintendent of the park, reported that he heard an aircraft flying close by shortly before 10:00 p.m. and that it was snowing. At approximately 9:45 p.m., the plane struck the mountain in the vicinity of the Bald Knob area. Rescue help arrived, and the two survivors were found within minutes after the crash. The five bodies were all recovered the next morning. Within days, the Air Corps was conducting a complete investigation on the crash and began moving the wreckage off the mountain. The plane skidded along the trees and ground, making a path about a quarter of a mile long. Later, this path would become a ski run, called the B-29 Trail.

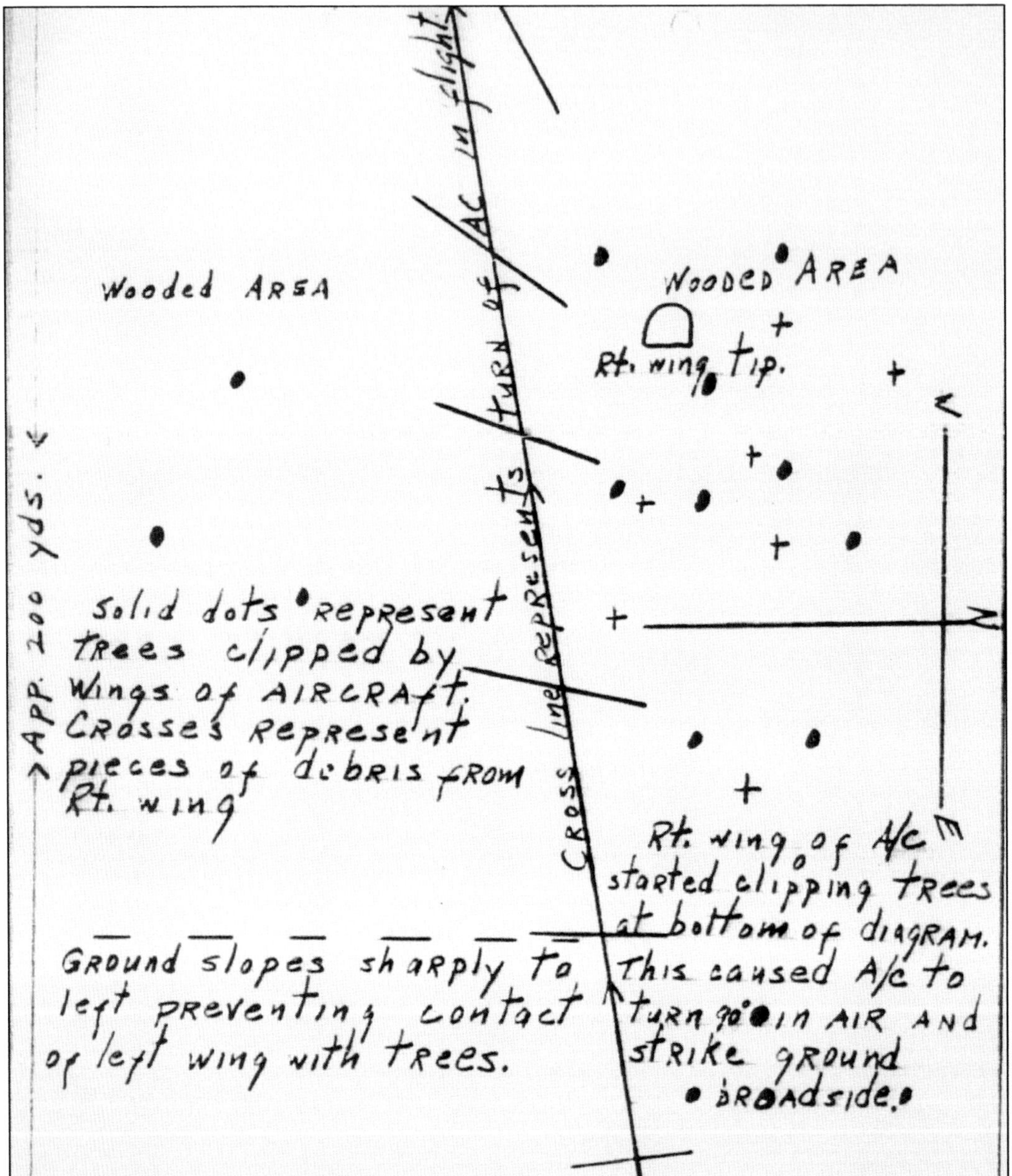

Of the many pages from the Air Corps accident report was this hand-drawn map, shown here and continuing on the next page. Here, one sees the line of course of the airplane, with handwritten notes from the investigation team. The report concluded that although weather was a factor, pilot error was the cause. The pilot or instructor pilot did not insure a minimum safe altitude; the plane should not have been flying that close to the ground or the mountain. (Haley.)

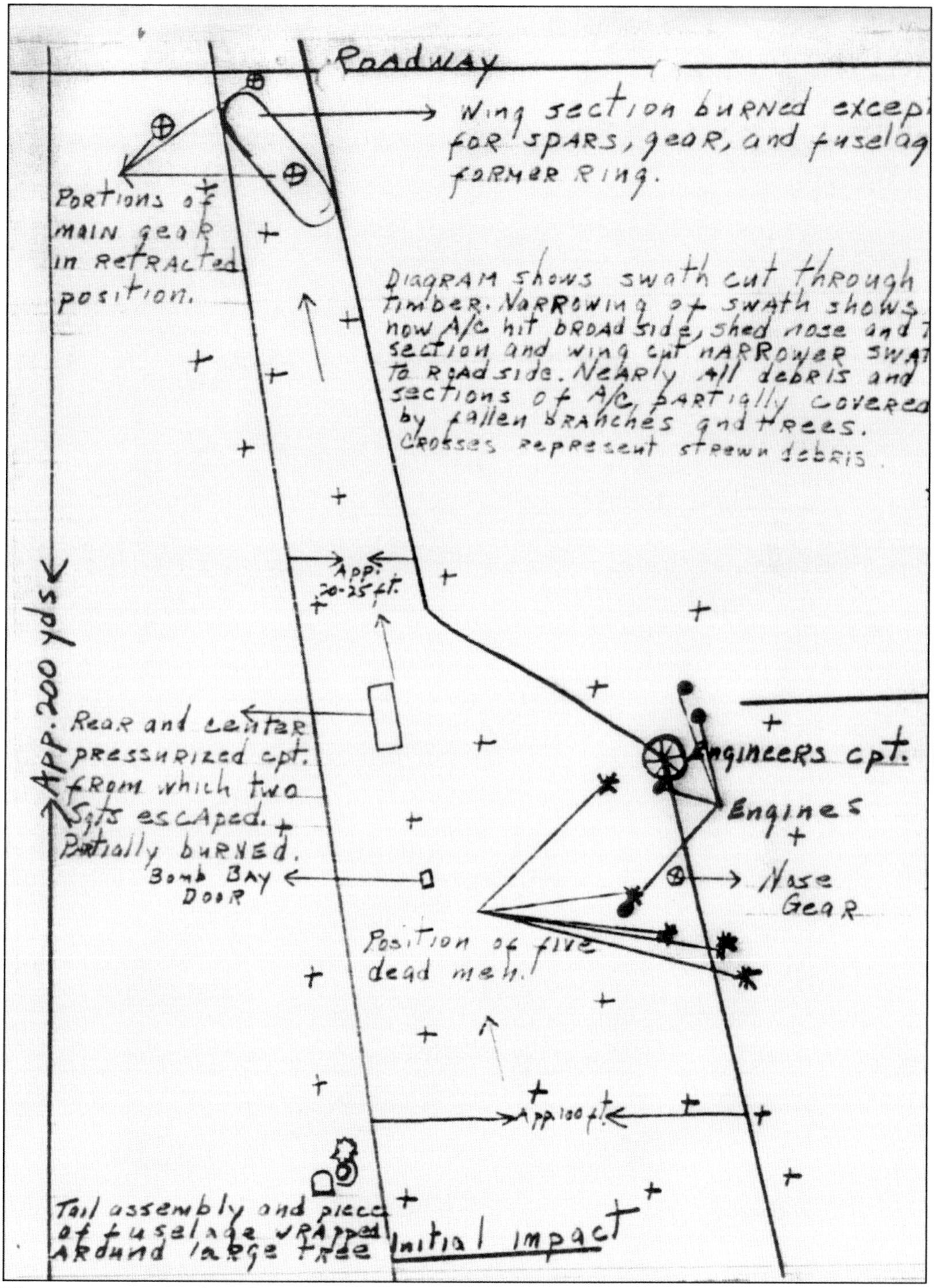

The report stresses that the investigation team did not have the pilot to interview, and all the controls and dials of the cockpit had been burned past recognition. The Air Corps personnel removed the wreckage as best as they could, but because of the winter conditions, they had to return in the spring of 1948 to remove any remaining debris that was found. (Haley.)

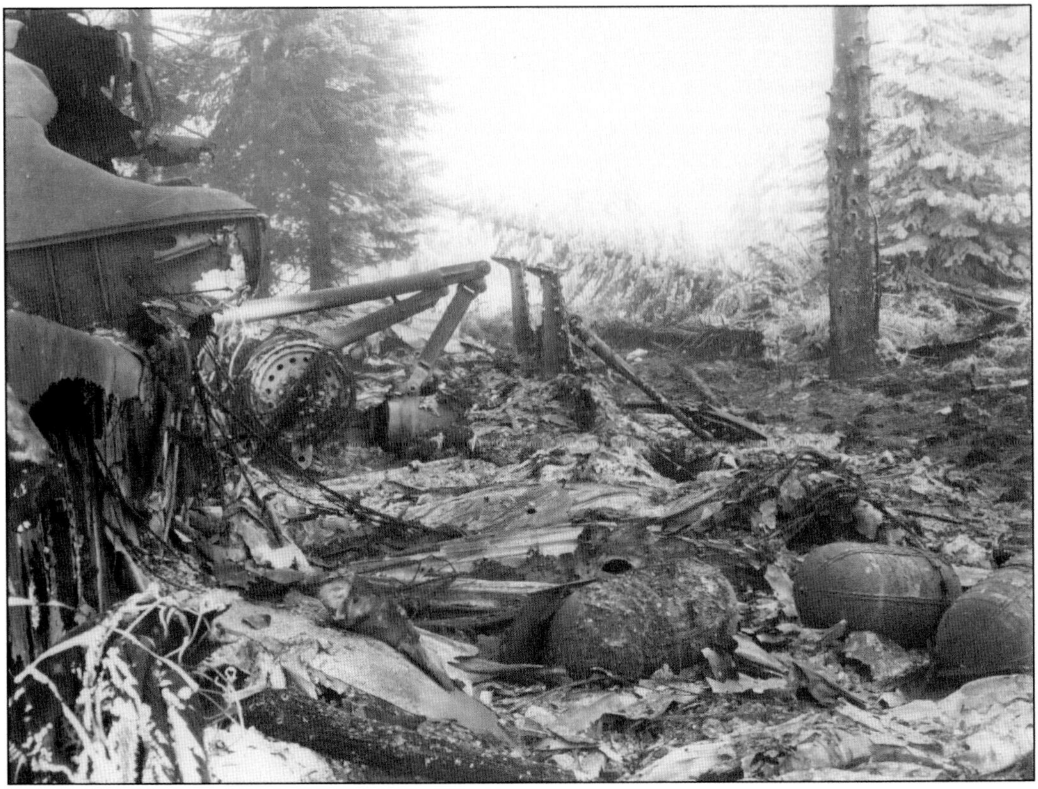

Wreckage of the B-29, including the retracted landing gear and tire rim, can be seen. Several pressure tanks are scattered, as well as one of the B-29 engines with a propeller blade sticking up. From the Air Corps investigation report, the right wing of the plane first clipped the trees for 600 feet, causing the fuselage to turn 90 degrees to the right before impact. The left wing and left main gear broke loose and burned. The fuselage cut a path through the trees, coming to rest in a ball of flames. The *Associated Press* reported that the B-29 may have been traveling at 230 miles an hour when it slammed into the mountain. Two feet of snow on the ground made the investigation difficult. (Both, Haley.)

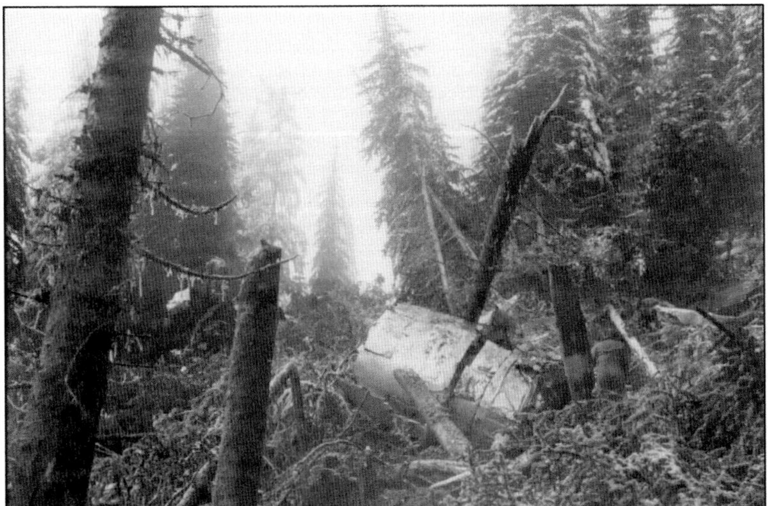

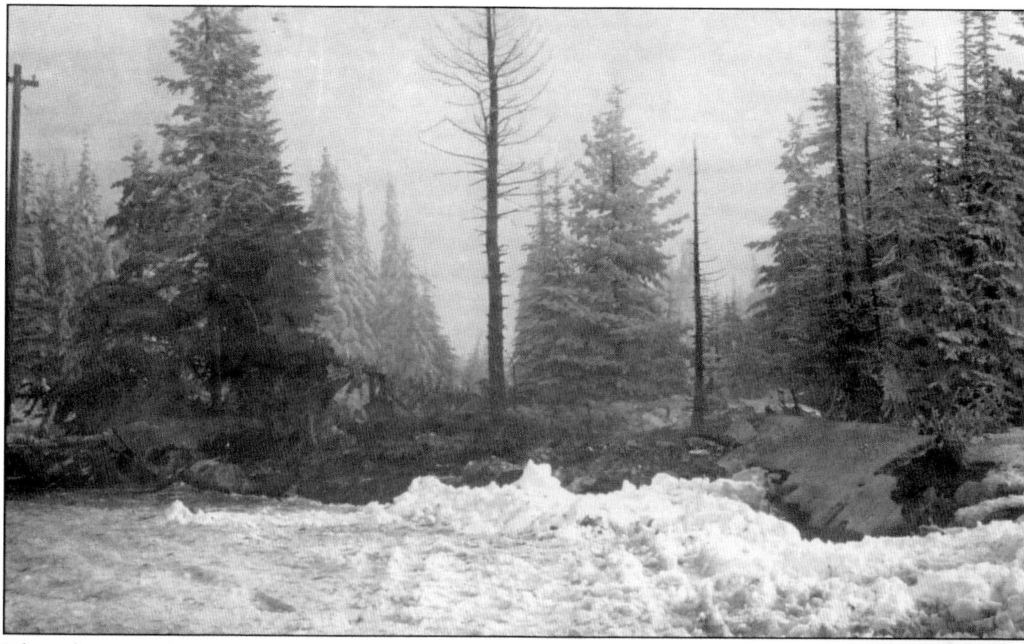

This photograph was taken from the road showing the swath cut by the wing and the burned-out section. John Linder and Tom Kinsler were operating the snowplow on the Deadman Creek Road near the Bald Knob at the time of the crash. Both men noticed flashes of light and found the wreckage engulfed in flames. Kinsler stayed at the scene, while Linder drove the plow back to the Mount Spokane Lodge to call for help. He returned with park superintendent Denton and his wife to help. Both survivors, Haley and Fine, were found and taken to the lodge to wait for an ambulance. They both recovered at Fort George Wright Hospital in Spokane. Shortly after the crash, an explosion from one of the airplane tanks caused minor injuries to two deputy sheriffs and one newspaper photographer. At right are the two sons of B-29 crash survivor Sgt. Truman W. Haley. Larry (left) and Charles (right) pose with pieces of airplane debris that they found while visiting the crash scene in 2010. (Both, Haley.)

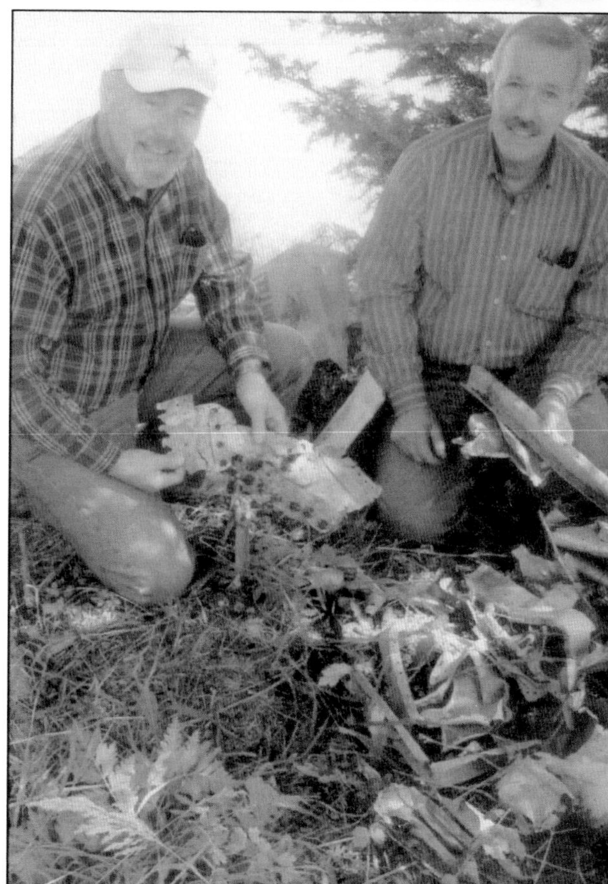

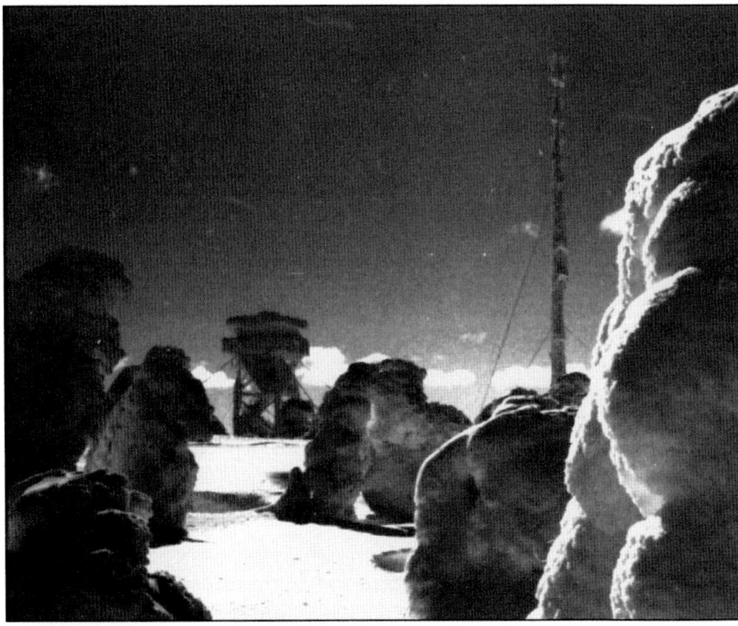

The KXLY-TV tower and antenna is on the right with the second-to-last fire lookout tower covered in snow and ice in the distance. This January 1974 photograph once again reminds one of the odd shapes that the ice-and-snow-covered trees can take on. (RK.)

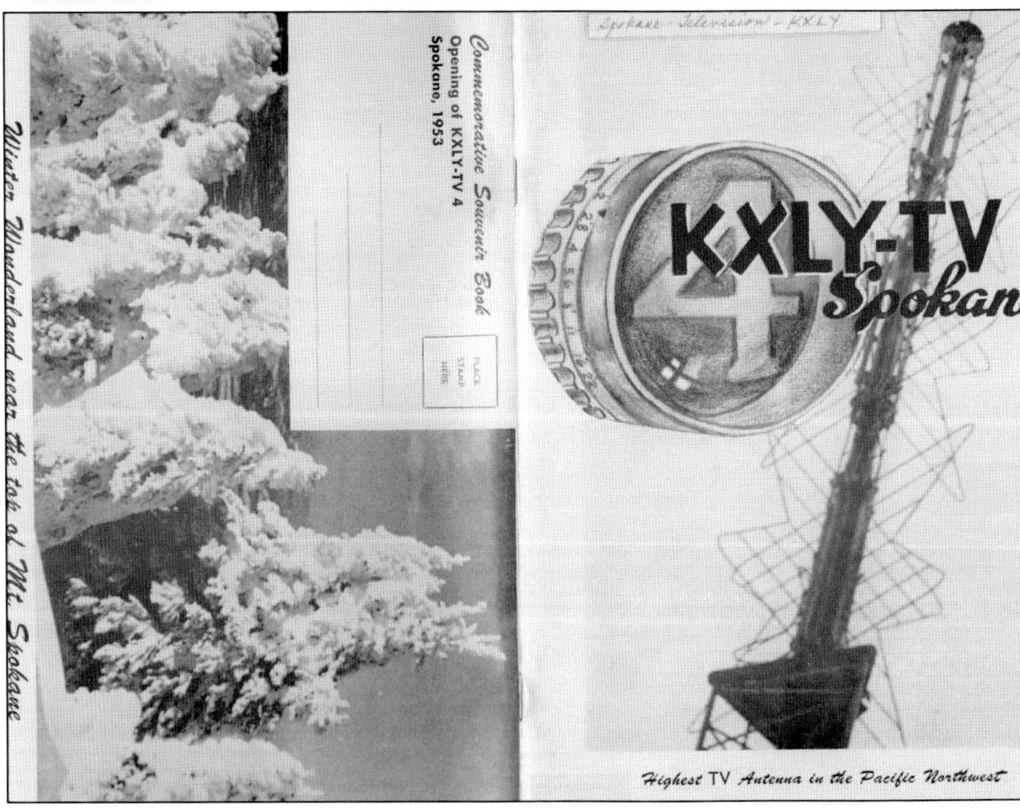

In the early days, KXLY-TV advertised heavily in newspapers and brochures regarding its transmitter being located on the summit of Mount Spokane. The station's sales department was successful in promoting this fact to television station advertisers, as well. Coverage reached hundreds of miles, giving it a large service area. Here is the cover of one such early brochure. (NWR-SPL.)

Nine

The Towers on Mount Spokane

Forest fire suppression was first and foremost in the 1930s, and the top of Mount Spokane was perfect for a fire watchtower. Right after the Vista House was completed, the Division of Forestry, later the Washington Department of Natural Resources (DNR), set up a fire lookout on the second story of the building in the summer of 1934.

There have been several towers on the summit of Mount Spokane over the years, each being replaced because of damage from winter snow and ice. In 2001, the fire lookout tower at Mount Spokane was removed permanently from the summit. During its 60 years of service, the lookout held the record for more reported wildfires than any of the other 657 fire lookouts in Washington.

KXLY-TV Channel 4 is a full-digital television and radio broadcasting center in Spokane, Washington, with its transmitter and tower on the summit of Mount Spokane. Coverage area includes Spokane, most of the interior Pacific Northwest, British Columbia, and Alberta, Canada.

In the summer of 1952, an application was filed by several businessmen, including singer and actor Bing Crosby, to construct a television station in Spokane using the top of Mount Spokane for the transmitter and antenna. By September 1952, approval was granted from the Federal Communications Commission (FCC) and the Washington State Parks and Recreation Commission.

Work started early in October 1952 on the KXLY-TV transmitter and tower. The studio was linked to the transmitter via microwave. By mid-November 1952, the two-story transmitter building, tower, and antenna had been completed, and crews began moving equipment into the building.

On January 12, 1953, wind gusts at Mount Spokane were reported at hurricane force. The wind ripped a section of roof off the transmitter building, sending snow inside the interior. Crews were able to protect the transmitter from the snow and water, but a portion of the interior walls and roof of the structure were badly damaged. By late January, the building had been repaired, and KXLY had test-pattern broadcasts.

On Sunday, February 22, 1953, KXLY-TV went on the air at 3:00 p.m.

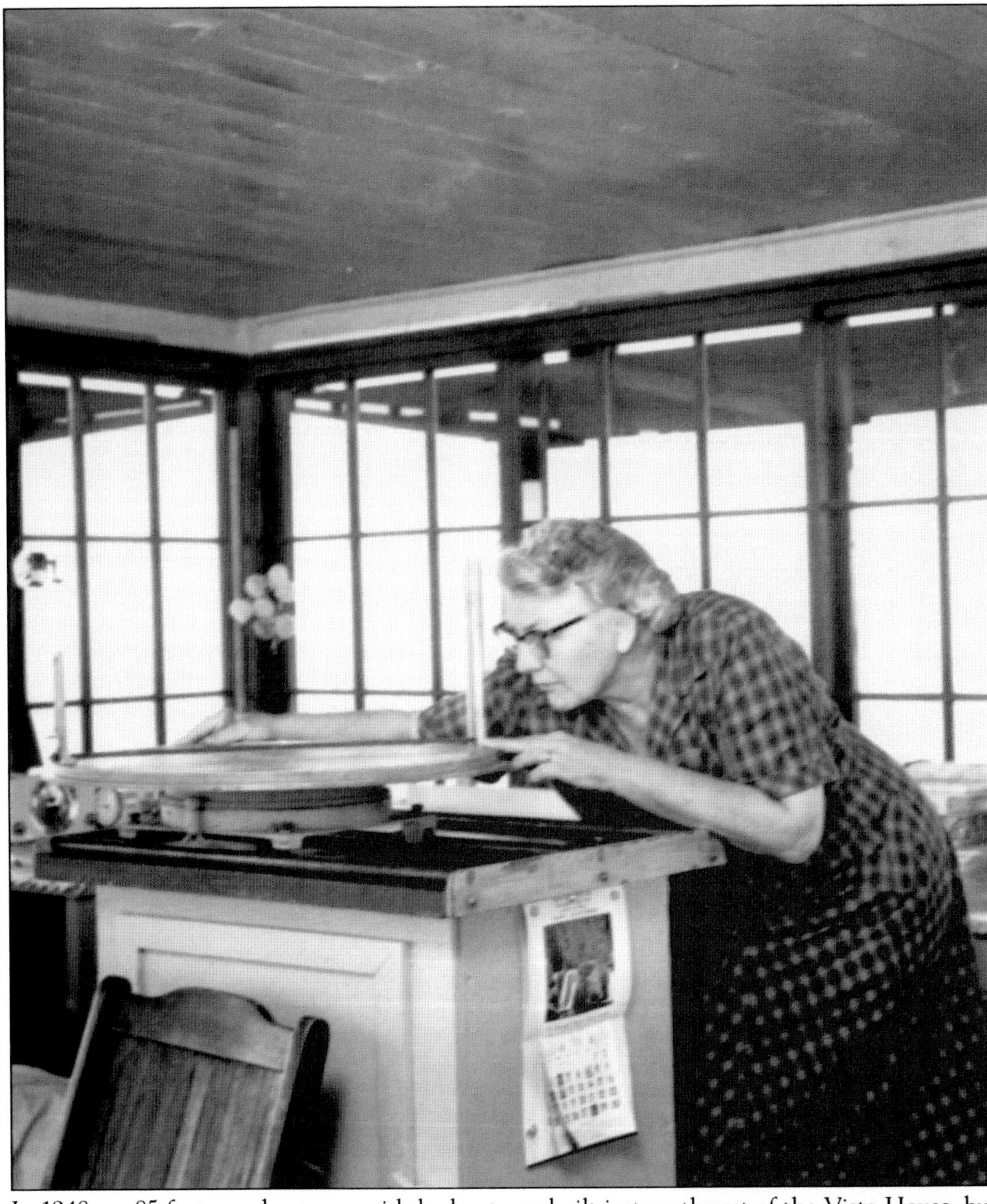

In 1948, an 85-foot wooden tower with lookout was built just southwest of the Vista House, but the weight of winter ice and snow collapsed the structure that first winter. Immediately after, a new 45-foot tower as well as a lookout was built on the same spot and used until 1963, when it was replaced with a 40-foot tower and lookout, constructed by the DNR. This photograph shows Adelia Blake sighting smoke at the Mount Spokane fire finder in 1955. She spent 17 years, starting in 1944, serving as the lookout fire spotter at Mount Spokane. Note the window shutters open on the outside of the lookout building. When fire season was over, the shutters would be lowered and locked into place for the winter. (RK, Wayne Rieper.)

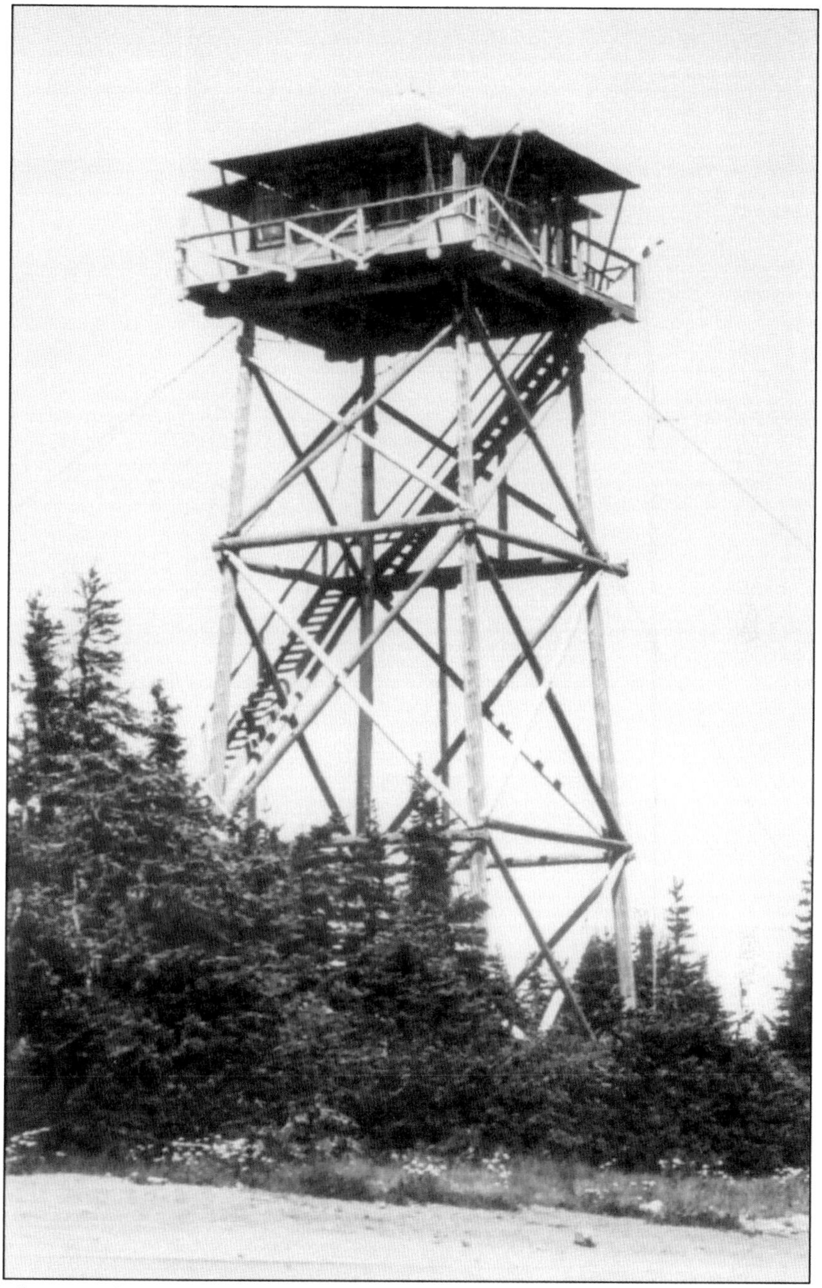

This 1955 photograph is of the 45-foot lookout tower on Mount Spokane. Summers were spent living in the lookout, and one of the most dangerous aspects of the job was lightning storms. The lookout and tower were protected with copper wire to shunt lightning off the structure to ground. Still the fire watchperson was in for a real tense and electrifying experience. After disconnecting the phone or radio, the watcher would wait out the storm by standing on a tiny stool that had glass insulators on its feet. Often the copper wire carrying the lightning charges to ground would hum, sizzle, and light up to a blue-green color—enough to scare anyone. Called "Saint Elmo's Fire," the air in the lookout became charged, and the watcher's hair would stand on end. This could last from several minutes to several hours. (RK, Wayne Rieper.)

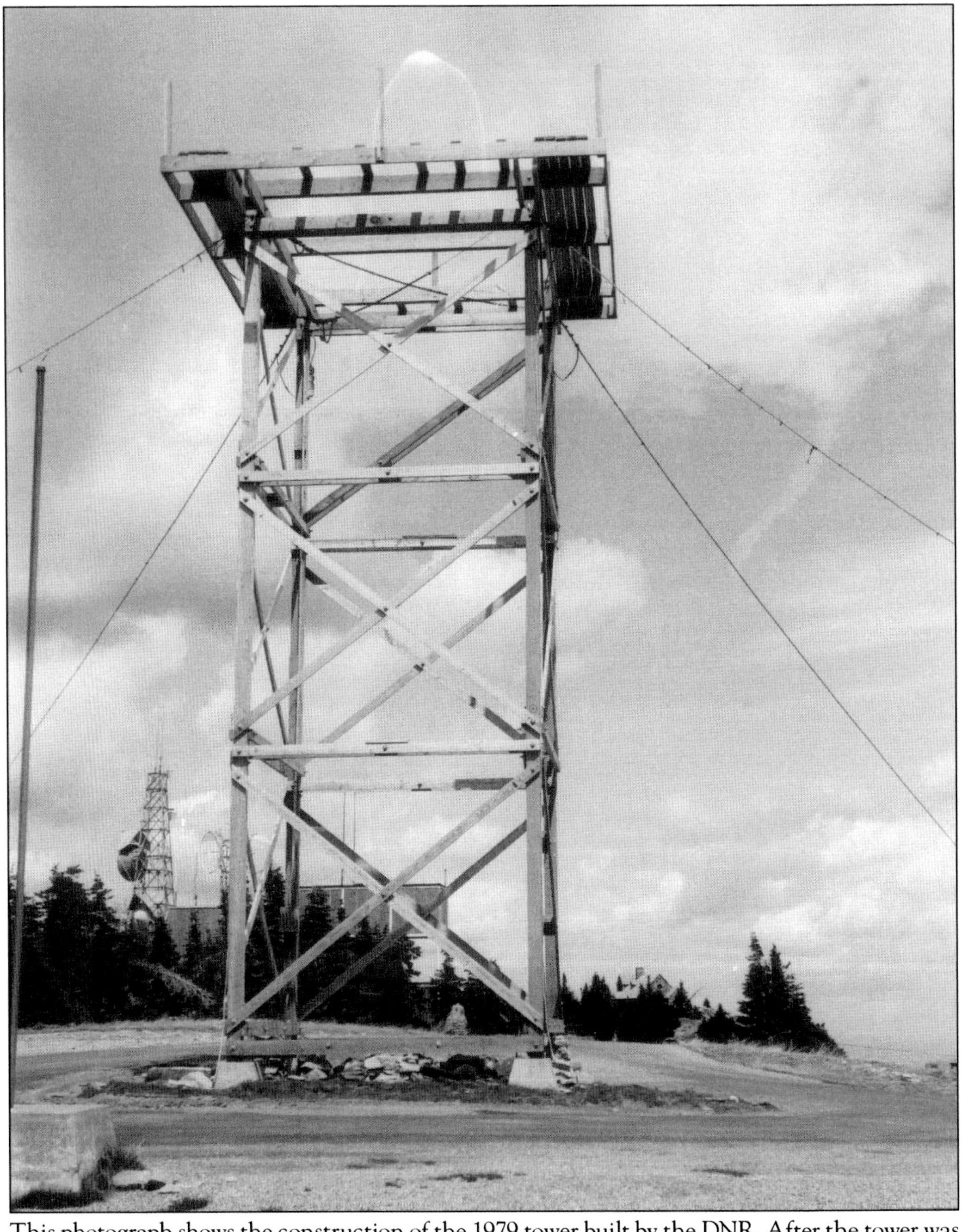

This photograph shows the construction of the 1979 tower built by the DNR. After the tower was completed, the glass-wall lookout room was built on the top. Note the beams for the floor of the lookout already in place as well as two sections of the catwalk almost completed. This lookout was in operation until 1994, after which it was used only for emergencies. This photograph also gives a view of the other summit buildings on Mount Spokane. Directly in back of the lookout tower are the communication building and microwave tower of Avista, formally the Washington Water Power Company. Avista has used the summit site for many years. To the right is the Vista House. (RK.)

The Mount Spokane lookout with its 40-foot tower was photographed in the summer of 1988. Note the guy wires anchored from the lookout to the ground to help support the structure during high winds. It was the last lookout used at Mount Spokane. (LS.)

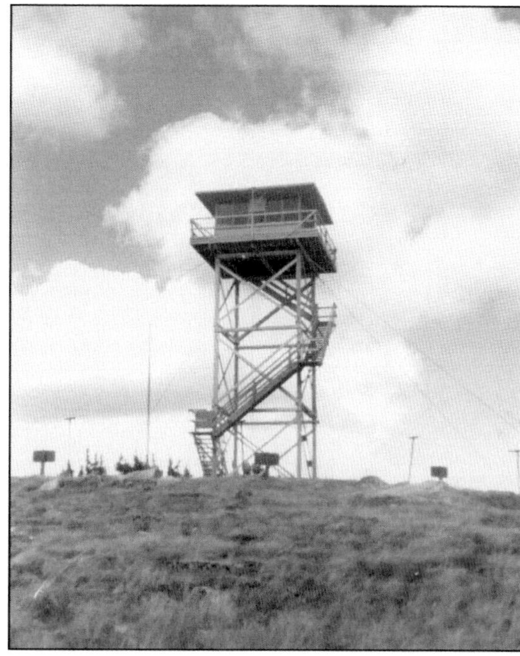

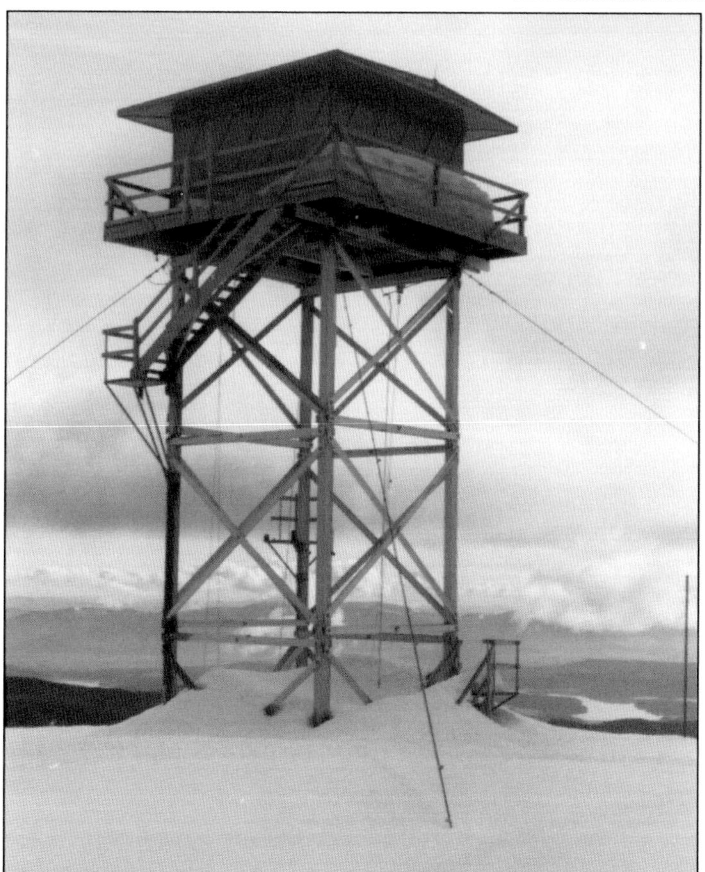

A portion of the steps was removed during each winter for safety concerns. The main reason why the Mount Spokane lookout had to be replaced through the years was due to the weather and icing on the tower and structure. If left without maintenance for any length of time, the lookouts at Mount Spokane would have collapsed. This photograph was taken in April 1988. (RK.)

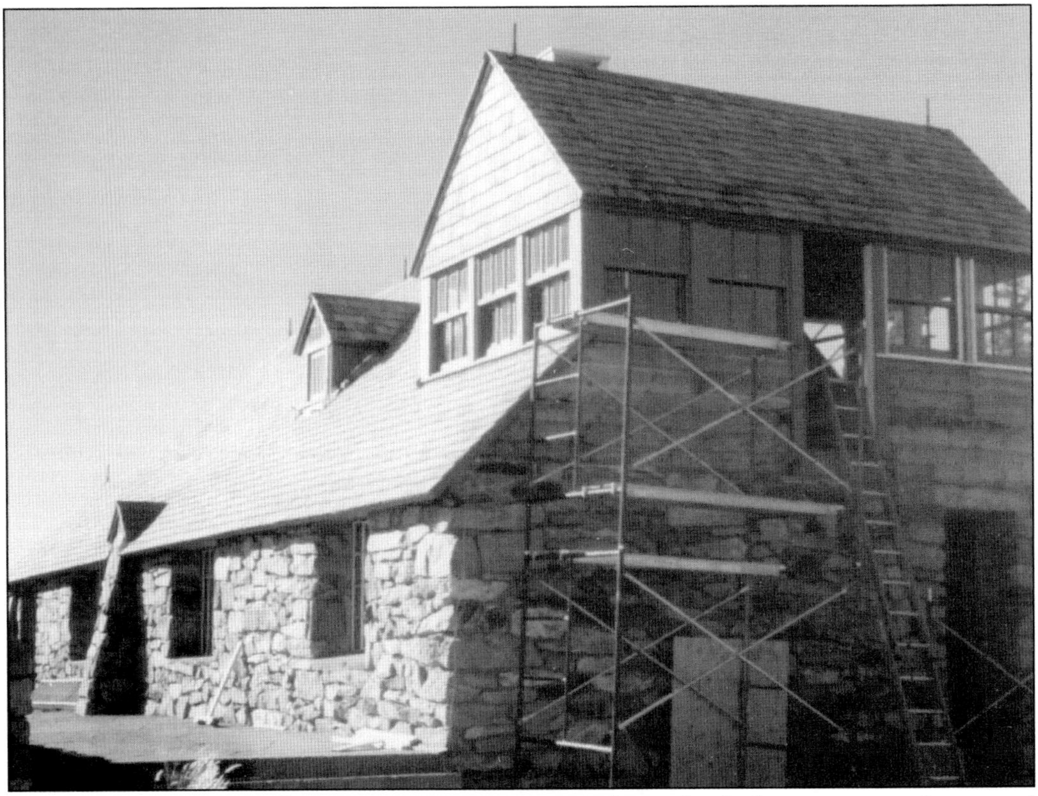

The Vista House was undergoing a restoration project for its fire lookout room on the second floor in 2002. In October 2002, the Washington State Parks authorized $151,000 to restore the second-story room back to a complete fire lookout room, with windows on three sides. Work was completed, but as of the date of this book, the state has not opened the restored second story. Below is an interior view of the second-story room during the 2002 restoration. The state has plans to open the second story to the public for overnight rental. (Both, RK.)

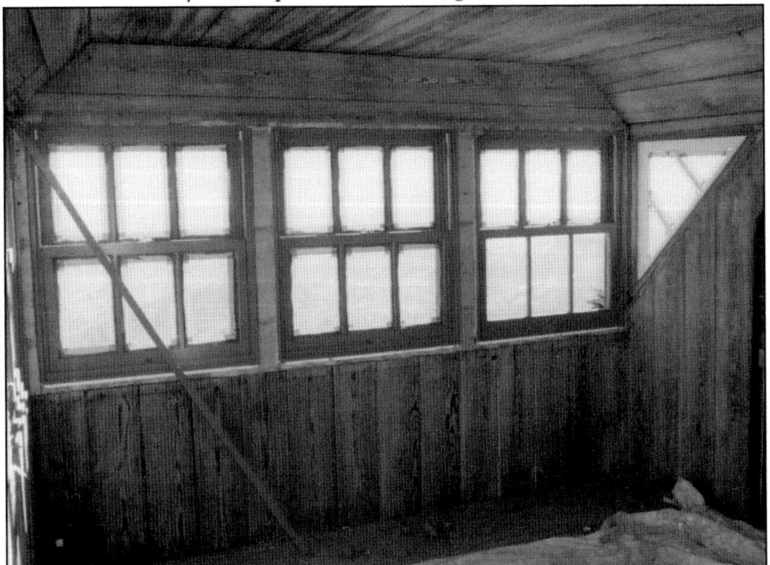

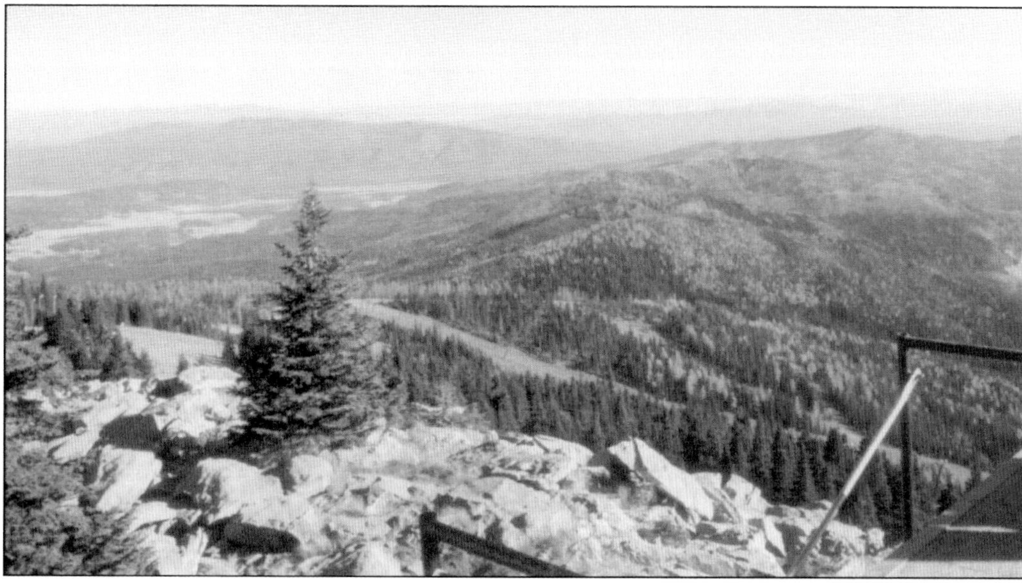

This is the view from the second story of the Vista House during the 2002 restoration. The view is tremendous. The photograph is looking to the north with the top of the ski runs on the lower right. (RK.)

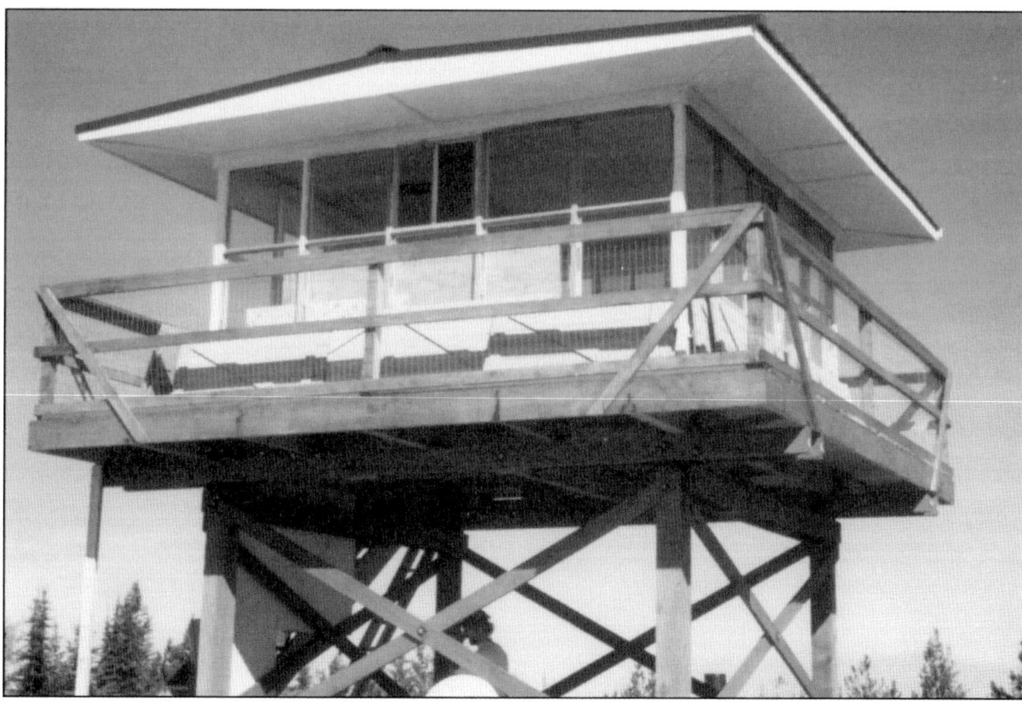

In June 2001, park officials and crews removed the last lookout tower at Mount Spokane with a crane and scrapped the tower. The lookout was moved to a storage area within the park until 2004, when state officials and volunteers adopted a plan to set the lookout on top of Quartz Mountain just southeast of Mount Spokane. It was set on a 10-foot tower and was restored for use by the public as a recreational rental cabin. With volunteer help, the lookout opened for rental in June 2005. (RK.)

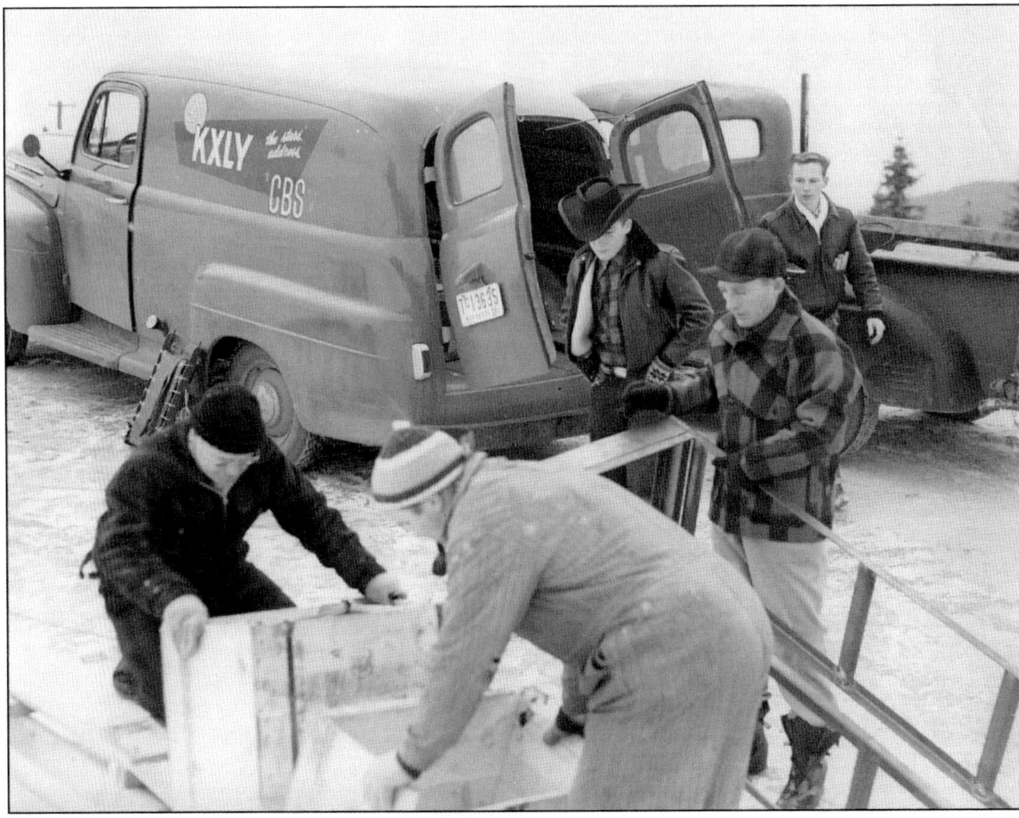

Bing Crosby had been involved with KXLY radio in Spokane since the late 1940s. Crosby is standing to the right of the trailer of the KXLY radio van and wearing a flannel coat. The license plate date on the van is 1951. On June 27, 1952, it was announced that Crosby had joined in partnership with KXLY to build and operate a television station in Spokane. (GUL-bcbc020502.)

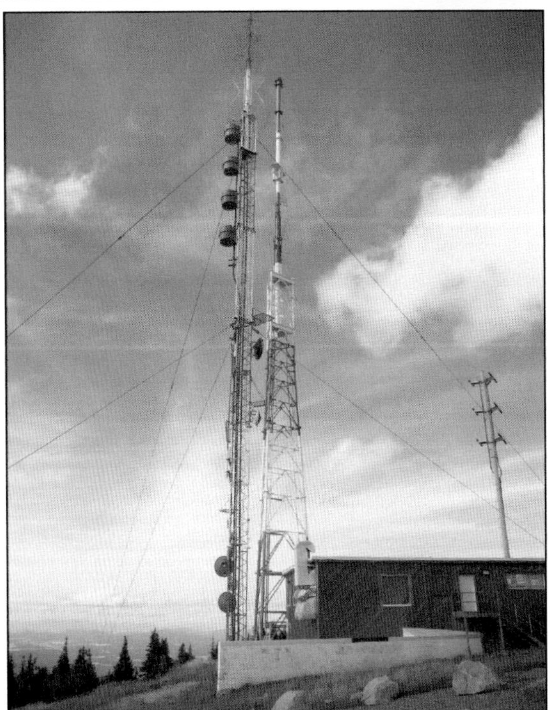

Plans at Mount Spokane called for the construction of a two-story, 40-by-80-foot concrete building to house the transmitter and supplies, with a 100-foot tower with a 45-foot antenna mounted on top. Provisions were planned so that television crews could ride out any severe storms on the mountain during the winter months. A second-story access to the transmitter building was installed to allow access in times of deep snow. (Terri.)

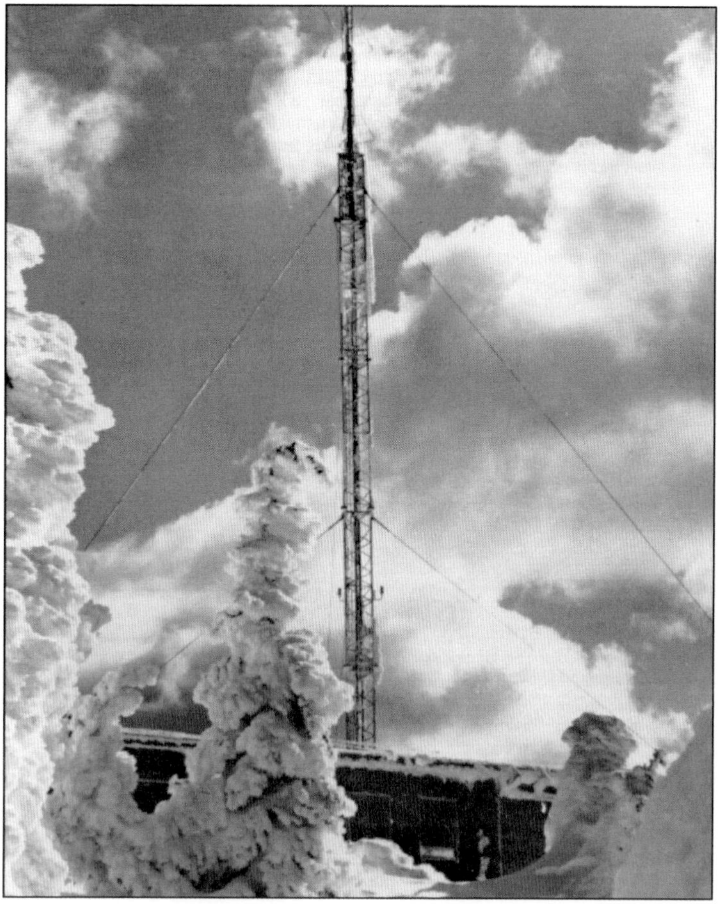

When crews were installing the television equipment, they could not connect the transmitter to the antenna because of icing on the tower and antenna. Originally, the station hoped to be on the air by December 1952, but because of weather delays, it was not until the first week of January 1953 that the transmitter and tower were finally connected. (Inland.)

After the station went on the air, problems continued during that same winter with snow and ice on the overhead power lines servicing the transmitter. Often the lines would break, forcing the station off the air. During KXLY's first winter at Mount Spokane, the power lines had been completely replaced twice. (NWR-SPL.)

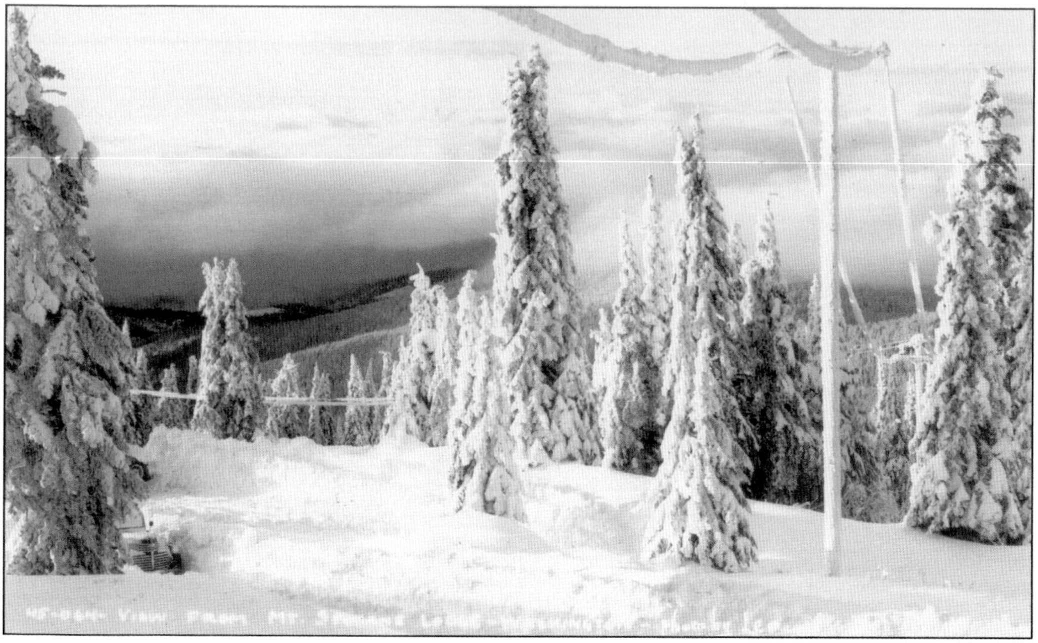

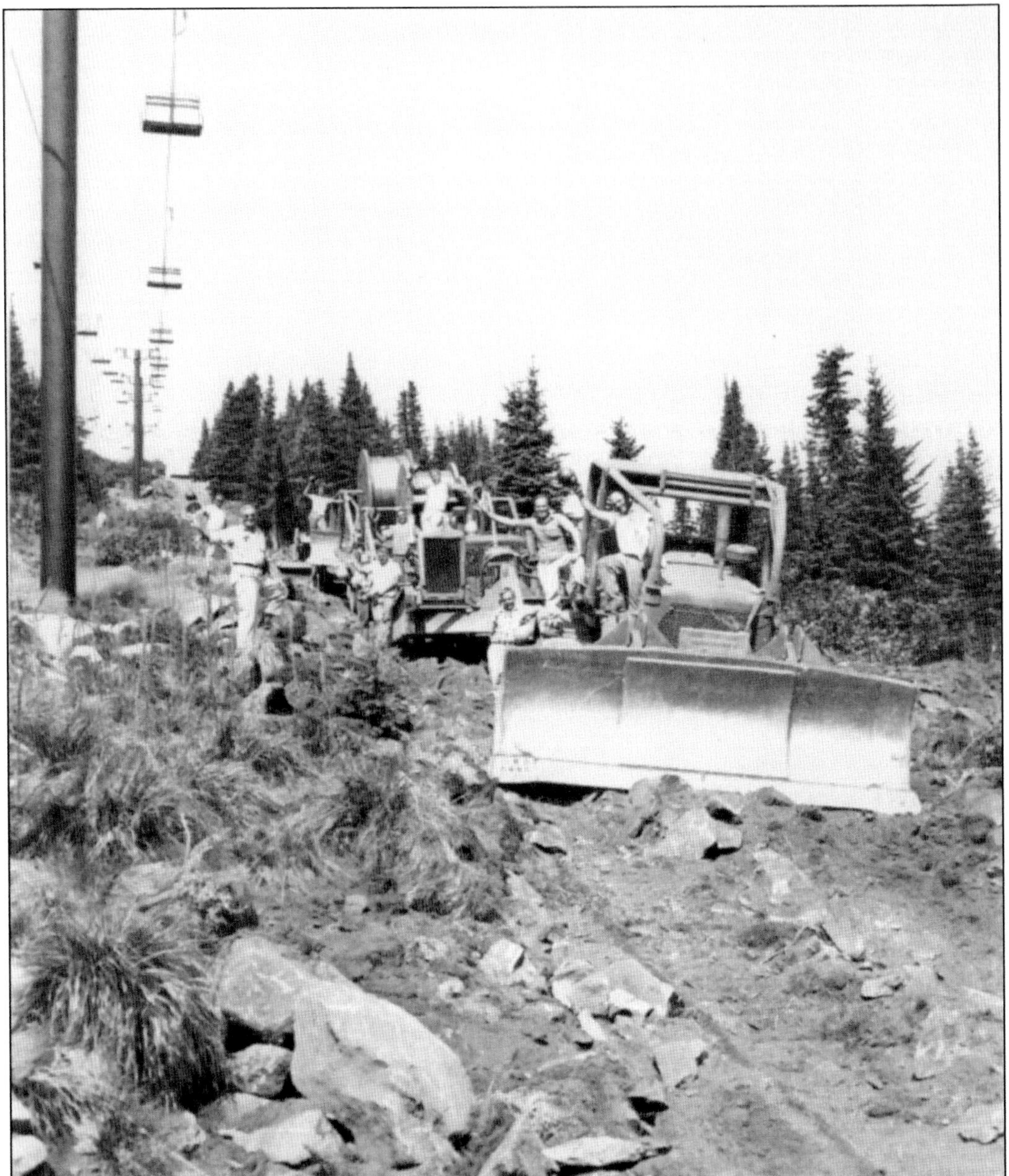

Another problem during the spring of 1953 was the overhead power lines being plagued by strong winds and lightning strikes that forced the station off the air for hours at a time. By the end of June 1953, power outages caused by the weather knocked the station off the air three times in four months. Most all of the weather-related problems with the power lines were encountered near the summit. The solution was a $30,000 underground power cable project from the site of the Mount Spokane Lodge up the western face of the mountain to the summit. Construction began in May 1953. Plans called for a 2,400-foot-long, four-inch-wide cable, with a 12,500-volt capacity, to be buried 18 inches underground. All of the work was completed by early fall before the first snowfall. It was agreed to leave the existing overhead power line in place. After the underground cable proved reliable, the overhead line was removed in the spring of 1954. A later Inland Power and Light underground power line construction project is shown alongside the chairlift. (Inland.)

The KXLY-TV transmitter building with its tower was photographed in the summer of 1988. The station leases the land and the right of use from the Washington State Parks. On September 24, 1952, the lease agreement between KXLY-TV and the state was approved and continues today. The state specified that the tower be constructed so that it would not interfere with present recreational facilities or possibilities in the area. In the photograph here, note the technicians on the tower. (LS.)

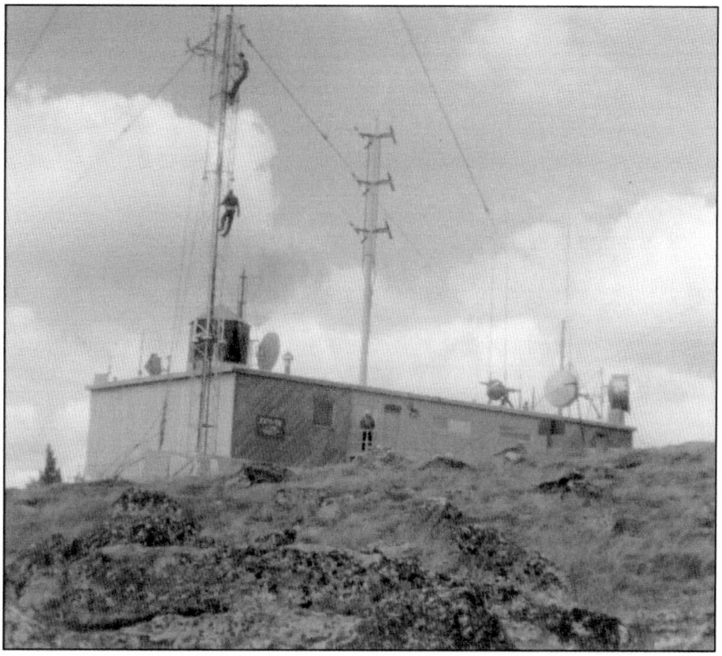

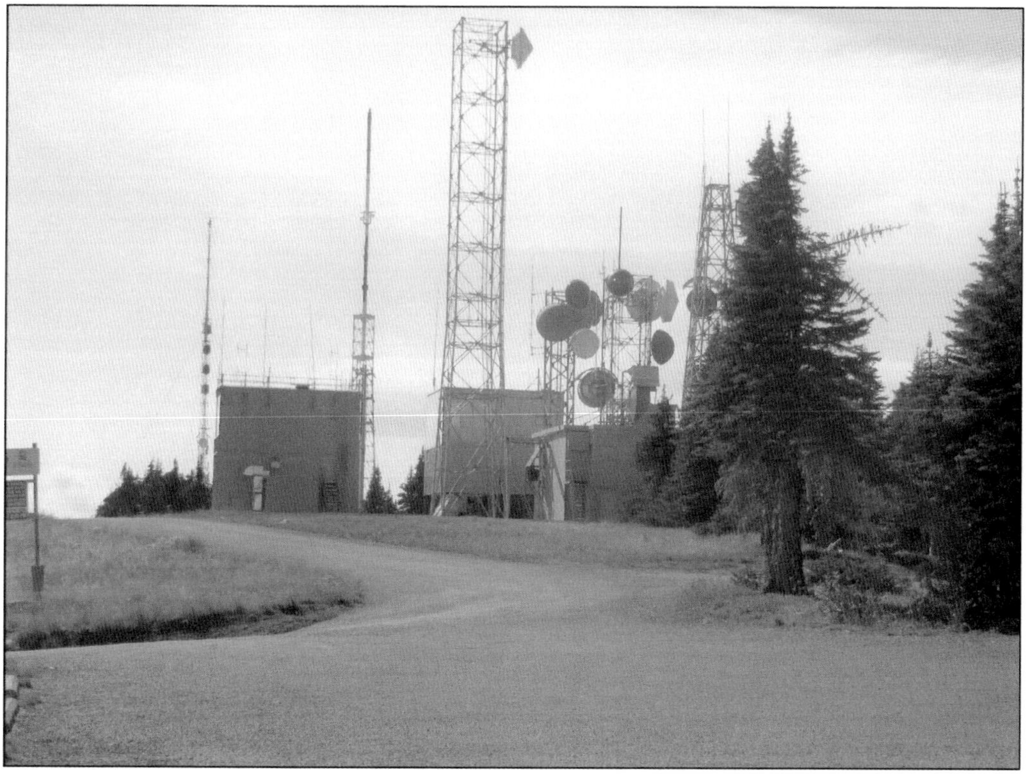

In 1952, the Bonneville Power Administration built a microwave radio repeater station at the summit. Later, the Washington State Patrol and the Washington Water Power (Avista) set up communication sites at the summit, as well. Today, winter maintenance is easily performed here with the help of tractors and snowcats that can reach the summit with ease. (Terri.)

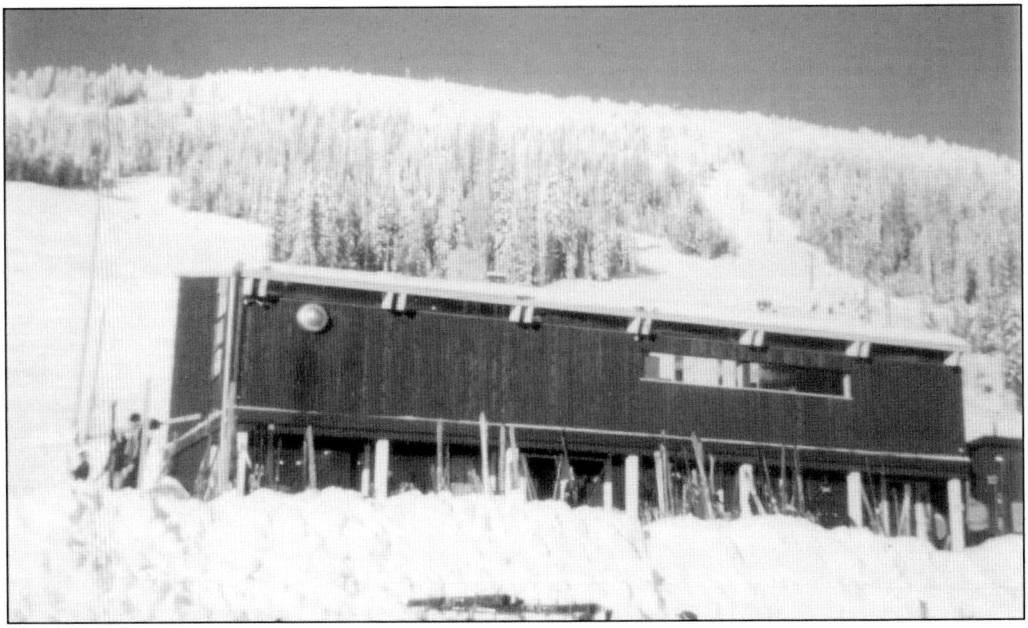

For $32,400, the 30-by-60-foot, two-story Lodge No. 1 was built in 1955 by Hefte Construction Company of Spokane. This photograph was taken before the addition in 1957. Riblet Tramway of Spokane designed and supplied the materials to build the chairlift, shown at right. At the time, the 4,400-foot chairlift was the longest and had the greatest amount of vertical lift (1,500 feet on a 15-percent grade) in the Northwest. (WK.)

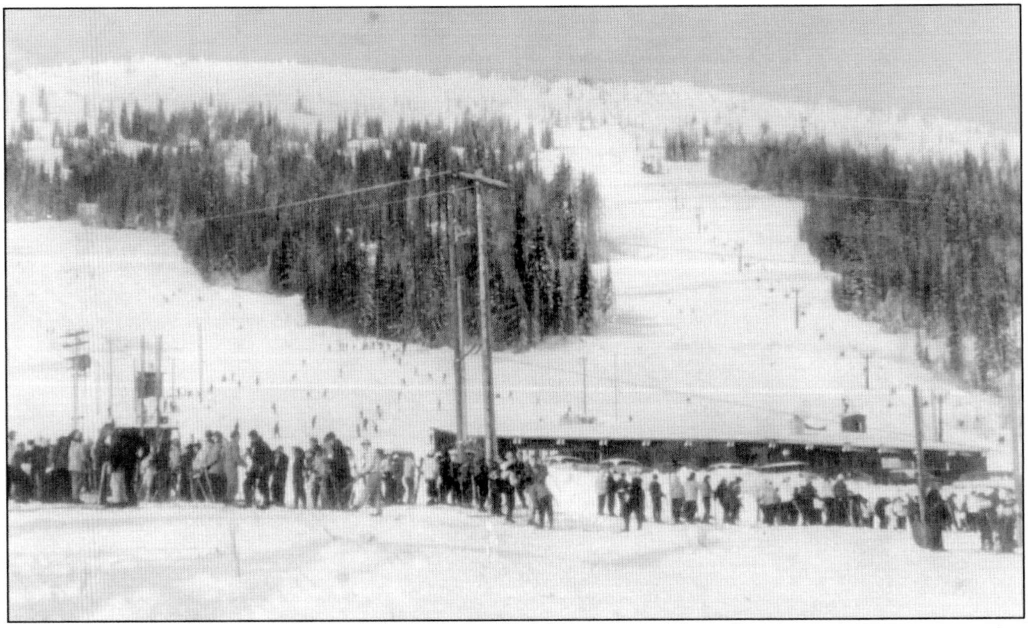

With record attendance and overcrowding at Lodge No. 1, the state built an addition onto Lodge No. 1, which was completed for the 1957–1958 season. This photograph shows Lodge No. 1 with its addition after it was reopened to the public. The addition was 30 by 65 feet and built on the end of the existing lodge. When completed, the structure would resemble a V shape. Built by Hefte Construction, the cost of the addition was $29,700. (SSP.)

Ten

The Skiing Continues

In 1952, the state announced plans and location for a new comfort station with water service and parking at the Bald Knob area. Estimated to cost $30,000, the one-story structure would provide a warming area and cafeteria for skiers in the winter and a picnic/camping area in the summer.

On November 16, 1953, Washington State Parks and Recreation Commission announced plans to relocate the skiing facilities to the east side of the mountain. A new lodge would be built, and a road would be constructed to the new area. The rope tows were moved over from Cook's Cabin. The lodge (now called Lodge No. 1) was completed and opened on November 26, 1955.

Al Mettler, the concessionaire at Mount Spokane, formed the Mount Spokane Chairlift, Inc., to finance a chairlift for the lodge. Chairlift construction was started during the summer of 1955 but would not be completed until the following ski season. In October 1956, the chairlift was completed, with its opening dedication on December 1–2, 1956. Many people, including state officials, attended the dedication. The chairlift was an instant success, taking skiers from Lodge No. 1 to the summit and Vista House. During the summer of 1957, the lift was operated as a sightseeing tourist attraction with riders taken to the top and back. A Spokane charter bus company, Spokane Suburban Lines, got into the action by offering round-trip charter bus rides from downtown Spokane to the Mount Spokane chairlift.

The January 13, 1958, edition of *Sports Illustrated* featured a photograph and article of the new chairlift and great skiing conditions at Mount Spokane. The article mentions the price of an all-day lift ticket being $3.25, which covered both the chairlift and rope tows.

With the first lodge and chairlift being successful, Chairlift No. 2 was constructed in 1961, followed by Lodge No. 2 and lights in 1968. The skiing area was enlarged again with more space opened up for skiing and three additional chairlifts. Chairlifts Nos. 3, 4, and 5 were constructed in 1970, 1972, and 1977, respectively.

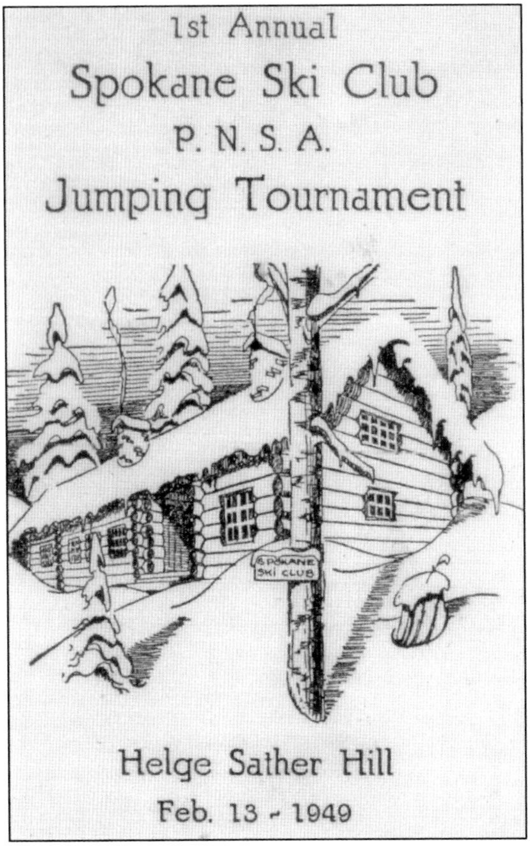

In 1948, the Helge Sather Ski Jump Hill was opened a short distance above the Spokane Ski Club cabin. The Spokane Ski Club and the Athletic Round Table sponsored Class-A jumping events, with jumps up to 300 feet. Many world-class ski-jumping tournaments were held at the jump. A parking lot, several food vendors, and public restrooms were provided at the bottom of the hill. Interest in the jumping hill waned after 1956, and a few years later, the area began to be covered over by natural vegetation. Today, the area is forested, with no visible signs of the old ski jump. (Both, SSP.)

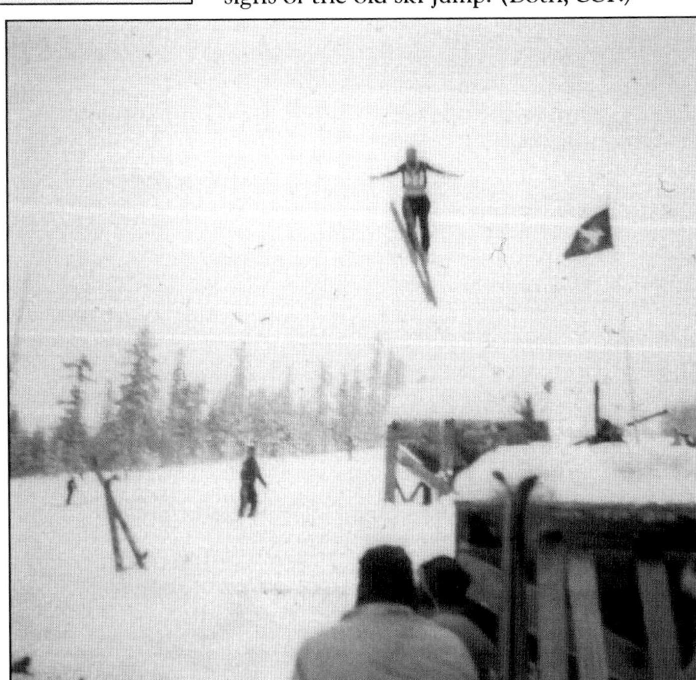

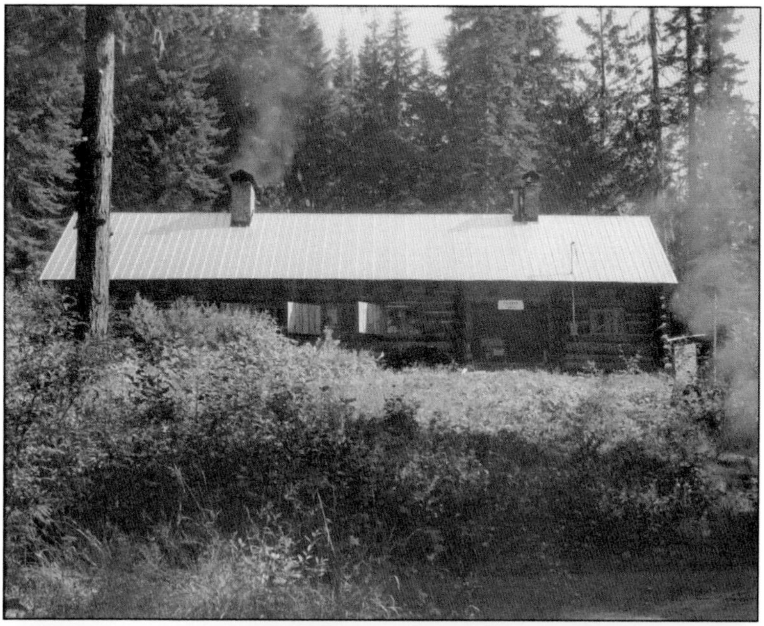

The Boy Scouts of America purchased land from the old Spokane Ski Club and set up camp at the ski cabin. The Scouts named the area Camp Fosseen in honor of Neal R. Fosseen, longtime skier and supporter of Mount Spokane skiing. Neal R. Fosseen was at one time the mayor of the city of Spokane. (BSA.)

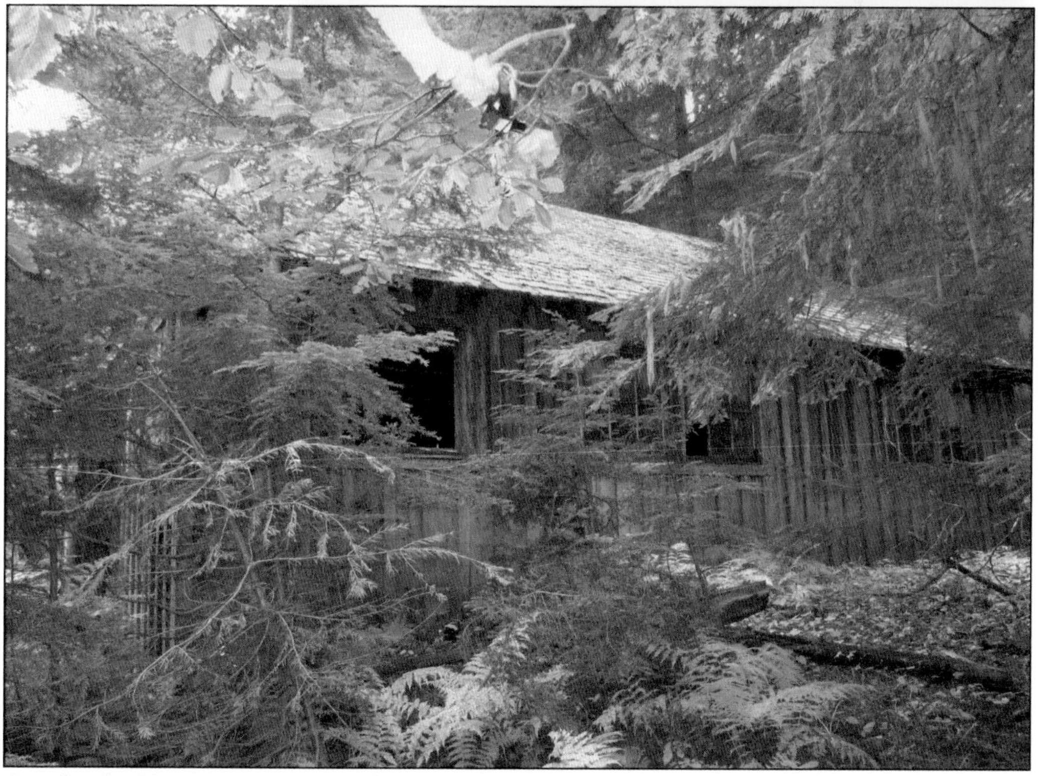

Another building was constructed and used by the Scouts at Camp Fosseen. This was located just a short distance from the original Spokane Ski Club cabin. The Scouts used the camp until 1979. Today, the land is part of the state park. The old ski cabin is gone except for the remaining chimney. The second building used by the Scouts, shown here among the vegetation, is partially collapsed. (Terri.)

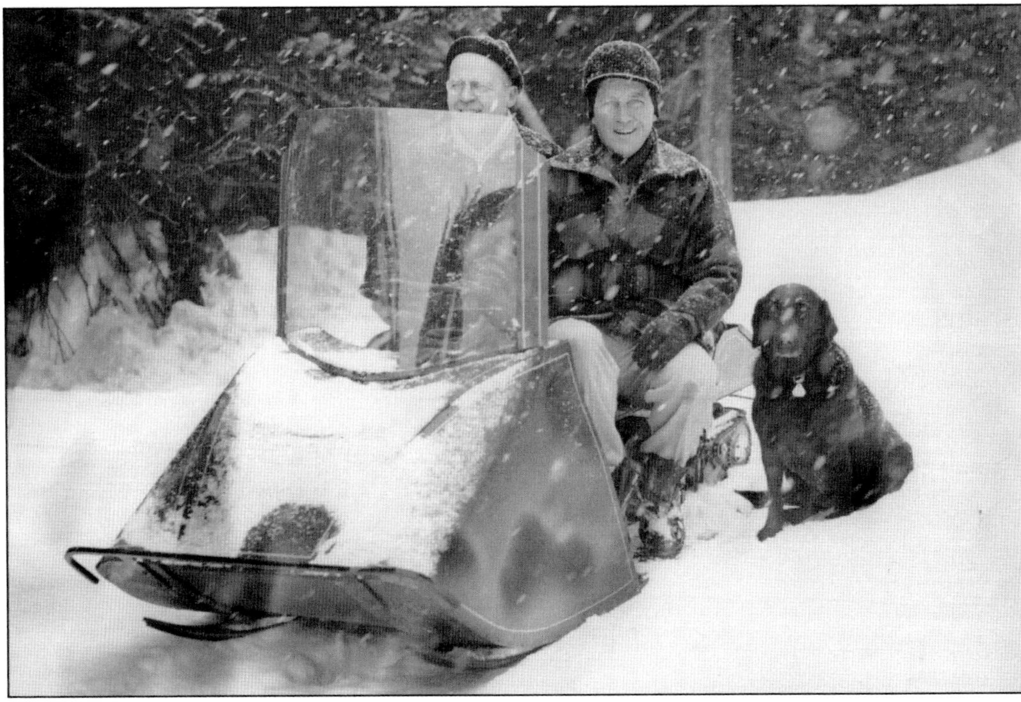

The above photograph shows Bing Crosby (right) snowmobiling on Mount Spokane in 1951. Snowmobilers have used Mount Spokane for many years. By 1963, the Spokane Snowmobile Association had formed, and in 1968 their name changed to Spokane Winter Knights Snowmobile Club. The Washington State Parks and the state legislature agreed to permit snowmobile use at Mount Spokane State Park in 1966. Trails groomed by snowmobiles wind their way through areas within the park. The old CCC camp area and this cabin serve as locations for snowmobile riders to gather and warm up. Snowmobiling, whether with a club or individually, has grown into a very popular winter activity at Mount Spokane. (Above, GUL-bcbc020501; below, Terri.)

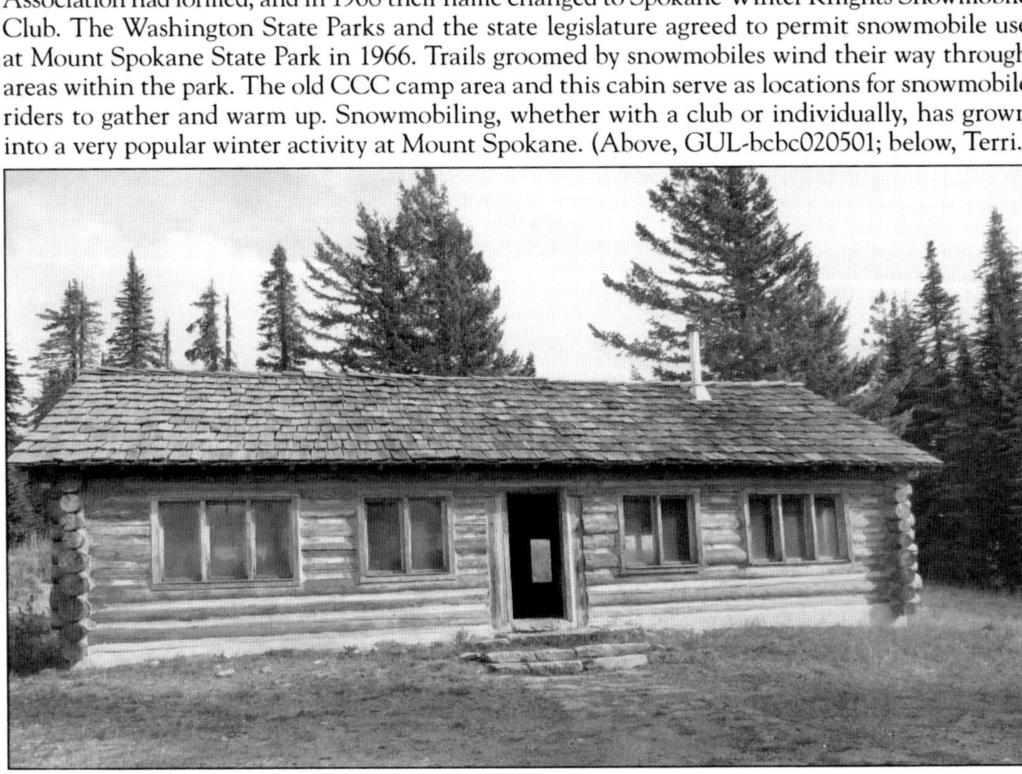

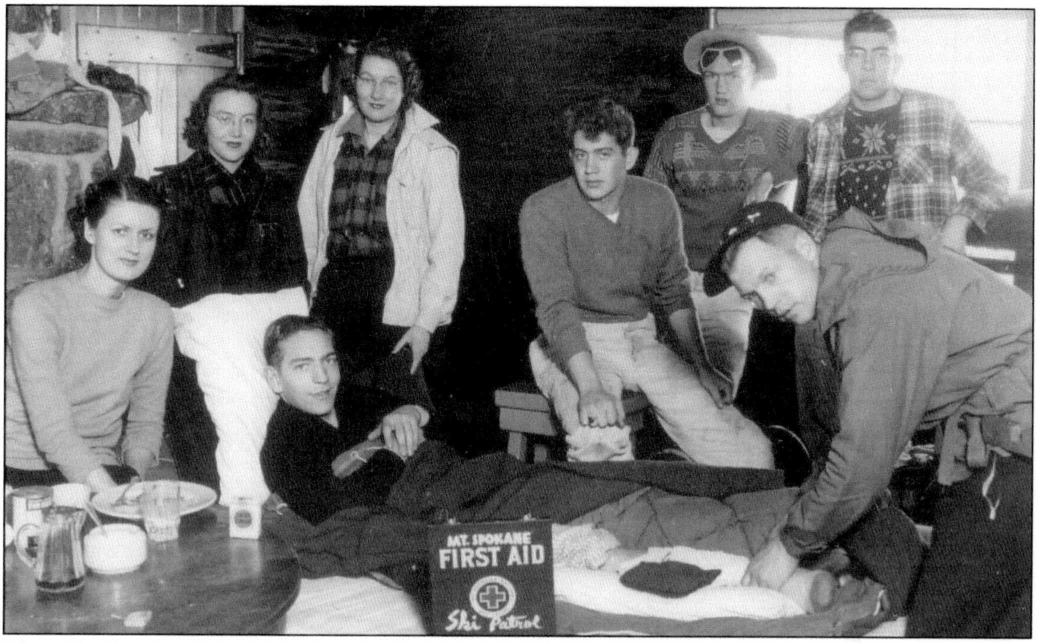

The all-volunteer Mount Spokane Ski Patrol, formed in 1938, provides first aid to injured skiers and removes accident victims from the mountain. Day-to-day patrols cover the downhill runs, ski area boundaries, and the Nordic trails. Volunteers are on duty continually while the runs are in operation. At the end of every shift, a patroller sweeps every run to make sure there is no one left on the mountain. If there is a lost skier, no one goes home until the skier is found. Starting in a small room at Mount Spokane, it has grown and expanded with a modern facility. The Mount Spokane Ski Patrol Building was built and financed by the ski patrol. Many members volunteered time to work on the building. Most of the construction was financed by proceeds from the annual Ski Swap, a fall sale organized by the patrol. The patrol also solicited and received donated building materials from several Spokane businesses. (Both, SSP.)

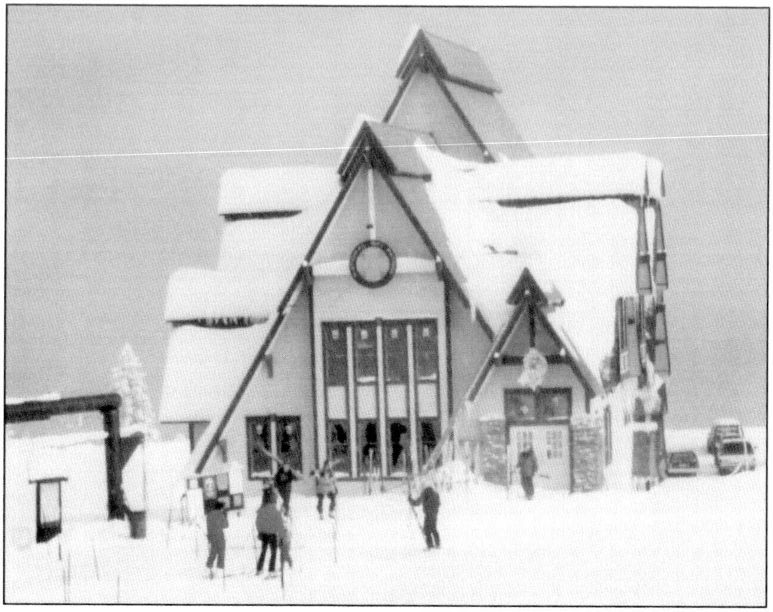

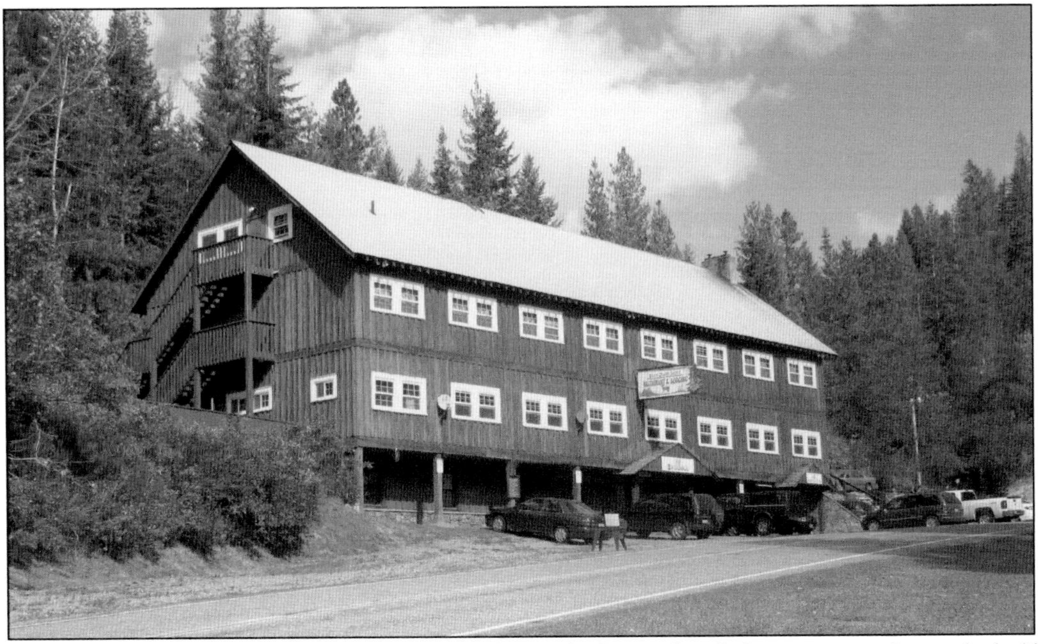

The Linder family operated the Linder Store alongside the road and chain-up area, located a half mile from the park boundary. John Linder cleared the area hillside, installed rope tows with lights, and opened a ski facility across the road from the store on December 26, 1952. Linder constructed and opened an impressive three-story lodge in front of the ski hill. The first floor had a lunch counter and warming room, with overnight accommodations on the second and third floors. The Linder's Ski Bowl was open for many years. Having changed owners, the lodge is still open today. It was remodeled and briefly operated by the Kirk family and called Kirk's Lodge. The lodge was renovated recently and is now called Bear Creek Lodge. It is open year-round with overnight lodging, a restaurant, and outdoor activities. (Both, Terri.)

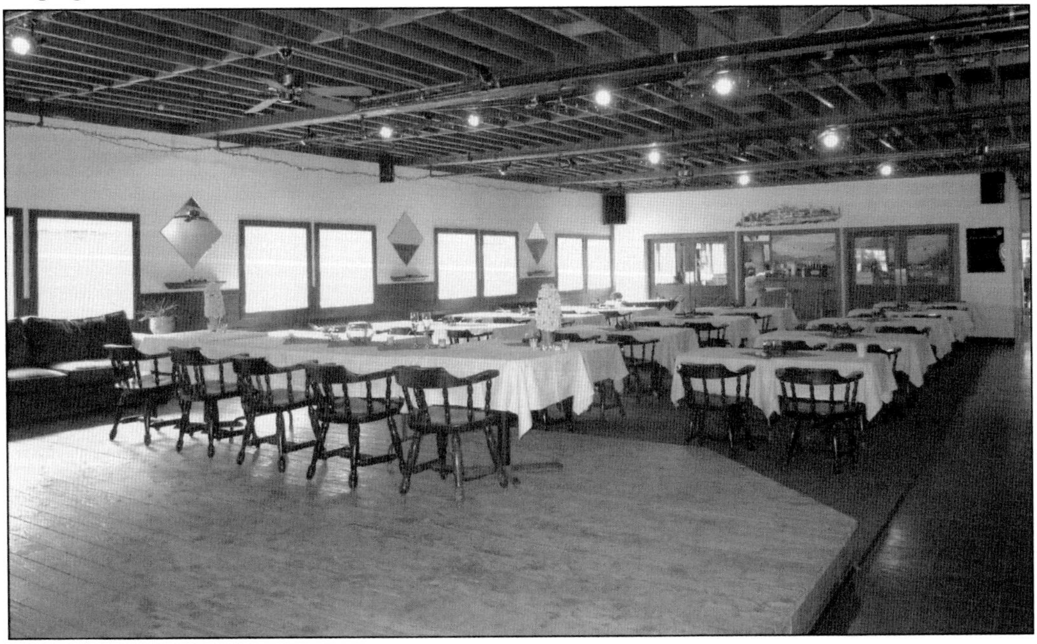

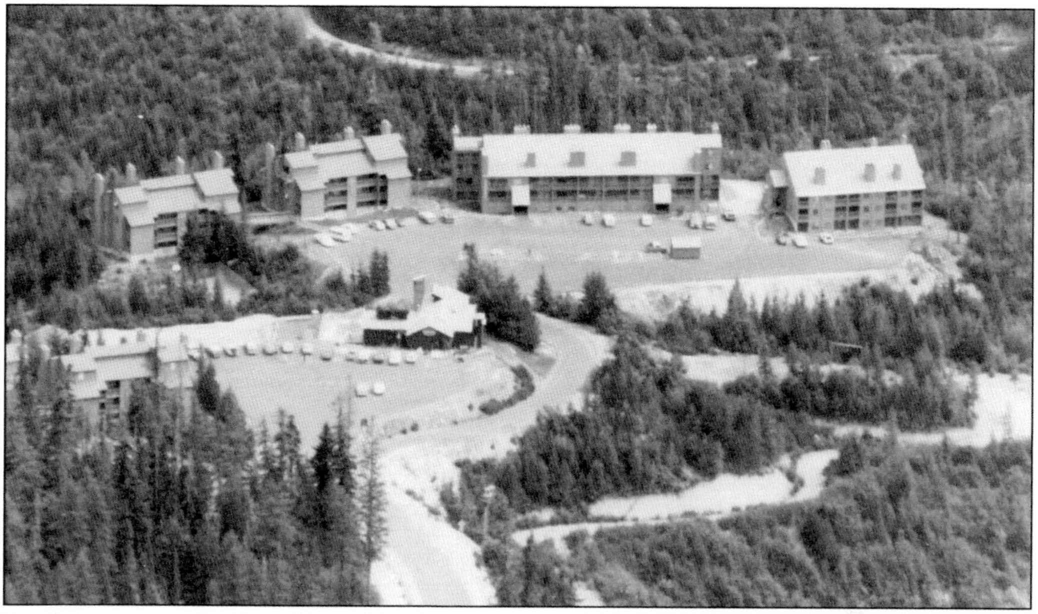

Work began on the Snowblaze Condominiums in May 1972. Five buildings, which had 67 condominiums, were built just below Lodge No. 1, with 65 of the condos sold by November 1972. Soon after, not only the condominiums but also the entire ski facility were being called Snowblaze. A $1 million project, which involved building 52 more condominium units, was under way by the summer of 1973. A skating rink, swimming pool, tennis court, and outdoor activity area were completed and in use by that summer, as well. The above photograph shows a portion of the condominium units. More units are to the left and not shown. Also shown here is the Snowblaze Lodge, which opened by 1973 and featured a restaurant, retail shops, and a cocktail lounge with live music. Later called Grambos, the lodge was open for several years. Tough economic times fell upon the lodge and the Snowblaze condominiums. Filing for chapter 11 bankruptcy, Snowblaze was financially restructured. Today, the lodge is now a private residence, and the condo units are still active. (Above, LS; below, JB.)

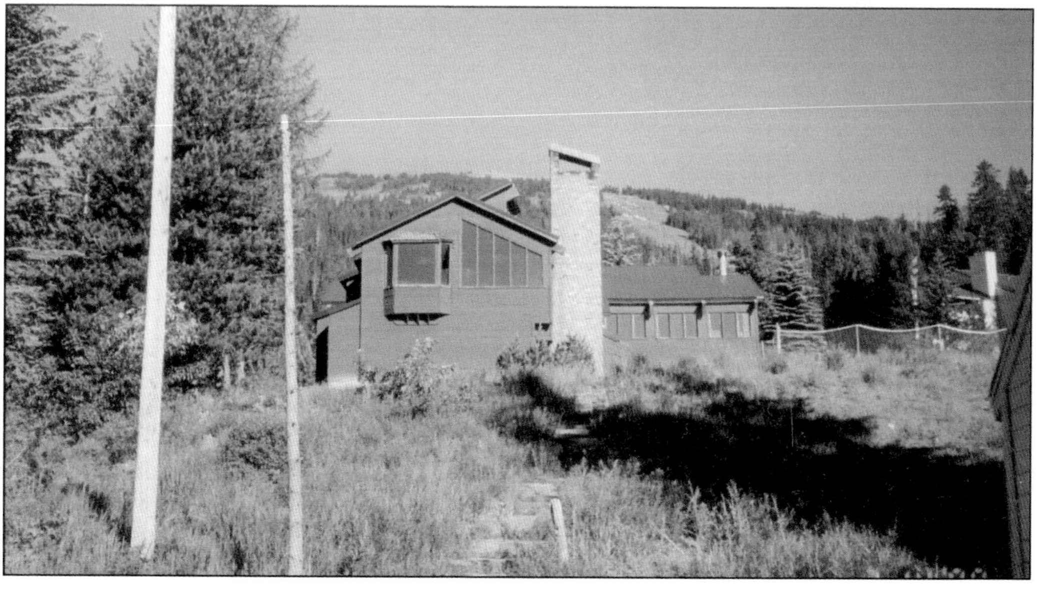

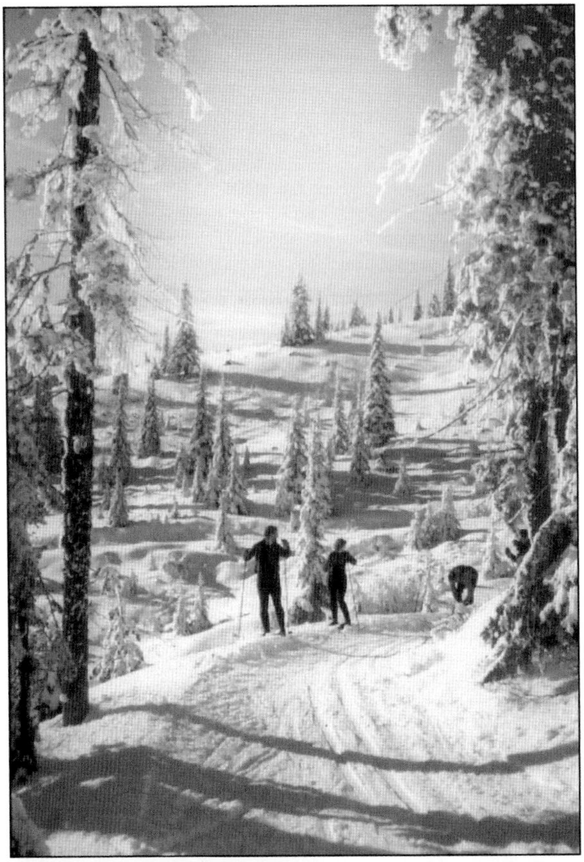

Shown at left, Nordic cross-country skiers are, from left to right, Ron McDonald, Roxie Miller, and Carl Miller on the Shadow Mountain Trail in the winter of 1988. In cooperation with Mount Spokane State Park and other agencies, the Spokane Nordic Ski Education Foundation (SNSEF) develops and maintains the Mount Spokane cross-country ski trails. The foundation teaches adults and children the techniques and fun of Nordic cross-country skiing, as well as informs the community about developments in the sport, and hosts ski competitions. Shown below is the 1995 Bill Koch Youth Ski League at the Nordic Kids' Olympics on Mount Spokane. (Left, JM; below, TF.)

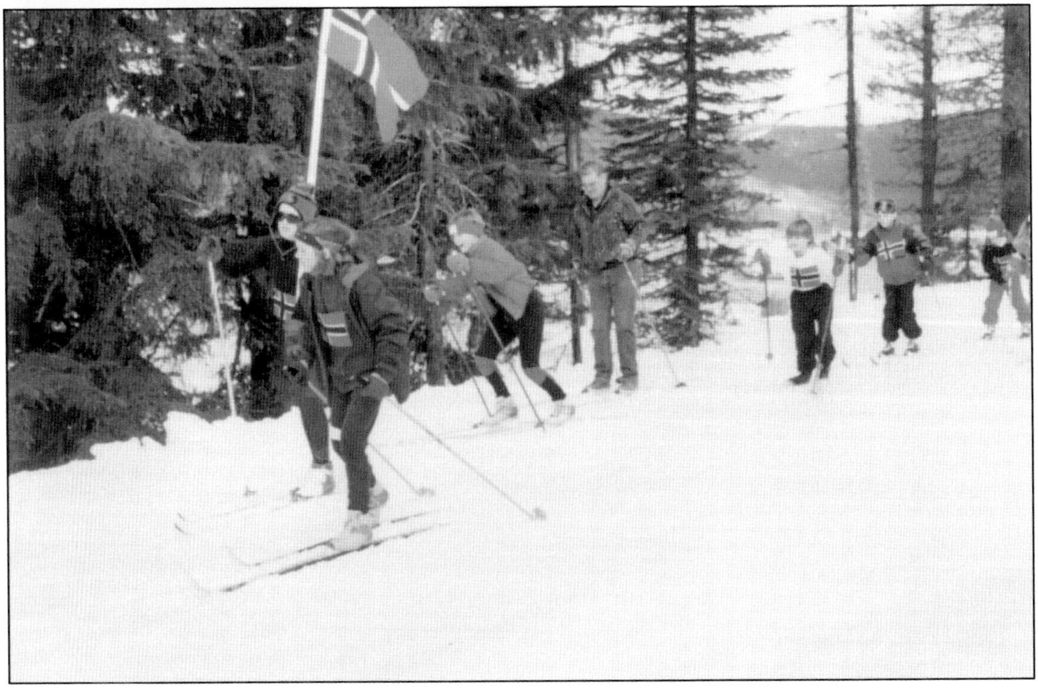

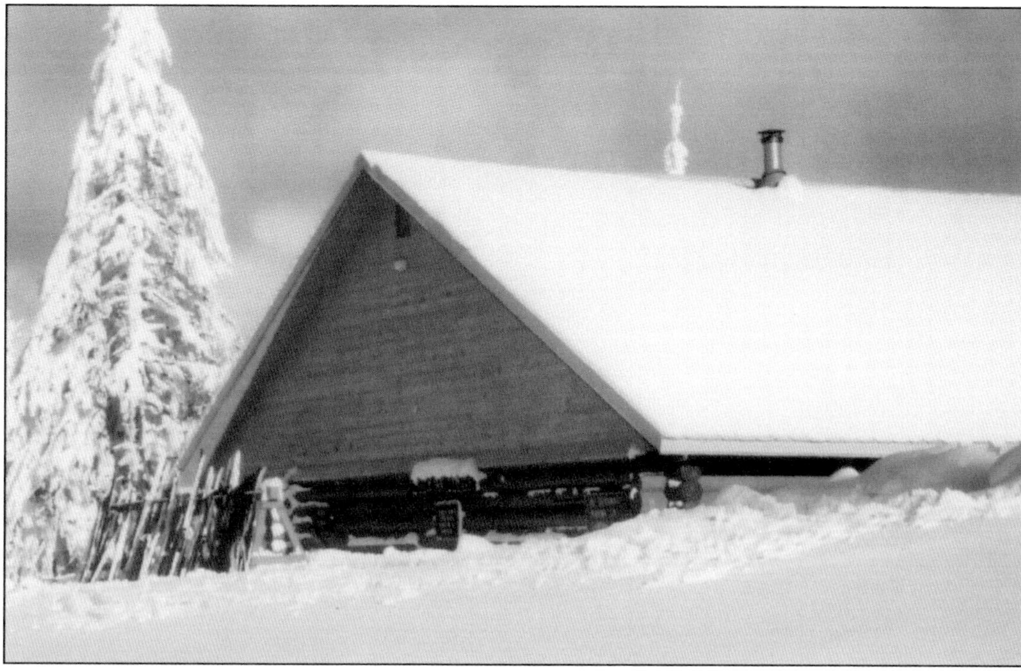

The Selkirk Lodge, also called the "warming hut" by Nordic skiers, was built by the club in 1989, with over 2,000 hours of volunteer time donated by the many members and other groups. The open spacious interior welcomes the cross-country skier to warm up by the wood stove and have lunch. The main driving forces behind the Selkirk Lodge were Carl and Roxie Miller. They had a lot of help from Washington State Parks, Inland Empire Nordic Club, 659th Engineers (Army Reserve), Winter Knights Snowmobile Club, and the outdoor retail store REI. The introduction of the Selkirk Lodge added greatly to the use of the ski trails and prompted the expansion of a number of trails. With the Selkirk Lodge and the expanded trail system, the Mount Spokane Nordic area has become very popular. A part of the US Nordic Ski Team trained on Mount Spokane in 1991 and 1996. (Both, JM.)

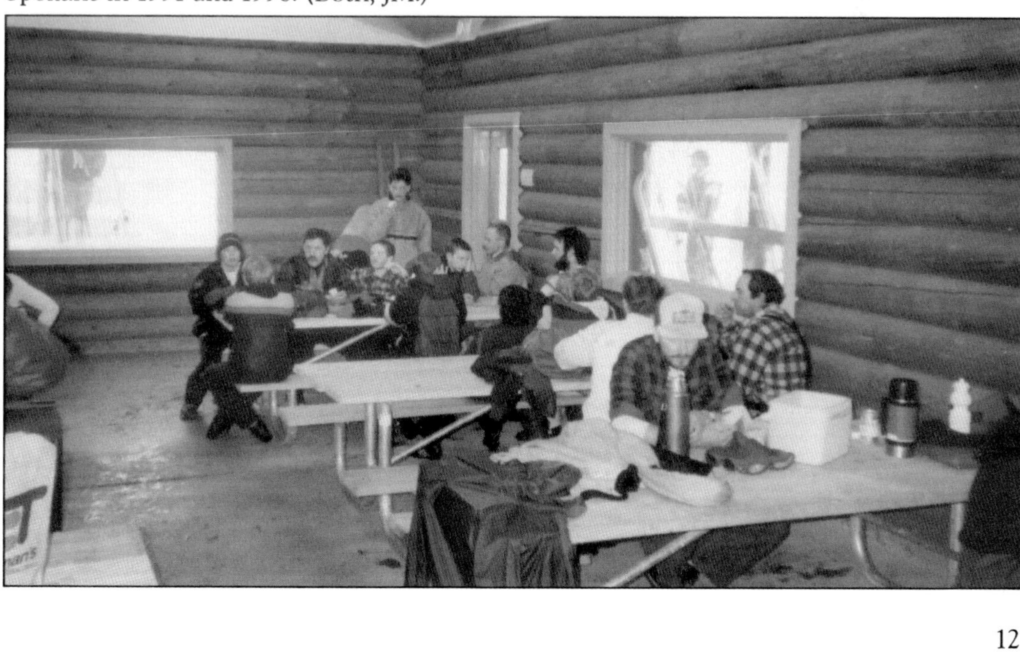

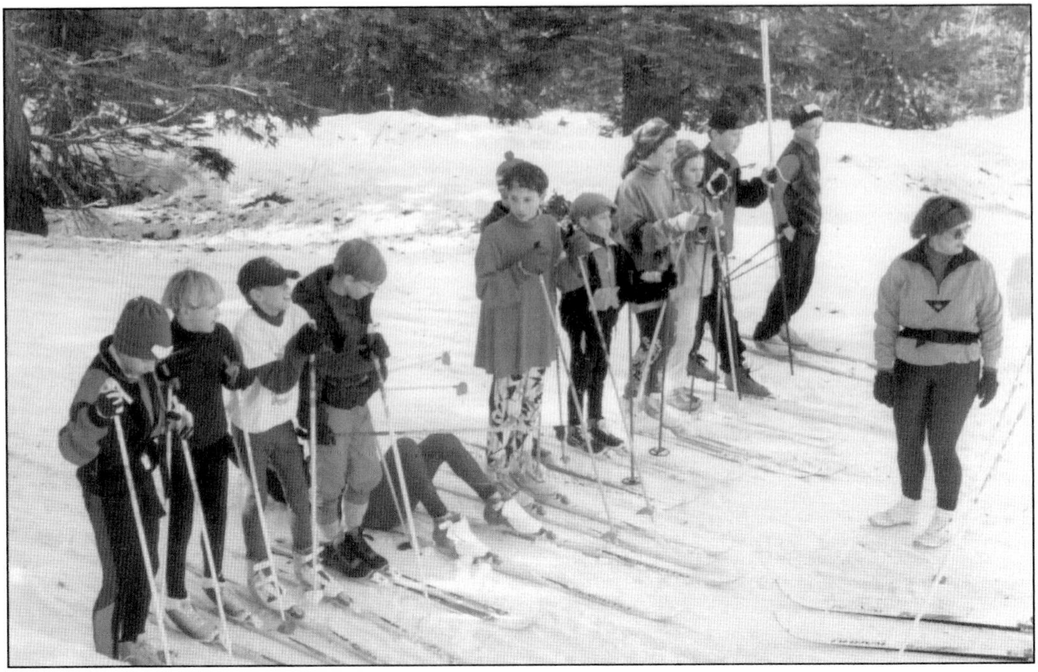

The Spokane Nordic Ski Education Foundation is member funded. Membership helps maintain and expand the Mount Spokane cross-country ski trails. Member involvement promotes the foundation's efforts to bring the community together to enjoy health, fitness, family, and the great outdoors. (TF.)

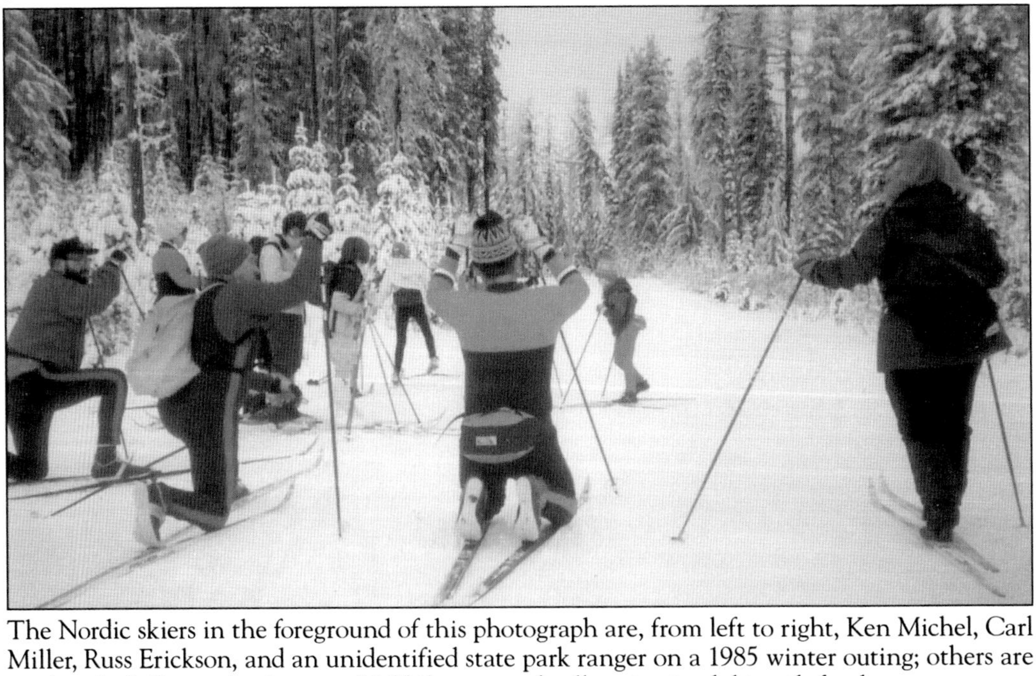

The Nordic skiers in the foreground of this photograph are, from left to right, Ken Michel, Carl Miller, Russ Erickson, and an unidentified state park ranger on a 1985 winter outing; others are unidentified. Currently, there are 36.5 kilometers of well-maintained ski trails for the cross-country skier, with members extending the lengths and adding other trails during the maintenance programs during the summer. (JM.)

This groomer is seen on the cross-country ski trails in the winter of 2000. The trails were originally groomed by the Inland Empire Nordic Club snowmobile, which pulled a variety of implements, one of them being bedsprings. This was replaced by a professional-quality groomer obtained by a Sno-Park grant. In 1988, the state parks took over grooming. With Sno-Park funds, officials purchased a new groomer in 1995. In 2012, approval was made for $300,000 from Sno-Park funds to purchase a new larger groomer. (JM.)

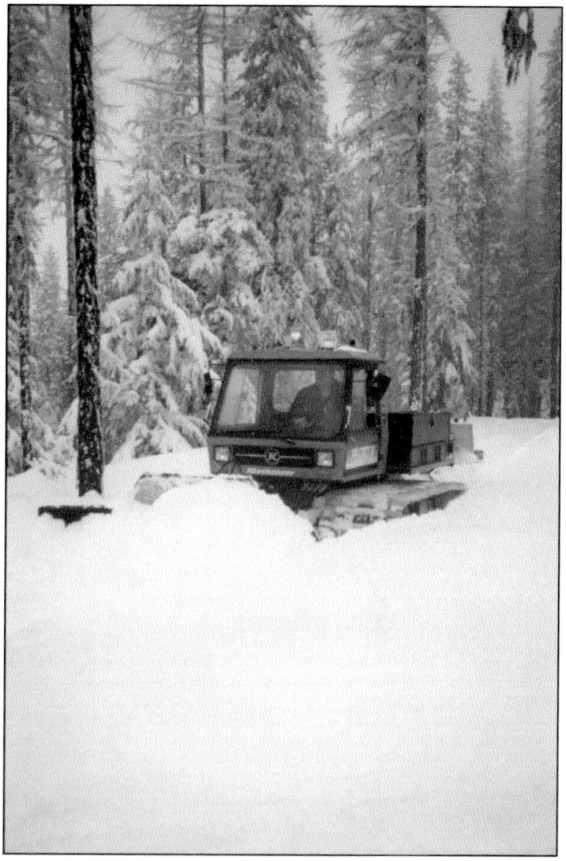

The Mount Spokane Ski Patrol is adjusting safety padding on the chairlift poles in this photograph. Pictured are, from left to right, Ryan Wickre, Bryceson Tenold, Dave Krause, Elaine Cairns, and Seth Fletcher. Ski patrol volunteers stay current with refresher courses on lift evacuation, search and rescue, first-aid procedures, toboggan use, and advanced skiing. The ski patrol is active in promoting public awareness on skiing safety and ensuring the ski boundaries are visibly marked. (SSP.)

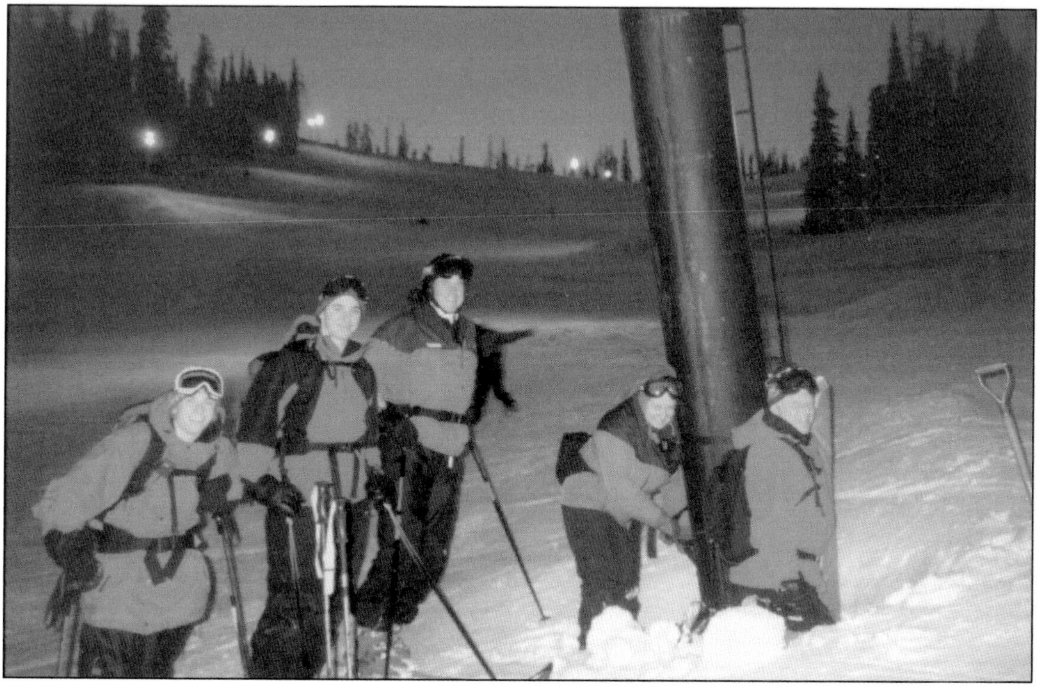

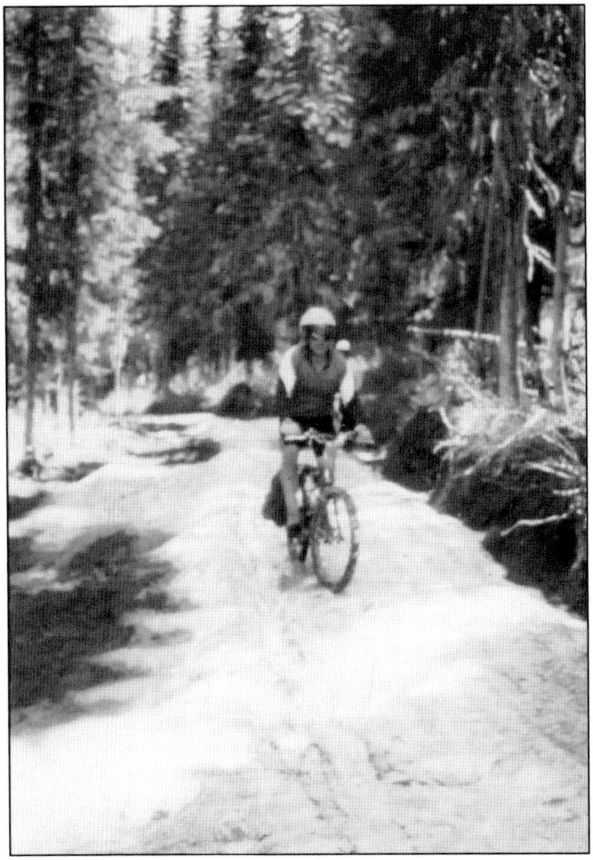

Carl Miller is riding through a sheltered trail in the early summer of 1989. Mountain biking has become extremely popular in the last several years at Mount Spokane with racing and backcountry leisure riding. Also shown here is a photograph of the 1994 National Off-Road Bicycle Association (NORBA) race on Mount Spokane (Both, JM.)

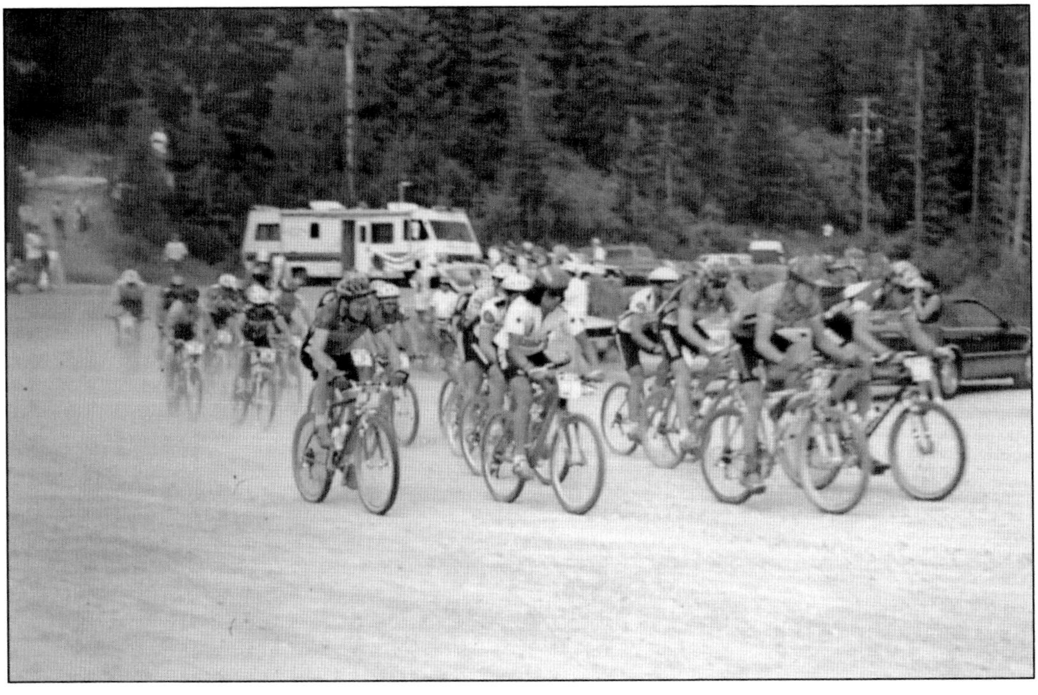

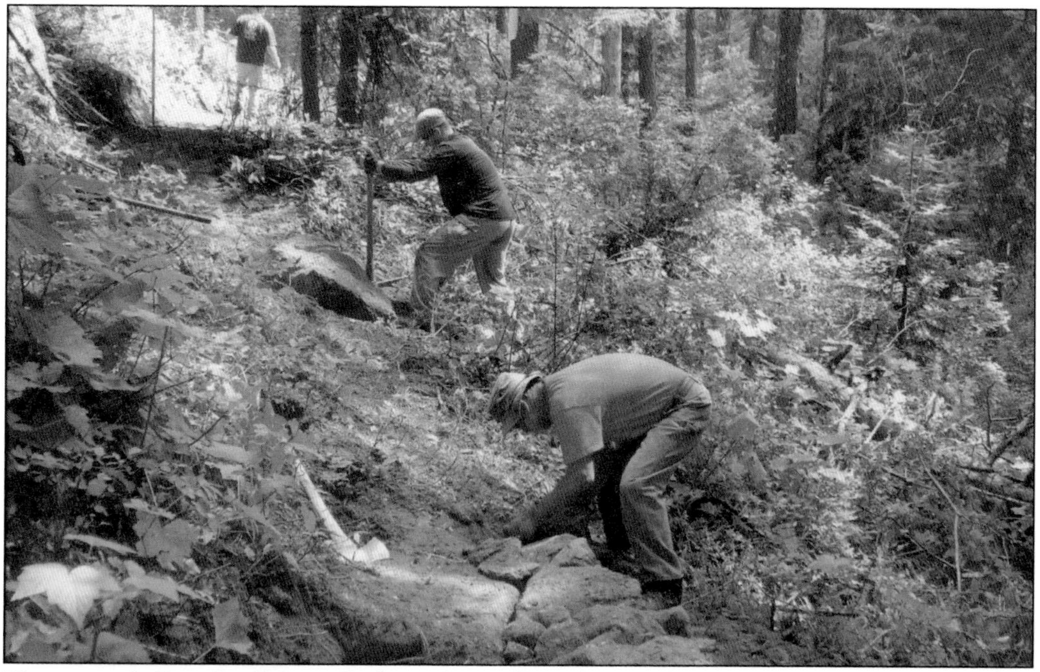

The nonprofit Friends of Mount Spokane Group (Friends Group) was started in 1995 in conjunction with the Mount Spokane State Park Advisory Committee. Members were appointed by the director of the Washington State Parks and Recreation Commission. The advisory committee guides the state in management planning, and the Friends Group raises funds and organizes projects to preserve and promote the park. Shown in the above photograph are, from left to right, unidentified, Eric Ryan, and Lynn Smith. They are participating in a 2010 Friends Group–organized trail project from Smith Gap to Kit Carson. Future projects include building a new hut for snowshoers and more trail maintenance. The Friends Group is also involved with assisting educational research. Shown below in the summer of 2011 are members of the Washington Butterfly Association; they are documenting the butterfly populations on Ragged Ridge. The ridge is a Natural Area Preserve and is only open for pedestrian day use and scientific research. (Both, CC.)

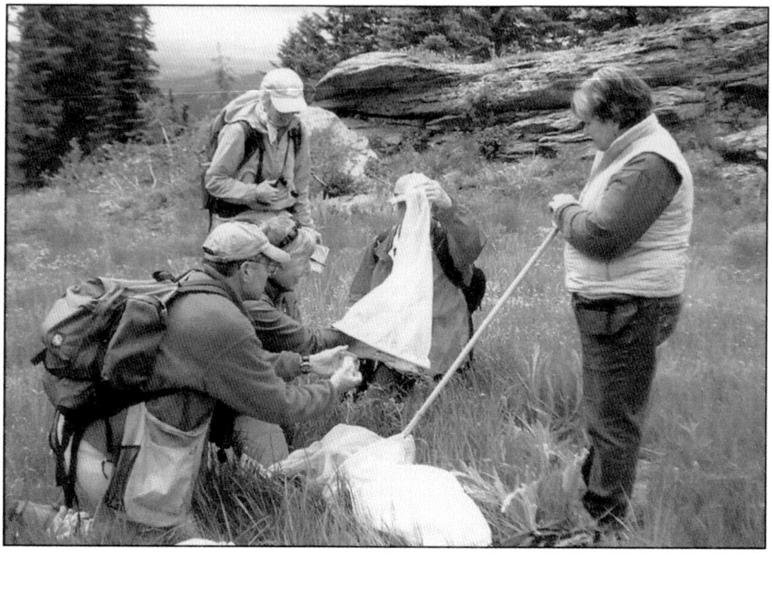

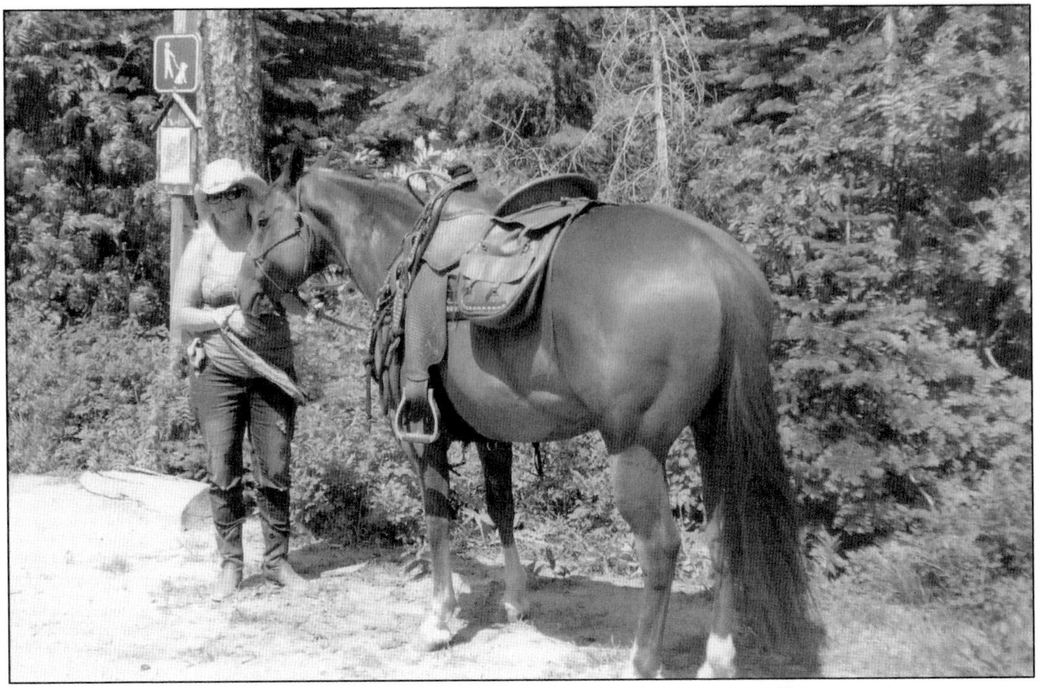

Today, horseback riding at Mount Spokane is as popular as ever. On any given summer day, several horse trailers can be seen at parking trailheads. The rider in this photograph is unidentified. (CC.)

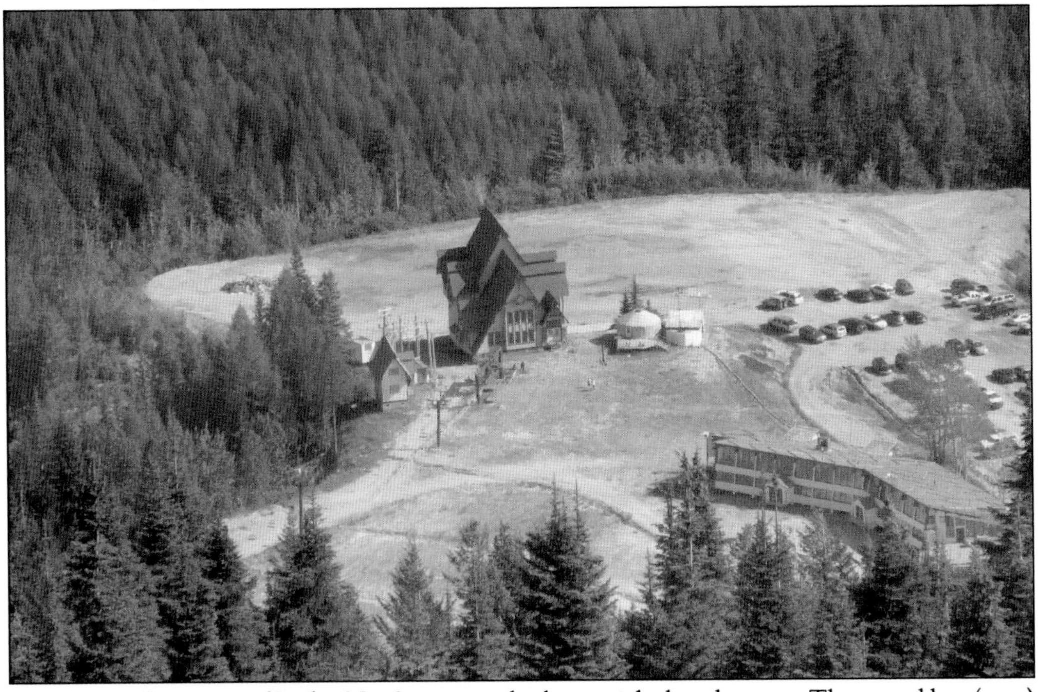

This is a modern view of Lodge No. 2, seen in the lower right-hand corner. The round hut (yurt) in the center is used by the ski instructors. Mount Spokane Ski Patrol's building is also in the center. The small building at the far left is the disabled skiers' building. (Terri.)

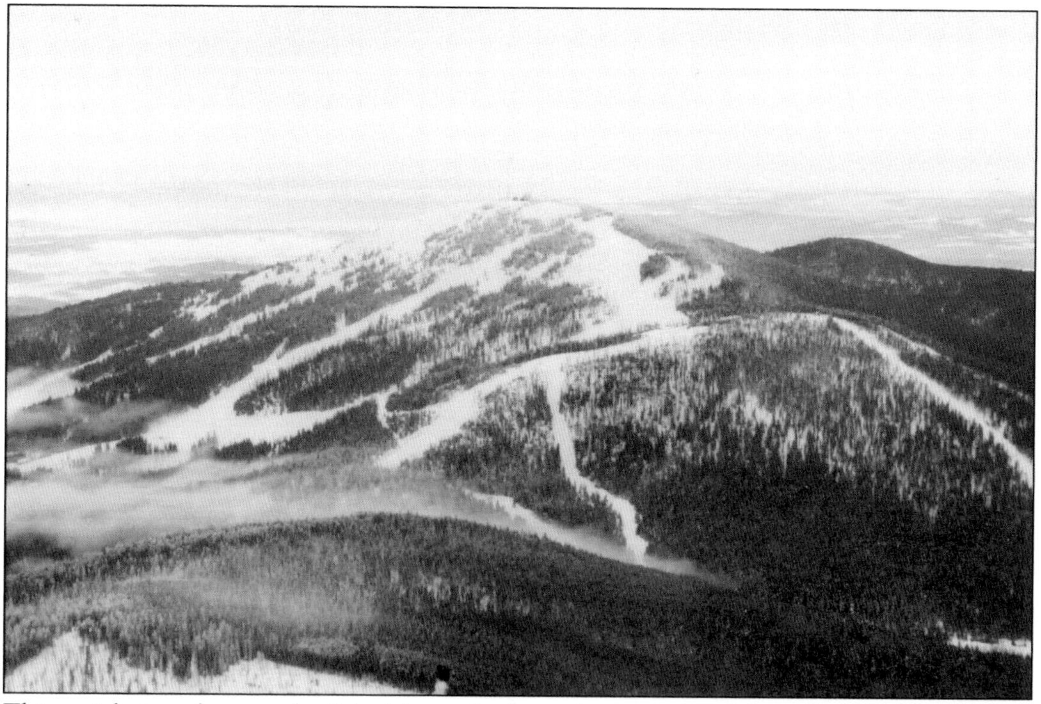

This aerial-view photograph of the Mount Spokane ski runs was taken on January 11, 2004. As of 2012, officials from the Washington State Parks in partnership with Mount Spokane 2000 have proposed the development of a new four-season lodge to be constructed near the present ski facilities. Funding is in the legislative process with tentative plans. A proposal to expand the ski area with a new chairlift is underway, as well. (Gene Crissey.)

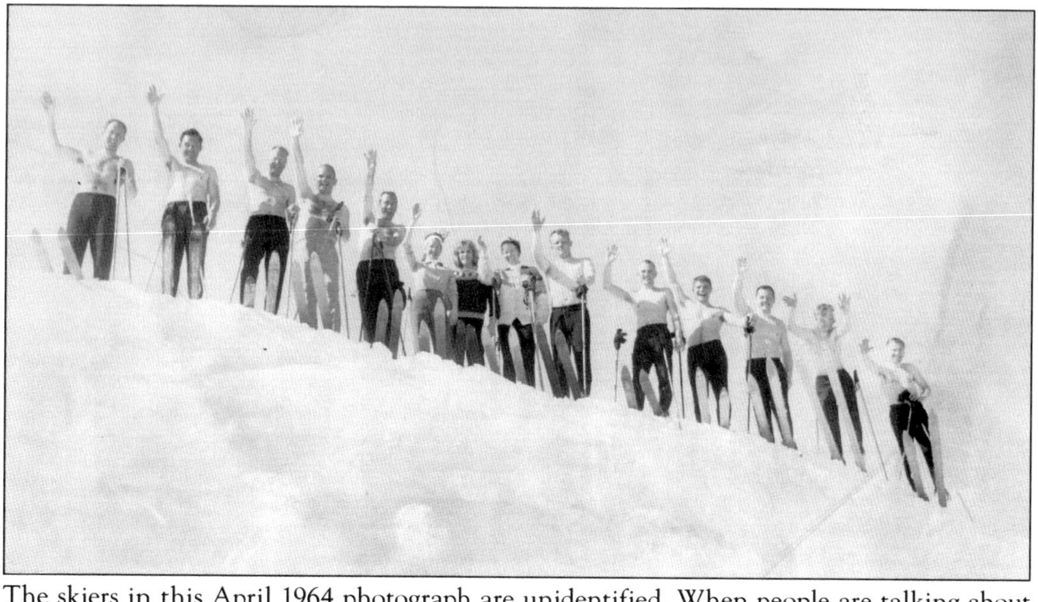

The skiers in this April 1964 photograph are unidentified. When people are talking about Mount Spokane or skiing there, everyone over the years, for whatever reason, seems to end conversations with "see ya on the mountain." So with that in mind, "see ya on the mountain." (Pat Rotchford.)